Scotland Yard's Murder Squad

DICK KIRBY

PEN & SWORD
TRUE CRIME

First published in Great Britain in 2020 by
Pen & Sword True Crime
An imprint of
Pen & Sword Books Ltd
Yorkshire – Philadelphia

HB ISBN 978 1 52676 5 338

A CIP catalogue record for this book is
available from the British Library.

Printed and bound in the UK by TJ International Ltd, Padstow,
Cornwall.

Pen & Sword Books Limited incorporates the imprints of Atlas,
Archaeology, Aviation, Discovery, Family History, Fiction, History,
Maritime, Military, Military Classics, Politics, Select, Transport, True
Crime, Air World, Frontline Publishing, Leo Cooper, Remember
When, Seaforth Publishing, The Praetorian Press, Wharncliffe Local
History, Wharncliffe Transport, Wharncliffe True Crime and White
Owl.

For a complete list of Pen & Sword titles please contact

PEN & SWORD BOOKS LIMITED
47 Church Street, Barnsley, South Yorkshire, S70 2AS, England
E-mail: enquiries@pen-and-sword.co.uk
Website: www.pen-and-sword.co.uk

Or
PEN AND SWORD BOOKS
1950 Lawrence Rd, Havertown, PA 19083, USA
E-mail: Uspen-and-sword@casematepublishers.com
Website: www.penandswordbooks.com

To Ann

Little deeds of kindness, little words of love
Help to make earth happy, like the heaven above.

Julia Carney (1823–1908), *Little Things*

Praise for Dick Kirby's Books

'His style of writing pulls no punches and he tells it the way it is. Highly recommended.' *POLICE HISTORY SOCIETY MAGAZINE*

'These are the real-life accounts of a tough London cop.' *DAILY EXPRESS*

'All of the stories are told with Dick Kirby's acerbic black humour in a compelling style, by a detective who was there.' *AMERICAN POLICE BEAT*

'New Scotland Yard legends are vividly brought to life by a man who had walked the walk, the Flying Squad's own Dick Kirby.' JOSEPH WAMBAUGH, AUTHOR OF *THE CHOIRBOYS*

'It's a rollercoaster ride; detectives who took crime by the scruff of its neck and wouldn't let go.' *EAST ANGLIAN DAILY TIMES*

'I am delighted that Dick Kirby has written this book. I am sure those who read it will realize how very hazardous the life of a policeman is.' MICHAEL WINNER

'Kirby looks to untangle facts from speculation and questions everything.' *GET WEST LONDON*

'Ex-cop Dick Kirby has now laid bare the Krays' empire.' *DAILY STAR*

'A vivid and fascinating account of policing some of the era's most serious crimes, written by an experienced and retired police officer.' *THE LAW SOCIETY GAZETTE*

'Real *Boys Own* stuff, this. Tinged with a wry sense of humour makes this an excellent read.' METROPOLITAN POLICE HISTORY SOCIETY

'This is a fast-paced, riveting read, made even more enjoyable by Kirby's trademark humour.' *TANGLED WEB*

'This is simply the best book about police gallantry ever written and arguably the best book about any sort of gallantry awards. It comes with our highest possible recommendation.' *HISTORY BY THE YARD*

'A sensational and gripping account.' *PEGASUS YEARBOOK*

'Dick Kirby pulls no punches as he looks in depth at some of the most infamous names from the criminal underworld.' *MEDIA DRUM WORLD*

'Murder, torture and extortion all feature prominently as Mr Kirby investigates some of the most famous incidents of the post-war era' *THE MAIL*

'Old-school, but effective – how the Met took the fight to the underworld.' *THE SCOTSMAN*

Contents

About the Author

Dick Kirby was born in 1943 in the East End of London and joined the Metropolitan Police in 1967. Half of his 26 years' service as a detective were spent with the Yard's Serious Crime Squad and the Flying Squad.

Married, with four children and five grandchildren, Kirby lives in a Suffolk village with his wife. He appears on television and radio and can be relied upon to provide forthright views on spineless senior police officers and other politicians, with their insipid and mendacious claims on how they intend to defeat serious crime and reclaim the streets.

He contributes regularly to newspapers and magazines, is employed as a consultant by television and film companies, reviews books, films and music and writes memoirs, biographies and true crime books, which are widely quoted – this is his nineteenth.

Kirby can be visited on his website: www.dickkirby.com.

Acknowledgements

First and foremost, my thanks to my friend, Flying Squad colleague and fellow author, Paul Millen, the former Scientific Support Manager for Surrey Police and arguably the world's finest crime scene investigator, for his exceptionally kind and thoughtfully written foreword to this book.

My thanks also to Brigadier Henry Wilson for his unflagging support, together with my deep appreciation for the staff at Pen & Sword Books: Matt Jones, Lori Jones and others too numerous to mention. A special thank you to Jon Wilkinson for his superlative and imaginative designs for the jacket covers which undoubtedly sell the books and to George Chamier, whose sharp-eyed editing is easily a match for those old-time First Class Detective Sergeants who wielded a red pen – only he does it with much more humanity.

I owe a debt of thanks to all those backroom people without whose help I should have stumbled at the first hurdle: Bob Fenton QGM, Honorary Secretary of the Ex-CID Officers' Association; Susi Rogol, Editor of the *London Police Pensioner* magazine; Mick Carter, secretary of The ReCIDivists' Luncheon Club; Chloe Guy-Pearson, Searchroom Assistant, Suffolk Record Office and Alan Moss of *History by the Yard* (whose encyclopaedic knowledge of the Metropolitan Police leaves my jaw permanently dropped).

I'm deeply obliged to the following who gave so unselfishly of their time in the compilation of this book: Stuart Bailey; Geoff Cameron; Kenneth Davies; Bernie Davis; David Hewett; Maurice Marshall; Geoff Parratt; Alex Ross; Graham Seaby; John Spears; John Troon; the late Lou van Dyke; and Tony Yeoman.

I'm most grateful to those who provided me with photographs: Bernie Davis; Mick Gray; David Hewett; Maurice Marshall; Geoff Parratt; Alex Ross; and John Troon. Other photographs are from the author's collection, and whilst every effort has been made to trace copyright holders, the publishers and I apologise for any inadvertent omissions.

My thanks go to my daughter, Sue Cowper, and her husband Steve for rescuing me from the minefield of cyber cock-ups, as well as the love and support I have received from their children,

Harry Cowper, Emma Cowper B. Mus, Jessica Cowper B. Mus – plus my other daughter, Barbara Jerreat, her husband Rich and their children, Sam and Annie Grace, my sons Mark and Robert, but most of all my wife, Ann, who for over 55 years has stood by me.

Dick Kirby
Suffolk, 2019

Foreword

*Paul Millen FCSFS, formerly Vice-President
of the Forensic Science Society*

How far we have come, how far we must continue to go. The exploits so carefully detailed in the pages that follow explore the drive, determination, skill and tenacity of those detectives at the forefront of recent policing history.

Far, because predominantly men with little resource to science used witness testimony, detailed questioning, reason and deduction to bring murderers to justice. They were at the forefront of their craft. Far also, because they paved the way for their skills to spread and develop as new scientific tools aided their task. The practice of investigation is much smarter now, much more disciplined, but that is progress. Science is a tool, it is not the solution on its own.

So this tradition of male detectives from Scotland Yard has given way to skilled detectives throughout the land and beyond. Joined by female detectives and supported by a range of experts, both police and civilian, sometimes employed by the police organisation, but often not. The situation we see today might to some be barely recognizable from that of less than 100 years ago. But that is not the case, and there is a lot we should remember and learn from those early pioneers. The tools available to investigate murder might have changed and continue to develop, but they are useless without the ability to question, probe and challenge.

When I was asked by Dick Kirby to provide a foreword for this book, I considered it an honour and duty. The request in itself was an indication of how far we (yes, we) have come since the first episodes described in the early chapters.

I first met the author over thirty years ago, when I was posted as civilian Scenes of Crime Officer to the Flying Squad, where he was a very active detective sergeant. Over a period of four or so years I supported him and many other fine colleagues. Supported is an important description, because I did not work for him but for the investigations he was charged with undertaking. Truth needs to talk to power sometimes and disappoint an established view. A true detective seeks the truth as lines of enquiry close and focus towards not only that which can be eliminated but that which can be proved with strength. Dick Kirby exemplified all the fine attributes of the detectives he describes in this book. Thoroughness, determination, guile and a sense of responsibility were the tools used to bring those who committed the most serious of crimes to justice; his descriptions are often expressed in language for its purpose and of its time. I challenge anyone not to be moved by the scene faced and the response given by Jack Capstick, when confronted with the savage murder of a child. The motivation to bring the perpetrator to justice was not coloured by emotion, but driven by duty. The duty is to our system of justice, but the victim is never forgotten.

The scientific tools these early pioneers had were extremely limited. But even thirty years ago, pre-DNA technology, just, it wasn't really much different. In the early 1980s there was a much greater range of scientific tools than in the past, and they were gallantly applied. They were nothing compared to the discriminatory tools available today. Things such as DNA, light sources for the recovery of evidence, digital, mobile phone photography and CCTV were but dreams then. What would Jack Capstick have given for such tools? He had fingerprint technology, but even that was in its infancy. Fingerprints at the Yard were the domain solely of police detectives. It would be a few years before civilian experts were trained. So there was a temptation for the few experts in one field to dabble in others. Such was the pressure to seek confirmation of a view, often disguised, rather than answers. The pathologist, Spilsbury or Simpson, might be asked to comment on fibres or foot or shoe marks, but the good doctor might not be the right expert, not then and certainly not by today's standards without specific expertise. The fingerprint expert Detective Inspector Fred Cherrill asked to examine handwriting is most likely stretching his actual expertise rather than applying it. Later in my career, and as a Scientific Support Manager for a provincial force and one who was responsible for commissioning external experts, I would have prevented such practice, save for safeguards. An expert must have an understanding of their limitations and those of the subject they study. In essence, they must understand what they don't know.

Although perhaps outside the scope of this book, but alluded to, is how the Met has developed its own organisational teams in more recent times. The fact that Geoff Parratt successfully led the investigation teams in over eighty murders in London is not only a personal testament but an organizational one in the face of such demand.

So the men and women of the Yard are still needed to apply their expertise in distant lands and situations where the tools are not available locally. But their 'murder bag' really contains a lot more and is replicated throughout the UK.

The availability of such resources comes at a time when pressures are put on the financial use of them, the volume of available material and the recruitment, development and retention of sound investigators. Once the chain is broken, the opportunity to pass on such important skills is lost.

So we must not forget but celebrate the investigative and detective skills that the Yard's Murder Squad demonstrated and are so eloquently described here. Progress is only progress if those charged with the responsibility to investigate continue to apply the same skills developed, honed and supported by the science available for their task.

Introduction

Following the formation of London's Metropolitan Police in 1829, the plain-clothes Detective Branch was introduced in 1842. It consisted of two inspectors (each paid £200 per year) and six 'serjeants', and all of the officers worked from Scotland Yard. No other detectives existed, either in the Metropolitan Police's divisions or any of the country's constabularies. It was those eight officers who were called upon to investigate serious crimes anywhere in the country or the British Empire; it was not until 1868 that their numbers were increased to twenty-eight.

The following year, the new Commissioner, Colonel Sir Edmund Henderson KCB, RE, decided to introduce detectives to the Met's (then) twenty divisions. It was a disastrous move, because it permitted the autocratic superintendents (who ran their divisions like small fiefdoms) to get rid of their most incompetent, lazy and barely literate officers into the detective branch. In 1871, when the Commissioner thought another good idea was for the newly-formed detectives to keep a daily record of their activities, the head of the detectives, Superintendent Frederick Adolphus Williamson, was obliged to point out that due to their lack of education, 'They would find it impossible to make a daily comprehensive report of their proceedings.'

That being the case, the 197 detectives, and the twenty equally useless sergeants who failed miserably to supervise them, just drifted along, being left much to their own devices.

But following what became known as 'The Trial of the Detectives', when three crooked officers were sent to hard labour for two years each, in 1877 Sir Charles Vincent KCMG, CB created the post of Director of Criminal Intelligence. He was responsible for the creation of the Criminal Investigation Department, which he had modelled on the workings of the French *Sûreté*, and within months this new department boasted 280 men, of whom 254 were divisional officers. This meant there were two fewer at Scotland Yard than nine years previously (although three had gone to prison, another had been posted there), but much-needed changes were made to investigative skills and discipline.

In those early days, the CID had little or no technical equipment. In 1894, Bertillonage (the unreliable system of identification of criminals by measurement of their body parts) was introduced, and Galton's system of fingerprint evidence was tentatively used the following year; it was not until Sir Edward Henry Bt., GCVO, KCB, CSI was appointed Assistant Commissioner (Crime) in 1901 (and later, Commissioner), that he established the fingerprint bureau and introduced and encouraged other innovations in investigative work. Nevertheless, when police were called to the scene of a crime, the best a pathologist could unhelpfully say with regard to any bloodstains discovered was that they were probably human; either that, or from one of the great apes.

In 1904, officers with not less than three years' service who wished to enter the CID had to apply in writing and pass an examination. They were interviewed by the Assistant Commissioner and, if selected, were on probation for three months.

One of the biggest problems facing the detectives sent on murder enquiries to the constabulary forces was that often a great deal of time had elapsed between the murder being discovered and the Yard being summoned; also, the body had often been moved and the bloodstained scene cleared up.

Therefore, in April 1906, following agreement in principle with the Commissioner, the Home Secretary, Herbert Gladstone, sent a circular letter to all of the country's Chief Constables telling them that to assist in the investigation of serious crime a small number of Scotland Yard detectives ('of special skill and experience') were available, and that 'application should be made without loss of time and while clues were fresh and to be accompanied by an assurance of the fullest co-operation from the Chief Constable applying and from his officers.' Those detectives were five chief inspectors, who became known as 'The Big Five', and they were based in the Central Department, later known as 'C1'.

It was a good concept and one which was well overdue; not that the parochial Chief Constables necessarily adhered to those strictures. Even though many of them still had no detective officers of their own to investigate murders, there was often great resentment at what they perceived as interlopers arriving to tell them what to do, and a great deal of tact was necessary on the part of the Yard officers. And for decades after those Home Office guidelines, bodies were often moved and sometimes buried before the arrival of the Scotland Yard detectives; on one glorious occasion, the main suspect had been tried at court and acquitted.

In fairness, there were blunders on both sides. Detective Chief Inspector Percy Savage of Scotland Yard, who boasted he had more acquittals in murder cases than any other officer – they included two where Savage had actually witnessed the offence! – also came to notice after he was castigated by the pathologist, Sir Bernard Spilsbury, for picking up pieces of rotting human flesh with his bare hands. He admitted that Sir Bernard had told him that 'No medical man outside a lunatic asylum would dream of doing such a thing and that I ought at least to have worn rubber gloves.' Savage rather gormlessly replied that police were not provided with rubber gloves, but from then on, the murder bag was carried by the senior officer's assistant, a detective sergeant who was colloquially known as the 'bag-carrier' and who ensured that it contained the necessary rubber gloves. Two Gladstone bags made of cowhide were in use from 1925 (by the 1950s they had increased in number to eight); as well as the rubber gloves, they contained magnifying glasses, instruments for measuring the depth of liquids, tape measures, test tubes and containers for holding samples of fluids, hair or other materials for scientific examination, equipment for fingerprinting and taking casts of footprints, first-aid equipment and stationery. The bag-carriers had to be fit; each bag weighed 34lbs, and those who were thoughtful often inserted a bottle of whisky to ward off the freezing temperatures experienced at cold, windy murder scenes.

As well as improving their musculature and offering alcoholic solace to their senior officers, the bag-carriers also had to introduce local officers to the Yard's 'system' of indexing and cross-indexing; and it must be remembered that the Yard officers were there to assist only – not to grab the glory or to show their constabulary counterparts how clever they were in making arrests, because they didn't; arrests and charging were always carried out by the local officers. However, the reports to the Director of Public Prosecutions (who would be responsible for considering further charges and directing his representatives and barristers to attend court) and the updates to the local Chief Constable in a protracted investigation were always submitted by the Murder Squad.

In fact, the description – The Murder Squad – was not entirely accurate. Its proper title was The Reserve Squad – No. 1 squad of C1 Department – because those officers dealt with a number of serious offences, not necessarily murder; but for the purposes of this book, it will be referred to as the Murder Squad.

As the years went by, the chief inspectors were replaced by superintendents, then chief superintendents. And as the bag-carriers rose through the ranks they gleaned expertise from their senior officers, so that when they too became senior investigating officers they possessed a wealth of experience.

A rota system existed known as 'The Frame', a literal description of an appliance in the Murder Squad office. Into the frame at No. 3 went the name of an investigating officer and his bag-carrier; this gave them a certain amount of notice, nominally two weeks. When a call for assistance came, they moved up into No. 2 position, thereby giving them one week's notice, and fresh names were inserted at No. 3. When the next call for assistance arrived, the officer now in No. 1 position had to be ready to go at a moment's notice. His every movement had to be noted in his absence from the office, even a trip to the lavatory; and when he booked off duty he would tell the officer on reserve duty (which was manned 24 hours per day) that if he was going to stop for a drink on the way home, he should provide the name and telephone number of the pub concerned, plus his expected time of arrival at his home address.

As experienced investigator Maurice Marshall told me, 'Of course, it seldom moved along so smoothly. You could go in at No. 3 and move up to No. 1 the same day; alternatively, you could reach No. 1 and sit there for weeks.'

Additionally, the calls for assistance were irregular and unpredictable. The nominated pair of officers over the notice period was not set in stone; sickness, annual leave, court appearances and so on could take one or both of them off the rota, in which case another officer (or officers) were substituted.

Probably, the most commonsense directive regarding the workings of C1 came in 1950 from retired Assistant Commissioner (Crime), Sir Norman Kendall, CBE:

> It is obvious that when a murder is committed in a remote or rural area, there can be no question about the Yard's Murder Squad being called in. This principle need not be carried out in all cases of murder, outside the Metropolitan Police area, but it most certainly should be when the district in which the murder is committed is not in possession of the experienced brains, manpower and resources of the Yard.

Following those rather caustic (albeit accurate) comments, some of the investigations carried out by members of that elite unit are now recounted. They reveal, without doubt, the high level of expertise that those investigators employed, which led, in those halcyon days of police-work, to Scotland Yard being accurately referred to as having the greatest detectives – especially those of the Murder Squad – in the western world. Many of them became household names, achieving almost film star-like status.

Their names appeared on newsagents' billboards together with brief details of their current investigations. The public followed their exploits in the newspapers which were always accompanied with photographs and often included the officer's biographical details; it made thrilling reading.

With special constables and holders of university degrees being currently considered to join these exalted ranks, this book represents a nostalgic view of those bygone times.

CHAPTER 1

The Stratton Brothers

Throughout this book, the detection of murder by the killer's fingerprints features time and again. The first time that a conviction was obtained through fingerprint evidence was on 13 September 1902 at the Old Bailey, when 42-year-old Harry Jackson – also known as Robert Williams – was found guilty (following an uphill struggle) of burglary after his fingerprints were found on a freshly painted windowsill. The fact that Jackson was stopped in possession of a jemmy and a quantity of property stolen from another house may have contributed to the jury's verdict, and the fact that he was the possessor of five previous convictions may have influenced the judge's decision to send Jackson to penal servitude for seven years.

But acceptance of fingerprint evidence was not cut and dried, not by any manners of means. A letter to *The Times*, from 'A Disgusted Magistrate', read:

> Sir,
>   Scotland Yard, once known as the world's finest police organisation, will be the laughing stock of Europe if it insists on trying to trace criminals by odd ridges on their skins.

Doubtless that appalled Beak would have been happy to rely on blurted-out admissions of 'It's a fair cop, Guv'nor' and hotly disputed property found in the prisoner's possession to secure a conviction, but the fact remained that not everybody was convinced of the reliability of finding fingerprints in a place where an accused person ought not to have been. Three years after Mr Jackson was packed off to Dartmoor for strenuous exercise in the quarry, matters were put to the test when for the first time fingerprint evidence was used in a murder trial.

★   ★   ★

Deptford is situated just south of a 'U'-shaped bend of the River Thames, almost opposite Millwall. By 1905, what had been the shipyard site of the Royal Dock had been transformed into the City of London Corporation's foreign cattle market, which provided employment for the girls and women of the community who butchered the 234,000 sheep and cattle imported annually. Deptford's inhabitants were mainly lower working class; unemployment was low, but wages were meagre.

The local Divisional Superintendent's report stated:

> The conditions of the inhabitants round about was very poor, casual and in chronic want. It was the resort of bad characters and many crimes of a serious nature happened occasionally in the district, and were to be expected.

That report rather sets the scene for the happenings of 27 March 1905.

* * *

The manager of Chapman's Oil and Colour Store at 34 High Street, Deptford, South London was 70-year-old Thomas Farrow, and he and his 65-year-old wife Ann lived in a flat above the shop, whose opening hours were from 8.00 am to 9.30 pm. Every Monday morning, it was the practice of the shop's owner, George Chapman, to come and collect the previous week's takings from Mr Farrow. These takings, which usually amounted to £12–£13 were wrapped in a brown envelope and surreptitiously passed across the counter, an action that would not necessarily have been noticed by any customer who happened be in the shop. But someone *was* aware of it, because it was brought to the attention of two local workshy brothers, Albert Ernest Stratton – also known as 'Ockney' – who was aged twenty, and Alfred, two years older. Neither had a criminal record but they were known to the local police as a couple of layabouts: Alfred, because he was living off the earnings of a pregnant prostitute (who features largely in this account), and Albert, as a merchant seaman who had deserted his ship.

On Monday, 27 March 1905, the brothers arrived at the shop at about 7 o'clock in the morning. Mr Farrow, who was still in his nightclothes, answered the knock on the door and was attacked with a blunt instrument. There were two separate pools of blood; it was clear that Farrow had gone after his attackers, was beaten again and, having received a total of six blows, had been fatally wounded. His wife was struck twice on the head while she was in bed; she lost consciousness, was taken to the Seamen's Hospital but died five days later.

At approximately 7.15 am, the Strattons, having washed their bloody hands in a basin, left the shop and were seen by witnesses, who stated that one of them was wearing a dark brown suit and a cap, the other was in a dark blue suit and a bowler hat. Two of the witnesses were Alfred Jennings, a milkman, and his 11-year-old assistant, Edward Alfred Russell; they saw them leave and slam the door, which flew open again.

'You've left the door open', called out the milkman.

One of the men replied, 'Oh, it's all right. It don't matter', and they both walked off in the direction of New Cross Road.

They were also seen by Ellen Stanton, who was on her way to catch the 7.20 train to London. She saw the two men running from the High Street into New Cross Road; one of them she already knew as Alfred Stratton.

But both had been seen earlier that morning by a professional boxer, Henry Littlefield, who identified Alfred Stratton as being the wearer of the dark brown suit. Littlefield had seen them at about 2.30 am; he knew them both, and Alfred had said, 'Hello, Harry. Out again?' Following some conversation, he noticed that Albert was fumbling with something under his coat and Alfred was looking up and down the street, before they set off in the direction of Farrow's shop. They were also seen about half an hour later by Mary Amelia Compton outside the Broadway Theatre, Deptford. She knew Alfred, and there was some conversation between them; Albert she did not know, but she later correctly picked him out at an identification parade.

After the Strattons had left the shop, two passers-by, Alfred Purfield and Edith Rose Worth, both saw Mr Farrow at the door of his shop, covered in blood and with what was described as 'a vacant look on his face', before he went back inside, shutting the door.

At 8.30 am, the shop's assistant, William Jones, arrived and was surprised to find the front door locked. He looked through a window and saw that chairs had been overturned. Alarmed, he got assistance from the shop owner's assistant, Louis Kidman, and they managed to gain entry and discovered the two victims, whereupon the police and a doctor were called. The first officer to arrive was Police Sergeant 8 'R' Albert Atkinson; he discovered an empty cashbox on the bedroom floor, as well as two facemasks made from ladies' stockings in the parlour. To ensure that the doctor would not fall over the cashbox, he pushed it to one side with his bare hands. Detective Inspector Arthur Hailstone and Sergeant Alfred Crutchett arrived shortly afterwards, the latter carefully moving the cashbox with pieces of paper to avoid getting his fingerprints on it. There was no sign of forced entry, but the matter – murder and attempted murder plus robbery with violence – was so serious that the Yard was asked to attend.

Three heavyweights to the investigation arrived. First was the Assistant Commissioner (Crime), Sir Melville Macnaughton CB, KPM, whose career at the Yard had commenced in 1889; he had been a member of the Belper Committee that examined the use of fingerprint evidence and then, following the setting up of the Fingerprint Department at the Yard on 1 July 1901, he had actively encouraged his officers to be 'fingerprint-aware'. There was a usable print on one of the cashbox's drawers, and this was handed to Inspector Charles Stockley Collins, who had been a member of the Fingerprint Department since its inception. He compared the mark with the fingerprints of both the Farrows and Sergeant Atkinson, but they did not match.

The third luminary from the Yard was Detective Chief Inspector Frederick Fox, who was one of 'The Big Five' referred to in the Introduction. Described rather flamboyantly in the *Daily Mail* as 'an investigator of tragic mysteries', Fox had joined the police on 20 October 1873 and earned a reputation as a fine detective. In 1900 he had overseen a case in which three immigrants had carried out a series of burglaries and had shot and wounded police officers. When the gunmen were each weighed off with eight years' penal servitude, with six and twelve months' hard labour for their receivers, at the Old Bailey on 16 March 1900, Fox and the other officers were commended by Mr Justice Ridley. These accolades were repeated four years later, when Fox arrested two men for burglary after a violent struggle which prompted the magistrate to record on the charge sheet:

> Chief Inspector Frederick Fox is worthy of commendation for a clever capture in a dangerous neighbourhood under difficult circumstances.

It's likely that the Beak's admiration was not shared by James Edwards or James Taylor, who were sent to penal servitude for ten and five years, respectively.

So with Collins returning to the Yard to see if a match could be found for the print on the cash box, Fox got to work to gather together the incoming information.

On 2 April, Alfred Stratton was drinking in the tap room of the King of Prussia pub in Albany Street, Deptford, when he was seen by Detective Sergeant Frank Beavis, who said, 'Alf, we want you'.

He replied, 'What for, Mr Beavis, for poncing?'

'No', said Beavis, and Alfred continued, 'I thought it was for living with Annie.'

'No. Where's your brother?' asked Beavis.

'I've not seen him for a long time', said Alfred, adding, 'I think he's gone to sea.'

Having told Stratton that he would be taken to Blackheath police station, Beavis said it was a very serious charge and Inspector Fox would tell him what it was when he got there. When he was searched, Alfred had a total of 18s 2½d in his possession, and Fox told him he would be charged with the murders, plus stealing money. Alfred asked him what evidence Fox had against him.

'A milkman and his boy saw you and another man come out of the shop at 7.30 on Monday morning', replied Fox, 'and a young woman who knows you saw you and another man running from the top of High Street, Deptford across New Cross Road towards Wilson Street at about the same time.'

Alfred stated that on the morning of the murder he had stayed in bed at 23 Brookmill Road with Annie Cromarty until 9.15 am. Miss Hannah Mary 'Annie' Cromarty – she described herself as 'an unfortunate'[1] who was 'in the family way', courtesy of Alfred, and who was prone to 'take a little drink and had been in trouble about it' – was duly interviewed by Fox the same day; she told him that she could not be sure that Alfred had stayed with her the entire night of Sunday 26 March and that he was fully dressed when she got up. She mentioned that he had previously asked her for an old pair of stockings and that on the morning of the murder she had noticed a smell of paraffin on his clothing – the inference was that this had come from the murder scene. In fact, that was not all she said. She mentioned that on the Sunday – the day before the murder – there was no money in the house. That evening, there had been an upset between her and Alfred, and he had punched her in the eye. After they had gone to bed, at about midnight, there had been a tap on the window, and Alfred had spoken to the person outside; she heard him say, 'Shall we go out tonight, or leave it for another night?'

She was unable to identify the visitor, but Francis Bayne and Rose Wood, who lived in the same house, did – they had looked out of their window and identified the caller as Albert Stratton.

Miss Cromarty had heard about the murder later that morning from a neighbour, to whom she replied, 'Oh! What a terrible thing!'

---

[1] A Victorian euphemism for a prostitute

but Alfred, who was present, had nothing to say. When he acquired an evening newspaper, she read the description of one of the murderers and their clothing and asked, 'Isn't it like you?' to which he replied, 'Do you think I should do such a thing and take you out, and walk about Deptford, knowing I had done such a thing?'

'I shouldn't think so, Alfred,' replied Miss Cromarty, but she was far from convinced.

The newspaper had reported that one of the suspects had been wearing a jacket and boots both of which were brown in colour; coincidentally, since the murder, Alfred had applied black polish to his brown boots, his brown jacket was now missing and when questioned about its disappearance, he said he had given it away. Her suspicions were even more aroused when he told her, 'If anybody asks you where I was on Sunday night and Monday morning, say I was in bed with you and I went to get some work at Braby's at 9.15 and came back at ten.'

She would later take the police to Ravensbourne, a nearby waterworks where she had previously gone with Alfred, who told her there was some money buried there; three or four inches below the surface, the police discovered a piece of material wrapped around two sovereigns and a half-crown.

The following day, Albert was arrested in Deptford High Street by Inspector Hailstone, who told him, 'I am an inspector of police and you must consider yourself in custody for being concerned with your brother Alfred in the wilful murder of Mr and Mrs Farrow at 34 High Street, Deptford and stealing £13 in money.'

To this, Albert replied, 'Is that all?' and Hailstone (who must have been rather surprised at such an offhand response) answered, 'Yes.'

'Thanks', replied Albert laconically and was taken to the police station; both men were fingerprinted, and Collins was able to get an exact match of Alfred's right thumb print with the mark on the cash box.

When Albert was charged, he replied, 'All right.'

On 3 April, Henry Jennings and Edward Russell attended an identification parade at Blackheath Road police station but both failed to pick out the brothers as the men they saw leaving the Farrows' shop on the morning of the murder; however, Ellen Stanton did.

The brothers were charged with Thomas Farrow's murder and appeared at Greenwich Police Court on 3 April, shortly after the identification parade. Alfred told the magistrate, Mr Baggallay, 'If this comes to anything, I suppose we can have a solicitor?'

to which the magistrate replied that this was only a preliminary investigation and there would be ample time to consider questions of their defence, and remanded them for eight days. The case was transferred to Tower Bridge Court, due to the limited accommodation at Greenwich, plus the fact that some forty witnesses would be called.

On 18 April, whilst the brothers were on remand in adjoining cells at Tower Bridge police court, Albert beckoned to Police Constable 357 'M' William Gittings, the assistant gaoler. Gittings went over to Albert's cell door and was asked, 'How do you think I'll get on?'

Gittings replied, 'I don't know.'

Then, referring to Alfred, Albert asked, 'Is he listening?'

'No', replied Gittings. 'He's sitting down, reading a newspaper.'

Albert then made this astonishing statement: 'I reckon he'll get strung up, and I'll get about ten years. He's led me into this, he's the cause of me living with a woman. Don't say anything to him. I shall not say anything until I can see there's no chance, and then . . .'

At that point, he stopped talking and walked around his cell before coming back to the door and continuing, 'I don't want to get strung up. He has never done any work in his life, only about a month and then they tried to put that Brixton job on him but they found out at the time he was at work. I've only been out of the Navy for seven months.'

Gittings did mention this to the gaoler, Police Constable 14 'M' Harry Allchurch, who did not think Albert's statement was 'of sufficient importance to have made a written report of it'. A week later, the matter was brought to the attention of Detective Inspector George Godley. Since he had been DCI Frederick Abberline's right-hand man during the hunt for 'Jack the Ripper' he did decide that those remarks were of 'sufficient importance', and a report was immediately called for.

The witnesses were duly heard, including Sarah Tedman, Albert's landlady, who gave evidence that he and a certain Kate Wade had lodged at her house at 67 Knott Street until the middle of February. Mrs Wade said that Kate's paramour's brother Alfred had asked her if she had any old pieces of stockings; she replied that she had none to give him. At the time the room was vacated, Mrs Tedman had also seen the brothers take from the top of a wardrobe a long chisel and a screwdriver. When this evidence was later given at the trial and was heard by Dr Dudley Burnie, who had carried out post mortems on both Mr and Mrs Farrow, he was heard to say that from Mrs Tedman's description of those implements, they could well have caused the injuries he had found.

After the brothers had left Knott Street, Mrs Tedman discovered three pieces of black stocking under the mattress which – although the term 'a mechanical fit' had not been used by forensic scientists (specifically because there weren't any) – bore a strong resemblance to the masks found at the murder scene. In fact, when she learnt from a newspaper report that stocking masks had been found at the scene, Mrs Tedman informed the police of her discovery.

On 20 April, a coroner's jury returned a verdict of wilful murder against both brothers, and they were committed to the Old Bailey to stand their trial on 2 May before Mr Justice Channell.

Mr Richard Muir (later Sir Richard Muir KC) led the prosecution – he had prosecuted in the case of Harry Jackson and had been an enthusiastic devotee of fingerprint evidence ever since – and was assisted by Mr Bodkin. Mr Curtis Bennett and Mr Rooth appeared for Alfred Stratton, and Mr Harold Morris, for Albert.

The fingerprint evidence was carefully explained to the jury by Inspector Collins:

> I have been employed in connection with the Fingerprint Department since the formation of the fingerprint system in 1901; previous to that I was employed for two or three years on the anthropometric system, which was a system based on certain body measurements and embodied, for part of the time, fingerprints. I have studied the works on the subject by Mr Francis Galton and Mr Henry; so far as I know those are the only works on the subject of fingerprints. At Scotland Yard we now have between 80,000 and 90,000 sets of fingerprints which means between 800,000 and 900,000 impressions of digits. In my experience, I have never found any two such impressions to correspond. In comparing the impressions, we proceed to classify them first by types and sub-types and then by counting and tracing the ridges; that is when we have complete prints of the whole finger. We then compare what are called the characteristics; in my experience, if the type or sub-type or the number or tracing of the ridges differ, they cannot be the prints of the same finger. If those matters agree, we then proceed to compare the characteristics. In my experience, the highest number of characteristics which we have ever found to agree in the impressions of two different fingers is three. That occurred, to the best of my belief in two instances; it may have been three but not more – we have never found as many as four.

He then pointed out eleven points of agreement and stated that the mark on the cashbox was made by Alfred's right thumb; this was confirmed by Detective Inspector Charles Steadman, head of the Fingerprint Department.

This was hotly disputed by Mr Rooth, who said that the case against his client was speculative and that the fingerprint evidence was unreliable. This was backed up by Dr John Garson, who had trained both officers and refuted their evidence. However, Garson was not an expert in fingerprinting but in anthropometry, which was its rival method of identification. During the hearing of the Belper committee, he had spoken out against fingerprinting.

Nevertheless, it was an argument that might have worked, but it didn't, after Muir revealed that Garson had written to the Director of Public Prosecutions and the defence, offering his services as an 'expert witness' to both, depending on who paid him the most, before he had even seen the thumb print.

'How can you reconcile the writing of those two letters on the same day?' asked Muir.

'I am an independent witness', declared Garson pompously, to which the judge replied, 'An absolutely untrustworthy one I should think, after writing two such letters.'

The defence had been advised by Henry Faulds, who disapproved of the way Scotland Yard used fingerprints, particularly when it came to basing identification on a single print. However, after the humiliating Garson debacle, the defence decided not to call him, in case Muir had something up his sleeve which might damage their case even more.

Albert did not give evidence; Alfred did, saying it was 'a put-up job', he had never been in the Farrows' shop and that Cromarty had made up those incriminating statements because he had ill treated her. He admitted meeting Littlefield and Miss Compton in the early hours, but claimed that he and his brother had returned immediately home to 23 Brookmill Road, had slept there the rest of the night and that he had let his brother out, just before 9.00 am, before Miss Cromarty was awake.

Mr Justice Channell summed up impartially, saying that although there were similarities between the two prints, the jury should not rely solely on fingerprint evidence, and he told them that Albert's comments at the police court – an important piece of evidence – were not evidence against Alfred. The strongest point in the prisoners' favour, he said, was that both the milkman and his young assistant had failed to pick them out on the identification parade. Then again, there was the testimony of Miss Stanton, who did . . .

On the second day of the trial, the jury retired for 2 hours 10 minutes before finding both brothers guilty.

Donning the black cap, the judge told them:

> The jury, after a patient consideration of the case have felt it their duty to find you guilty of the crime of murder. For that crime there is but one sentence. I can only implore you to make use of the time which remains to you in this world, for I cannot hold out any hope to you that the sentence will not be carried out. The sentence of the court upon each of you is that you be taken from hence to the place from whence you came and that there you be hanged by the neck until you are dead and may the Lord have mercy on your souls.

With the chaplain intoning, 'Amen', the brothers were led from the court to Wandsworth prison, where on 23 May the hangman John Billington was given two assistants, Henry Pierrepoint and John Ellis, since it was customary in the case of two executions for the same murder for the murderers to be hanged simultaneously.

With their arms pinioned and their legs bound, white hoods were placed over their heads. Albert called out, 'Alfred – have you given your heart to God?' to which Alfred replied, 'Yes.'

It appeared that the Almighty might have been engaged on other business, because while Albert was given a drop of 6 feet 6 inches, which caused death by dislocation of his neck, Alfred, 25 lbs lighter, was given a drop one foot longer. His neck was dislocated, too, but not cleanly as his brother's; Alfred was therefore strangled to death.

Then again, it was more merciful than the death sentence which the brothers had meted out to the unfortunate Mr and Mrs Farrow.

CHAPTER 2

The Man with the Monocle

From the time in 1895 that 15-year-old Harold Dorian Trevor stole and donned a gentleman's outfit, complete with cane and eyeglass, he became known as 'The Man with the Monocle', and he never looked back. He had little to look forward to, either, because in a criminal career that included 45 years' imprisonment, he would experience just eleven months of freedom. He was an opportunist thief and conman who never used violence. His contemporaries and cynical police officers believed he would spend his final days behind bars; instead, to everybody's surprise, he ended them on the gallows.

He affected the air of 'a man about town', attired in morning dress, with a cutaway jacket and striped trousers, white spats, a gold-topped cane and the inevitable monocle. Not that he was known as Mr Trevor, oh dear, no – he was Commander Crichton, Commander Herbert, Sir Francis Ford, Captain Gurney and, on one auspicious occasion, Sir Charles Warren, which was the name of the Metropolitan Police Commissioner.

It was as Lord Reginald Herbert that he arrived at a Windsor hotel; after an expensive luncheon, which he paid for with a dishonoured cheque, he invited the hotel proprietor and his wife to take a drive in his brougham; in their absence, he helped himself to the contents of their cashbox. He used the proceeds to fund a sumptuous dinner with a young actress; when she discovered that the purse was missing from her handbag, she called the police, and Lord Herbert ended up with six months' imprisonment.

He was just twenty-two when he received his first sentence of penal servitude[1] and he was the ringleader of a mutiny at Maidstone Gaol in August 1912 whilst serving a sentence of five years' penal servitude. The prison's governor was obliged to call in troops with fixed bayonets before order was restored.

---

[1] Penal Servitude was a term of imprisonment, ranging from three years to life, which was meant to punish rather than reform. For the first nine months of their sentence inmates were kept in solitary confinement, and then put to work carrying out hard physical labour, usually in quarries. It was abolished in 1948.

On his release, his brother met him at the prison gates and gave him money to go abroad, to avoid further dishonour being placed upon the family; predictably, Trevor used this beneficence to go on a crime spree in London and Brighton, obtaining goods by deception – and as always, with a high degree of savoir-faire.

In 1925, he stole £18 from the apartment of a woman in Tavistock Place; unfortunately, Trevor bore an uncanny resemblance to Major R. G. Shepherd DSO, the Deputy Assistant Director of Ordnance Stores for the London Command, and it was the Major who was arrested after witnesses identified him as the perpetrator. Although fingerprint evidence proved this not to be the case, it led to a court of enquiry held by order of both Houses of Parliament into Major Shepherd's unfortunate arrest. His solicitor demanded that Trevor should give evidence, but the chairman held that his evidence would not be relevant, as indeed it wasn't; it was sheer bad luck that the Major had been pinched, and nothing to do with Trevor. Following a prison sentence for that particular peccadillo, Trevor continued his normal practice of fleecing women hotel proprietors, boarding house keepers and tradespersons (these included his sister), usually at resorts along the south coast of England.

'The Monocle Man' got his comeuppance on 28 April 1936, when he appeared at the Old Bailey for a string of offences involving theft and fraud. At his many court appearances, Trevor inevitably made long and moving pleas for leniency. He did so on this occasion, to which the Recorder, Sir Holman Gregory KC, told him, 'I have listened with sympathy' before sending him to penal servitude for five years.

Released from prison, Trevor made straight for a flat at Elsham Road, Kensington, having discovered that the owner, 65-year-old Mrs Theodora Jessie Greenhill, the widow of an Army officer, wished to rent the flat furnished, since she wanted to move out of London because of the wartime bombing. On 14 October 1941, Mrs Greenhill opened the door to find a tall, grey-haired, distinguished-looking gentleman, complete with monocle, who introduced himself as Dr H. D. Trevor and who seemed to fit the bill of a suitable tenant completely. Having received the first instalment of rent, Mrs Greenhill sat down at the bureau in her drawing room and started writing a receipt. She got as far as 'Received from Dr H. D. Trevor the sum of s– ' before the writing trailed away; it appeared she had spotted Trevor helping himself to a silver cigarette box, and he, realizing that she had observed his larcenous behaviour, hit her over the head with a beer bottle, which shattered. The blow stunned her, and then, as Sir Bernard Spilsbury would later state, a ligature was placed around her neck and she died of strangulation.

Having demurely placed a handkerchief over the dead woman's face, Trevor retrieved his advance, entered the bedroom and with a nail file opened a cash box containing approximately £5. He then ransacked the flat, the contents of which he placed in a large trunk, before getting a labourer outside the flat to hail a taxi for him. From there, he went to King's Cross, where he pawned two of Mrs Greenhill's rings, then made for Birmingham, where he sold the cabin trunk and disposed of more of her property.

Meanwhile, one of Mrs Greenhill's daughters, who lived with her, had left the flat prior to Trevor's arrival; at 12.30 pm she telephoned her mother's number, but there was no reply; at 2.30 pm she tried again, still without success. But another daughter from Mr Greenhill's first marriage, Miss Tattersall, who had been living abroad, made an unexpected visit to the flat. When she received no reply to her repeated knocking, she used a duplicate key to enter, and found her mother's body.

* * *

The officer called from the Yard to investigate the case was Detective Chief Inspector William Abednego (he kept quiet about this second Christian name) Salisbury. Having served as a 2nd Lieutenant with the Royal Field Artillery since 1916, he joined the Metropolitan Police in 1920. He had been a member of the Flying Squad, where he served with Ted Greeno and shared his forthright approach: when the duo chased two burglars into a house, the miscreants attempted to escape through a bathroom window. Greeno pulled them back, and since they'd left their truncheons in their Flying Squad car, Greeno hit his prisoner with a lavatory brush, whereupon Salisbury floored his man with a sink plunger. Salisbury was a brilliant murder investigator – of his sixty-five commissioner's commendations, several were of the rare, and much prized 'high commendation' variety – and he was idolized by the young John Gosling, later to become a Flying Squad officer and one of the originators of the Ghost Squad. However, in this case, Salisbury found he had very little to do.

The sight which greeted Salisbury was of the woman's body, which lay where it had fallen. It appeared that she had not struggled; the pen was still in her hand, and no furniture had been overturned. The bureau drawers were open, and in the bedroom was the forced-open cash box.

Fred Cherrill from the fingerprint branch now arrived. He found the remains of the smashed beer bottle; some fragments were on Mrs Greenhill's head, a few more to the right of the bureau, but most had been gathered up by the murderer and thrown into a waste-paper basket. Cherrill took possession of those fragments – ninety-four altogether – and examined them for fingerprints; he found four. There was a small occasional table close to the body; on its top was a thumb-print made in blood; underneath it was more blood. Another fingerprint was found on the cash box in the bedroom.

And then Cherrill looked at the incomplete receipt and saw the name 'H. D. Trevor'. Of course he knew the name – every copper in London did. But could this be Harold Dorian Trevor, 'The Monocle Man'? If so, it was the first time he had ever used his real name during the commission of a crime. Cherrill immediately sent for all the fingerprint forms bearing the name 'Trevor', and when they arrived, a comparison was made with the prints found in the flat. Within minutes, Cherrill was able to announce to an astonished Chief Inspector Salisbury, 'The man we want is Harold Dorian Trevor.'

Trevor's details were immediately circulated in *Police Gazette*, the Scotland Yard publication sent to every police station in England and Wales, and he was traced from King's Cross to Birmingham and thence to Wales.

He was arrested as he stepped out of a telephone box on Saturday, 18 October in Rhyl, North Wales, and when he was later seen by Chief Inspector Salisbury, he said, 'It was not murder. There was never any intent to murder. I have never used violence to anyone in my life before. What came over me, I do not know. After I hit her, my mind went completely blank and is still like that, now. Something seemed to crack in my head. I would like to tell you all I remember about it when we get back to London.'

Trevor did make a statement upon his return, and after an initial appearance at West London Police Court he was committed from there, on 4 November, to stand his trial at the Old Bailey.

He appeared before Mr Justice Asquith on 28 January 1942 in No. 1 Court, where the facts, as presented by Mr W. L. Byrne for the Crown, were barely in dispute. Mr Derek Curtis Bennett ran a spirited defence of insanity, stating that his client's paternal grandfather had been certified insane and that Trevor's conduct had always been 'strange and erratic', but the following day, he was inevitably found guilty. When asked if he had anything to say before the court pronounced sentence, yes, Trevor certainly had something to say, and any pleas for leniency which he had made hitherto paled into insignificance compared to his rhetoric on this occasion:

> I would like to say, once and for all, finally to say this, that I, as a man who stands, so to speak, at death's door, would like to confirm all I have already said regarding this lady's death, that I have no knowledge of it. Even as I am speaking, the moving finger is writing on the wall and the words, once written, can never be recalled. I sincerely hope that each of you, gentlemen of the jury, and the judge, too, in passing sentence will remember these words – that when each of you, as you surely must, someday, yourself stand before a higher tribunal, you will receive a greater measure of mercy that has been meted out to me in this world . . . if I am called upon to take my stand in the cold grey dawn of the early morning, I pray that God in his mercy will gently turn my mother's face away as I pass into the shadows. No fear touches my heart. My heart is dead. It died when my mother left me.

Trevor knew that the sentence of death was inevitable but thought that by reciting this utter codswallop in ringing tones to a jury, who may (or may not) have listened to it dewy-eyed, the foreman might suddenly blurt out a recommendation for mercy; but he didn't.

With the hangman's noose metaphorically (if not actually) dangling over his head, Trevor appealed on 23 February 1942. It was a disaster. Firstly, the appeal was held before Mr Justice Humphreys, who had participated in the prosecution at a number of notable trials: Oscar Wilde, Dr Crippen, the Seddon poisoning case, the George Smith 'Brides in the Bath' case and the treason trial of Sir Roger Casement; he was pretty well prosecution-minded.

Next, Mr John Flowers KC for the appellant practically threw himself on the mercy of the court by informing them that the instructions given by the appellant to his solicitors and counsel were so erratic that, 'It is difficult to know how to present the matter to the court for his appeal.'

That very morning, said Mr Flowers, Trevor had told him that, as well as his grandfather, he, too, had been certified as insane when he was thirteen years of age in 1893. Flowers added that he felt bound to say that during the interviews held with his client Trevor had appeared quite irrational, before hurrying on to say that the doctor who had certified Trevor was now dead but that his successor probably had the necessary record of the certificate. In addition, said Mr Flowers, evidence could be obtained from the school which he had attended at the time and from the private mental home to which Trevor had said he had been sent. Therefore, he applied for the appeal to be adjourned in order that extra evidence might be called.

With that, Mr Flowers sat down.

Mr Byrne who now appeared for the Crown, as well as having prosecuted the case at the Old Bailey, was informed he need not stand up. It was now the turn of Mr Justice Humphreys:

> At the last moment, without any previous notice, counsel for the appellant is asking leave to call further evidence which might or might not be able to prove something. The verdict of the jury had been the only possible one on the evidence. No one has suggested until this moment that the appellant had been certified as insane in 1893.

Giving the luckless Mr Flowers a withering look, Mr Justice Humphreys continued, 'That matter must be left to those appointed to inquire into the state of a man's mind in such circumstances. The appeal will be dismissed.'

Nowadays, such a request for an adjournment would be unlikely to be refused, but this is now, and that was then. Doubtless, the Appeal Court felt that this was a typical bit of Trevor's manipulative behaviour to string matters out, and he was denied his last chance to deliver an impassioned speech.

It did not preclude him, however, from penning this emotive document from the condemned cell at Wandsworth prison:

> In all the years I spent in prisons, it never occurred to me that I might finish up on the scaffold. Indeed, when I went to Kensington on that fateful afternoon when I killed Mrs Theodora Greenhill, I still thought that I would be able to take my own life.
>
> After having left the flat in which I left her, I drove off to North Wales, where I had spent my boyhood years. At the back of my mind was the idea that I would have a last few days of glorious life, and that then I would kill myself by driving a car right over the edge of the cliffs into the waters of the Atlantic.
>
> Unfortunately fate, in the guise of a special constable, intervened. At a moment when I had already planned to have one more expensive lunch in a North Wales hotel, and then to end my life at sunset, a special constable trapped me.
>
> Still, I have lived my life, not as I would like to have lived it, but as it was forced on me by fate. I was educated at a first-class school in Birmingham and was the friend and playmate of men who are bishops today. Some of them are sitting in the

Episcopal Chairs, while I am facing the short walk from the condemned cell to the scaffold.

But I am not afraid to face death. I am an old man and, as I said to the judge at the Old Bailey, I still sincerely hope that when each one of the jury and the judge stands, as they will one day stand before a higher tribunal, they will receive a grater measure of mercy that has been meted out to me in this world. My life has been all winter and now I am face to face with the sunset.

And with that hypocritical piece of self-pitying whining, that was that. As he approached the scaffold, on 11 March 1942 at Wandsworth prison, he had nothing else to say; it had all been said. When he had apologised to Mrs Greenhill's daughters at the Old Bailey, he flung out his arms in a dramatic gesture and cried in ringing tones, 'If my life can be of any satisfaction to them, then take it!'

A few weeks later, the hangman, Albert Pierrepoint, did just that.

CHAPTER 3

Florence Ransom: Triple Murderess

When female murderers – or perhaps murderesses – in the United Kingdom who have been responsible for the death of more than one person are discussed, Rosemary West immediately comes to mind, because she and her husband Fred were accountable for the deaths of nine young women. There were sexual connotations in that case (as well as torture), as there were when Myra Hindley was convicted, with Ian Brady, of murdering five children of both sexes. Sexual implications did not arise in the case of the nurse Beverley Allitt, but she murdered four children and attempted to kill three others, as well as causing grievous bodily harm to six more, and her victims were both boys and girls. In recent times, there was Joanna Dennehy, who in the space of ten days in 2013 killed three men and pleaded guilty to their murders, plus two other attempted murders.

Missing from the list is the name of Mrs Florence Iris Ouida Ransom, who is largely forgotten nowadays. She did rather better, time-wise, than Ms Dennehy, because 73 years previously, it took her approximately five minutes to cold-bloodedly slaughter three women, one after the other; and unlike all of the other murderesses mentioned, she used a firearm. But perhaps it's not so surprising that Mrs Ransom's name is unknown to many. The case did not receive a great deal of prominence in the newspapers at the time, because the day following the murders in 1940, the Battle of Britain began, and people were more concerned with the prospect of a German invasion and the Luftwaffe's bombing raids. Nobody saw Mrs Ransom commit the murders, there were no forensic clues, she denied being responsible or even being in the vicinity, but the officer who investigated the matter (on his first provincial murder) amassed such a wealth of circumstantial evidence that she was convicted.

The state of affairs which led up to the triple murder are complex, and in some cases bizarre, but if the reader accepts from the outset that Mrs Ransom was as mad as a March Hare, and had previously been an inmate at hospitals and mental homes, it will make matters easier to follow.

★   ★   ★

It may seem odd that the detective chief inspector in charge of the Flying Squad was tasked to investigate a murder in the constabularies, but the reason was that on 9 July 1940, the Flying Squad was still part of C1 Department at the Yard; it would take another eight years before it became C8 Department and therefore completely devolved from C1.

Peter Henderson Beveridge was then the head of the Squad; joining the Met in 1919, following active service in France with the Seaforth Highlanders, he had served in London's East End and West End, as well as doing a stint on the Flying Squad. At half an inch under six feet, the 41-year-old Scot with flaming red hair was as hard as nails and had a wide knowledge of the underworld. He was also a martinet who insisted on his officers wearing hats, saying it would make them look 'more dignified'.

'I'll never wear a hat', retorted one of the more injudicious of his junior officers, at which Beveridge advised him to obtain one by the following day, 'Or I'll get one for you.'

When the bare-headed officer arrived in the office the next day, Beveridge was true to his word and presented him with what was colloquially known as 'a top hat'; in other words a police helmet, to complement his new blue serge uniform. The man, destined to spend the rest of his service pounding the beat, had in fact been quite a good detective, albeit a singularly imprudent one.

So on that July evening at 11 o'clock, Beveridge returned to the office with his friend, Detective Inspector Ted Greeno, only to be told that Captain J. A. Davidson, the Chief Constable of Kent, had requested that an officer be sent to investigate the murders of three women found in an orchard in Matfield, near Tonbridge.

'Good luck, Peter', said Greeno. 'I'll look after the Squad while you're away.'

This was not for long; exactly two months later, Greeno would be promoted to the rank of chief inspector and he, too, would lead a number of successful murder investigations.

Beveridge telephoned Detective Inspector Fred Smeed of the Kent County Police, who provided him with a brief outline of the case, although it was not altogether accurate. Earlier that day, the bodies of 47-year-old Mrs Dorothy Sanders Fisher and her 19-year-old daughter, Freda, had been found in the grounds of their two-bedroom cottage, together with the body of their maid, Charlotte Saunders. They were found by the gardener employed by Mrs Fisher's 80-year-old mother, Mrs Harriet Gibbs. She had been expecting her daughter for tea that day, and when she received no answer to her repeated telephone calls she feared the worst, because of the German bombing raids, and had sent her gardener to investigate. The gardener reported his discovery to the local special constable, who in turn informed Inspector Smeed, and by the time he and other officers arrived, it was 9.15 pm, dark, and the initial inspection had to be carried out by torchlight. Working in those difficult conditions, it was thought – at the time – that the women had been shot in the back with a revolver and that the maid had been bludgeoned around the head.

Mrs Fisher was already known to the local police, because her male friend, a Danish national named Westergart who lived in West London, had been refused permission to visit her since large portions of the South Coast were out of bounds to certain civilians. These included Danes; although Denmark had declared itself neutral at the outbreak of war, on 9 April 1940 it was occupied by Germany. No doubt Mr Westergart was as patriotic as the 1,072 Danish merchant seamen who died in the Allied cause; nevertheless, there were 2,000 other Danes who volunteered to become members of the *Freikorps Dänmark* and fought with the Germans on the Eastern Front, so the Government's exclusion of Mr Westergart was understandable.

Mrs Fisher had been annoyed at the ban on her friend and, what was more, so was her husband, Walter Lawrence Fisher, who had also protested to the authorities. But most important, said Inspector Smeed, was that neither Fisher nor Westergart had been seen by police; therefore interviewing both men was a priority for Beveridge.

He summoned his bag-carrier, Welsh-born Detective Sergeant Bert Tansill, a tubby, single man, then aged thirty-six, who had arrived at C1 one year prior to Beveridge. He had great experience, having been commended on twenty occasions, as well as receiving monetary awards for arresting a whole range of criminals for offences including conspiracy, corruption and drug dealing.

Together with his Flying Squad driver, Police Constable 305 'CO' George 'Jack' Frost, who had joined the Met on the same day as Beveridge and, with twenty years' service with the Flying Squad, was regarded as the best driver in the Force, they made their way to Westergart's address. His shock at receiving the news of the women's deaths was genuine; furthermore, he was able to give an account of his movements on the day of the murder when, he stated, he was nowhere near Matfield, which turned out to be truthful. Having searched his flat, Beveridge could find no trace of a weapon and was able to cross the Dane off his short list of suspects.

But because a blackout had been imposed due to the German air-raids – and because he knew he would have to move fast – Beveridge decided to use his own Flying Squad car and driver, and did so without bothering to inform the Yard. The following day, Superintendent Alexander Bell of C1 Department furiously demanded the return of both car and driver, because officers on provincial enquiries were expected to take a train to their destination and thereafter use a car and driver provided by the host Force.

However Beveridge, hardliner that he was, stuck to his guns and retained both car and driver; besides, he still had to interview the husband, Walter Fisher.

By the time he had finished interviewing Westergart and snatched a few hours sleep, Beveridge was on his way to meet Walter Fisher at Carramore Farm near Bicester, but in the interim he discovered that Fisher left the farm at 8.00 am to drive to Aylesbury, in order to catch the London-bound train to Marylebone station, since he had a business in the capital. Beveridge, having sent a message to stop Fisher's car on the main road, away from the farm, arrived a few minutes later, informed Fisher of the deaths and asked him to account for his movements the previous day, which he did, to Beveridge's satisfaction. It would then be necessary for Fisher to identify the bodies at Matfield, but before doing so, Beveridge asked to have a look round the farmhouse; also to inspect any firearms which Fisher might possess. But as they went through the house, Beveridge saw that in Fisher's bedroom there were two beds with a woman occupying one of them, and Fisher explained that the lady was a friend of his, Mrs Ransom, who was feeling unwell and had decided to stay in bed. Beveridge quickly came to the conclusion that Mrs Ransom's occupation of Fisher's bedroom was prompted by rather more than an ailment.

Tansill remained with Fisher, taking a few notes, while Beveridge strolled around the farm, in police parlance 'giving his eyes a treat'. He gave his ears a treat as well, because he got into conversation with the foreman, who didn't care for Mrs Ransom – whom he referred to as 'Mrs Fisher' – one little bit. She was domineering and dictatorial, he told Beveridge, adding that she had lived at the farm for some time; and this was later confirmed by Tansill's conversation with Fisher. Like any good detective, Beveridge let a possible witness talk about anything and everything; some of the information gleaned would be of no use whatsoever, but other chatter might well hold vital intelligence. So when the foreman told Beveridge that for the past few weeks the cowman had shown Ransom how to fire a shotgun, it was interesting, but that was all;

remember, Beveridge had been told that it was believed two of the victims had been shot with a revolver. And when the servant also mentioned that the woman had been learning to ride a bicycle but was not very good at it, that didn't seem important at all – but in fact, both pieces of information were stored in Beveridge's memory and would become vital to the investigation.

Returning to the farmhouse, Beveridge saw Tansill in conversation with Fisher and was rather surprised to see that he was accompanied by Mrs Ransom, who appeared to have made a remarkably rapid recovery. She was a striking looking woman, aged thirty-four, with a mop of red hair and brightly painted fingernails, dressed in blue slacks and a multi-coloured sweater; not the sort of person who could be easily missed in a crowd. Nothing was said to her about the murders, and as the two officers and Fisher drove off to Tonbridge, the very astute Tansill started talking to Fisher about the Dane, before moving on to the family's domestic details, which Fisher was happy to supply.

Fisher had been a successful businessman and had married Dorothy when she was aged twenty-one and he was twenty-seven, in 1913. It was not a happy marriage, and after the birth of their second daughter, Freda, their relationship broke down and, having moved to Rosslyn Road, Twickenham in 1932, each had taken a lover; in Mrs Fisher's case, the Dane, and in her husband's, Mrs Ransom, whom he met in 1934; she was a widow, and he referred to her as 'Julie'.

Today, such liaisons would be regarded as commonplace but eighty years ago, they were looked upon, in Cole Porter's words, 'as something shocking'. Nevertheless, Mrs Fisher and her lover often stayed at the Twickenham house in what appeared to be an atmosphere of equanimity, and later, Fisher took the cottage, 'Crittenden' at Matfield, and he and Mrs Ransom spent weekends there. Two years previously, the elder daughter, Joan, had married and moved to India, and at the same time, the house at Twickenham was sold; Fisher moved to the farm at Bicester and Mrs Fisher, her daughter Freda and the maid, 46-year-old Miss Saunders, moved into 'Crittenden'. It was all, said Fisher, an amicable arrangement. Matters were made even more complicated by the family's use of nicknames: as well as Mrs Ransom being referred to as 'Julie', Mr Fisher was known as 'Peter' and Mrs Fisher as 'Lizzie' or 'Mrs Kelly'.

So by the time they arrived at Tonbridge police station, Beveridge was in possession of some interesting information. Now that they were alone, Beveridge asked Tansill his opinion of Mrs Ransom.

'A good-looker, but tough', he replied. 'Her eyes are a bit queer – sort of vacant.'

At the murder scene, Beveridge saw the body of Charlotte Saunders. He had originally been told that she had been bludgeoned, but a brief examination revealed she had been shot with a shotgun, as had Freda Fisher, whose body was found 200 yards away in a corner of the orchard. Mrs Fisher, whose body was found 100 yards away in an opposite corner of the orchard had also died from shotgun wounds in the back. Both mother and daughter were wearing gumboots.

Sir Bernard Spilsbury was called to carry out the post mortem, and since the rooms in the cottage appeared to have been ransacked, the services of Superintendents Cherrill from the Fingerprint Branch and Percy Law from the Photographic Section were summoned. But although drawers had been pulled out and correspondence, jewellery and money were scattered all over the floors, it appeared that nothing was missing. And then there was the mystery of the tea-tray, found on the kitchen floor together with broken crockery. When these were pieced together, there were found to be four plates, cups and saucers, and of course, the inference was that Miss Saunders had prepared tea for four people. Would Miss Saunders have taken tea with her employers – or were there two other people calling on the Fishers? Or, in the event that Miss Saunders had been invited to take tea as well – she had been employed by the family for eight years – was there just one visitor?

Meanwhile, roadblocks were set up, ponds dragged looking for the missing weapon, and tramps and gypsies in the area questioned and checked out.

Beveridge gave his imagination free rein as to what had happened, and in all probability – particularly after he had heard Sir Bernard Spilsbury's views on the matter (which concurred with his):'These are not revolver wounds; they were made by gunshot' – he was not far wrong.

First, the murderer was someone well-known to all three women who arrived at the farm with a shotgun and, in all probability, went into the orchard with Mrs and Miss Fisher, ostensibly to shoot rabbits – hence the two women wearing gumboots. When the women were some distance from the house, Freda was shot first, in the back at close range. Seeing what had happened, her mother ran across the orchard, through weeds and grass, and leapt a wide ditch before falling upon a wicker gate and being shot herself, once in the back, then again in the neck. The murderer then returned to where Freda lay, almost certainly dead, but fired two more shots into her side. Then, on to the cottage, where at the back door, the killer came face to face with Miss Saunders, who dropped the tray of crockery and ran through the house and out of the front door. It was likely that Miss Saunders was going to run to the main road to summon assistance, but the murderer must have guessed that that was her intention and ran round to the front door, where Miss Saunders was shot in the head, between the temple and the right ear.

The weapon – a single-barrelled .410 shotgun – had been fired six times. This meant that it had had to be reloaded five times between killings. Between the bodies of Mrs Fisher and her daughter was found a lady's discarded left-hand white hogskin glove, which must have belonged to the killer. This was because when Freda was shot, and her mother ran for her life, the spent cartridge would have had to be extracted from the breech, but since it was such a tight fit it could not be removed by someone wearing gloves, so that glove had been taken off and dropped before reloading. Leaving the glove behind was a mistake on the part of the killer, but it was the only one. The spent cartridges had been gathered up and taken away; they were never found. It was more than murder – it was three cold-blooded executions.

Then there was a yellow bicycle found near the cottage in a ditch on the main road. It belonged to Mrs Fisher – hers were the only fingerprints found on it – and it was slightly damaged. It all seemed to be coming together; Mrs Ransom had been learning how to ride a bicycle – not too well – and had been practising with a shotgun.

The roadblocks and door-to-door enquiries paid off; on the afternoon of the murder, was it Mrs Ransom who was seen on three occasions peering through the hedge into the orchard? The witness, 14-year-old William Smith, described a woman with bright red hair and fingernails to match, wearing blue slacks and a coloured jumper, who was doing just that. That matched the description of a woman given by twelve other witnesses who were in the vicinity that afternoon. There were farm workers, a taxi driver and a ticket collector at the railway station, who stated that she was also carrying a long, narrow brown-paper parcel under her arm and that she boarded the 4.25 pm train to London, after she had been given a lift by a baker named Playfoot, together with his father. She informed father and son that her husband was in the Royal Air Force, her children had been evacuated to Cornwall and her mother was very ill.

And amongst the scattered contents of the cottage were a number of letters between Mrs Ransom, Freda and Mrs Fisher which dealt with a disagreement in June which had strained their relationships. The expressions 'touchy', 'unnecessary' 'peculiar' and 'mental strain' were used, and in a letter to Freda, Mrs Ransom had said that she and Mr Fisher had come to a decision and 'we are fully agreed that you should not come again'.

It was high time to have a word with Mrs Ransom, and at 6 o'clock in the morning of 12 July, Beveridge, Tansill and Inspector Sneed and his wife – she might be needed as an unofficial helper, due to the shortage of women police officers – drove to Bicester to interview her.[1]

But Mrs Ransom was not at the farm; Beveridge learnt that she had been driven to Aylesbury railway station, accompanied by the cowman's wife, Jessie, who was also the dairymaid, in order to see both her doctor and Mr Fisher in London – the same Mr Fisher who, following the interview with Beveridge on the Wednesday, had not returned to Bicester as Beveridge had believed, but had gone straight to London.

In 1940 there were a record number of telephone intercepts – 1,682 of them – granted by the Home Secretary, the vast majority going to Special Branch and the security services. But with the possibility of there being a multiple murderess on the loose, the Home Secretary was persuaded by Superintendent Bell to allot a couple of intercepts to the Flying Squad, and within the hour, Bell informed Beveridge that Mrs Ransom had spoken to Fisher on the telephone. She was very upset, telling him that the police were ransacking the farm, and she arranged to meet him at the York Road exit of Waterloo's underground station at 1.30 pm. Telling Detective Inspector John 'Jock' Black to cover the meet in the eventuality that he was delayed, Beveridge and the other officers raced to London, arriving there just before 1.30 pm. But the phone lines had been buzzing, and Black arrived and told Beveridge that the appointment had been changed to 4 o'clock – and then later, that it had been changed again, this time to 6 o'clock at a solicitor's office in High Holborn – and that Mr Fisher was sounding distinctly worried. He wasn't the only one; during a previous telephone call to the farm, Mrs Ransom had told Jessie, 'Someone's been to the cottage and taken the gun; I must see a solicitor.'

---

[1] Mrs Smeed's attendance was not unusual; police officers' wives often helped out in circumstances such as these. Twenty years previously, Kent's Chief Constable had stated that there was no need for women officers in the county, and at the time of this investigation, out of the 183 police forces in England only 45 employed women officers.

Beveridge entered the solicitor's office right on time, to find Mr Fisher there with the cowman's wife, but no Mrs Ransom who, he was told, was out shopping.

Within a short time, Mrs Ransom did appear, and Beveridge, who was waiting outside in the street with Tansill, politely lifted his hat.

'Mrs Ransom, I believe?' he said, but she denied she had ever seen him before.

This scene was snapped by press photographers, who were told to keep it under wraps because of the question of identification. Taken to the Yard, Ransom made a statement which was a complete denial, both of the murders and that she had been to Matfield. Instead, she said, she had been at the farm at Bicester during the whole of the day of the murder and, what was more, the servants would authenticate it.

But they didn't; and there were a few more amazing disclosures awaiting Beveridge, who told Mrs Ransom that she would be taken to Tonbridge, where she would be put up for identification.

* * *

The first shock came when Beveridge interviewed the cowman's wife, Jessie Guilford, who informed him that her husband Fred was Mrs Ransom's brother. The next came when she stated that the elderly housekeeper at the farm, Mrs Mary Guilford, was Mrs Ransom's mother. These matters were confirmed by the brother and mother; Mrs Ransom denied that she was related to either.

Her brother agreed that he had unsuccessfully shown his sister how to ride a bicycle and how to fire a shotgun. Some three weeks before the murders, and referring to one of the farm hands, she asked one of the servants, 'Is that gun of Dick's (probably a nickname for Fred) dangerous? Would it kill anyone?' and was told, 'Not at a distance. You would have to get close to anybody.'

A few days later, she asked her brother, 'How does your gun work? Would you teach me how to shoot rabbits with it?'

He did so, handed her a dozen cartridges and lent her the gun on 8 July. She returned two days later, telling him, 'Clean it. Be careful to clean it as it's been in the wet.' Asked if she had used all the cartridges, she replied, 'No, I was so scared, I threw them away.'

She participated in an identification parade, together with eight other similarly clothed women and was picked out by several of the witnesses. Although the most minute search had been carried out, both at the murder scene and in Mrs Ransom's belongings, no companion could be found for the discarded hogskin glove found in the orchard. When Beveridge asked her to try the glove on, she replied, 'Certainly, I'll try it, although I think it's much too small for me', but it was found to be a perfect fit.

Remembering the bicycle with slight damage to it, Beveridge asked a police doctor to examine Mrs Ransom to see if there were any signs of an injury consistent with a fall from a bicycle; he found a graze on one knee which could have been due to such a fall.

Then there was the stationmaster at Bicester station, who remembered a woman dressed in slacks and carrying a long parcel boarding the 8.56 am train for London on 9 July and said that she could have reached Tonbridge via London at 12.08 pm. Leaving there on the 4.25 pm train, she should have reached home by 7.00 pm.

On 15 July, one week after the killings and the day after the inquest, Ransom was charged with all three murders by DI Smeed, whereupon she replied, 'I didn't do it! I didn't do it! How could I? No, no!'

On 14 August, after a series of remands at Tonbridge Police Court, Mrs Ransom was committed to the Old Bailey to stand her trial. Originally she appeared before Mr Justice Hallett on 23 September, but Mr Stuart Horner for the defence requested that the trial be adjourned, stating that he wished to have his client examined by a neurologist, adding that he had only been briefed for the case one week previously.

Mr Justice Hallett (who had twice been severely criticised by the Court of Appeal for bad behaviour and advised by Lord Kilmuir that he should retire) was in his usual irascible mood and grudgingly agreed to the adjournment, saying, 'So that no one can be given the least possible chance to say he had not been given every chance.'

The trial at the Old Bailey commenced on 7 November 1940 before Mr Justice Tucker; but at the end of the second day's proceedings, a Friday, something unusual occurred. It had hitherto been the practice to send jurors in a murder trial to a hotel when a weekend intervened – but not on this occasion. New regulations, imposed a fortnight previously, permitted jurors to return to their respective homes over the weekend, owing to the preponderance of air raids.

Mr St John Hutchinson KC appeared for the prosecution and he produced an impressive array of witnesses, including those who had seen Mrs Ransom on the day of the murder. Some had seen her wearing white gloves before the murder; none, of course, had seen her wearing them afterwards.

The firearms expert, Robert Churchill, stated that the gun was heavy, with a stiff trigger and unlikely to go off accidentally; the cartridges fitted tightly and were difficult to extract. Having examined articles of the victims' clothing, he was of the opinion that the gun had been fired at close range, and from the pellets extracted for their bodies, Mr Churchill stated that they could have been fired from the gun which was produced in court.

Mr Fisher told the court that the night before the murder, he had seen a tobacco tin containing cartridges by the side of Mrs Ransom's bed. These fitted a .410 shotgun which he had purchased in Bicester some months previously, at the request of Fred Guilford, and in an adjacent bedroom was a canvas bag containing a gun's cleaning rod. It was Ransom's habit to meet Mr Fisher when he drove into the farm at 6.45 pm, but on the day of the murder, he did not see her until much later, at 8.50 pm. Mrs Ransom came in, distressed, said that she had chased a lost cat, fallen down and bumped her head and had gone to the Guilfords' cottage to lie down. Mr Fisher also stated that she spent the night awake, in the bed next to his. But when she arrived home that night, her sister-in-law stated that she was wearing the clothing so accurately described by the other witnesses.

Her mother described her daughter's behaviour that night as being 'crazy and bewildered' and then provided utterly damning evidence. She told the court that at breakfast time on the morning of the murder, her son had handed her a note from Mrs Ransom. It was in her handwriting and although it had since been destroyed, she remembered what had been written:

> Mrs G:
>   Will you come down and see to Mr Fisher and the farm and don't let anybody on the farm know I am out. I will try to be back before Mr Fisher arrives. If not, I shall be back soon after. Burn this.

Beveridge gave evidence of Mrs Ransom's statement in which she completely denied any knowledge of the murders. In part, this read:

> If there is any doubt about me or any suspicion that I was concerned with the death of Freda or the others, I am willing to do whatever is asked of me. I can assure you, however, that I am not concerned and I do not believe Mr Fisher is, either.

There was only one witness for the defence and that was Florence Ransom. She stated that she had suffered from loss of memory, giddiness and fainting, but she was positive and impressive when it came to cross-examination. She told the jury that she and Mrs Fisher and Freda 'were on very good terms' and denied that the note passed to her mother contained the words, 'Don't let anybody know I am out'. In fact, she added, 'I have never believed that Mrs Guilford is my mother', despite the fact that her own maiden name was Guilford.

After Mr Hutchinson asked her to put on the single glove, she did so but in answer to him asking, 'It fits all right, doesn't it?' she replied, 'Well, it's not a comfortable fit. It's not big enough.'

When Mr Justice Tucker asked her, 'You say you feel quite confident you did not go to Kent on the ninth?' she replied, 'I feel certain I did not. I cannot possibly imagine I could have gone.'

Telling the jury in his summing up for the prosecution that the evidence was 'absolutely overwhelming', Mr Hutchinson said:

> This is not a murder one could do in a moment of excitement. It was one of the most cold, deliberate and, I am bound to say, brutal murders that can be imagined.

In turn, Mr Horner, summing up for the defence, placed an empty cartridge in the gun's breech and said:

> It is not easy to get out, and there were supposed to have been six shots fired. Because a person practised with a gun at Bicester on July 8, and three people were shot with a gun of the same kind at Tonbridge on July 9, it is going a long way to assume it was the same person, especially when it was a woman, who obviously was inexpert with weapons. If it were all thought out with so much care – practising shooting, practising cycling, trying to keep where she was going from other people – do you not think she would have not prepared a really good alibi? Her story has stamped on it the sign of truth. There is not one shred of motive.

The Judge's summing up was completely fair, when he said:

> The prosecution relied upon a glove, but you should not put too much reliance on it, if the case did not rest on a great deal more than that. If, according to Mrs Ransom's story, she saw the 8.27 and 8.56 trains pass, she could not have been in Kent that day. You know that Mrs Ransom is of an hysterical type. She might rightly be described as an unstable type, and there

have been occasions when she suffered from loss of memory. Epilepsy has been referred to but no evidence has suggested that she ever suffered from it. The doctor who saw her on July 12 has not been called, nor the medical man who had opportunity to observe her while she was in prison.

It took just 47 minutes of deliberation on 12 November for the jury to find Mrs Ransom guilty; after the judge pronounced the death sentence, she had to be assisted from the dock, moaning, 'I'm innocent.'

The jury foreman asked the judge if they could be excused jury service for a year; in fact, the judge directed that they would be exempt for the next six years.

By now, the worst of the bombing of London was over, and the newspapers gave a little more prominence to the case, including the charismatic photo of Beveridge making the arrest, but little compassion was generated for Mrs Ransom, despite her courtroom histrionics. The American journalist, Quentin Reynolds, who had watched the trial, wrote:

> Sixteen thousand decent neighbours of mine have been killed since September 7th. Naturally, it was hard to find any sympathy or feel it was important that a half-balanced, degenerate woman had just been sentenced to die.

Her appeal against conviction, on the grounds that the trial judge had failed to give the jury a proper direction with regard to the evidence of insanity, was heard by the Lord Chief Justice on 9 December and was duly dismissed. However, the Home Secretary demanded that a medical enquiry be carried out, and on 21 December, she was judged to be insane, the death sentence was cancelled and she was sent to what was then called the Broadmoor Criminal Lunatic Asylum.

The musical comedy, *The Earl and the Girl* by Seymour Hicks, was first performed in 1903 in London's Adelphi Theatre; it was a tremendous success and ran for many years, both at home and abroad.

On 3 March 1948, a performance of the play was put on by inmates of Broadmoor. The part of Liza Shoddam, the sweetheart of Jim Cheese, a fairground dog trainer, was played by Daphne Brent 'with an aplomb that would have startled many experienced actors and actresses' the *Evening Standard* told its readers, although Peter Beveridge knew Miss Brent rather better as Florence Ransom.

Mrs Ransom was discharged in January 1967, aged sixty, having been incarcerated for over 26 years.

So what was the motive – or was there one at all? It's possible that Mrs Ransom disliked her lover's wife and daughter because they were on harmonious terms with each other; or perhaps she wanted Fisher to divorce his wife so that they could marry. Was Fisher himself involved? He was not there at the time of the murder, that much is certain, but was he aware of Florence Ransom's plans? She was keen to exonerate him from any culpability in her statement to Beveridge, and it's known that Beveridge was unhappy about Fisher, although to what degree it is difficult to say.

But whatever the case, it's interesting to note that Tansill was commended by the Commissioner for the Ransom case, but Beveridge was not. It appeared that Alex Bell had neither forgotten nor forgiven Beveridge's appropriation of both Squad car and driver.

CHAPTER 4

Lorry Ride to Death

George Horace Hatherill was a bit of an oddball; he joined the Metropolitan Police not wanting to become a detective, and for the first twelve years of his service, he wasn't. Then he changed his mind, ascended the ranks and for the last ten of his forty-four years of police service was commander of the Metropolitan Police's Criminal Investigation Department and appointed CBE. This is how it came about.

Born in 1898, Hatherill joined the Army in 1916 and, as a member of Queen Victoria's Rifles, was wounded whilst seeing active service in France. He was snapped up by the Metropolitan Police in 1920, not only because he was tall, at 6 feet $2\frac{1}{8}$ inches, and ex-servicemen were much in demand, but also because he had taken a course of shorthand and typing – and he had a natural aptitude for foreign languages, speaking six of them.

He spent ten weeks as a constable at St John's Wood police station before he was transferred to Special Branch, and there he spent the next twelve years, receiving commissioner's commendations and monetary awards for his work in cracking cases contrary to the Official Secrets Act, as well as spending seven years in Brussels as liaison officer to the Belgian police and security services. But in 1932 he decided he wanted a change of direction and took a four-month course in criminal investigation, before joining the CID as a detective sergeant (first class).

To be fair, Hatherill was no kicker-in of doors, runner of informants or the type of officer (common amongst his contemporaries) who effected arrests by grabbing hold of miscreants by their lapels, with the words, 'Now listen, mister . . .' No, he was a gatherer of sober facts, painstakingly putting together all the jigsaw-like pieces of a case – arson, fraud, forgery, corruption – before making an arrest. He would take his time, not hurrying, until every single possible piece of evidence was in place. For a detective chief inspector with the Yard's Murder Squad, there were some who said he took too long. As the following case illustrates, his critics might have had a point.

★　★　★

On Wednesday, 19 November 1941, two girls – Doreen Hearne aged eight and Kathleen Trendle aged six – left their school in the Buckinghamshire village of Penn at 3.30 pm and started to walk the half-mile home. There was an Army lorry parked at a crossroads, and the girls asked the driver if they could have a ride. This was witnessed by some other children; the girls got into the lorry, which then drove off.

When the girls failed to arrive home, their parents, understandably alarmed at hearing that they had last been seen in an Army lorry, telephoned the police, and searches commenced using the police, local villagers and Boy Scouts.

Four miles away, at nearby Haslemere Lodge, 341 Battery, a unit of the 86th Field Regiment of the Royal Artillery was stationed, and it was there that a local officer, Police Constable Coulson, took one of the girls who had witnessed the children get into the lorry. Asked if she could identify the driver, she looked at a 26-year-old driver named Harold Hill and said, 'That looks like the man.'

The following day, Hill was spoken to by a local inspector, John Tobin. 'I know nothing about the girls', said Hill. 'I saw your officer last night and I spoke to some of the men in the hut, when I returned. I made a remark: "There must be a bloody murderer in this hut".'

However, Inspector Tobin quite rightly told Hill, 'I've not suggested that any murder has been committed' as indeed he hadn't – the bodies had not by then been found.

When questioned about his movements on the day, Hill immediately said to a nearby soldier, 'You saw me at twenty past four' – and that was the exact time the girls had got into the lorry.

But on Saturday, 22 November, the girls' bodies were found in a copse known as Rough Wood, some four miles from the village. By then, the Army unit had moved on, Buckinghamshire police telephoned the Yard asking for their assistance and it was Hatherill who was 'in the frame'.

Telling the local officers to touch nothing at the scene, Hatherill set off the following morning at 7 o'clock with his bag-carrier, together with the eminent pathologist, Sir Bernard Spilsbury, and drove to Buckinghamshire's police headquarters at Chesham.

However, the girls' bodies *had* been moved, to the local mortuary; therefore the officers and the pathologist went first to the scene of the crime, then on to the mortuary, where Sir Bernard carried out the autopsies.

Although death was caused, in both cases, by stab wounds to the throat – in Doreen's case, three to the neck, including a large one which suggested the weapon had been twisted, plus six smaller puncture wounds to her chest; and in the case of Kathleen, eleven wounds to the throat, one of which had penetrated her spinal cord – both had been rendered unconscious by manual strangulation, almost certainly prior to being stabbed.

Sir Bernard believed that the same weapon might well have been used to inflict all the injuries, that it had both a blunt point and cutting edge and that it was five-eighths of an inch wide. Both girls' clothing had been pulled up under their arms, but their underclothing was undisturbed and there was no indication of sexual molestation. In analysing the food in the girls' stomachs it was clear that they had been murdered the afternoon of their disappearance.

Now, back to the scene, where rain from the previous day had left the terrain very soft. The bodies had been approximately 20 yards apart. A sock, identified as Kathleen's, was found hanging from the branch of a tree 4ft above the ground, as was her red leather gas mask case, and a hair ribbon belonging to Doreen was also found.

One of the most important finds was a khaki handkerchief bearing a laundry mark, 'RA 1019'. Close to an area of ground stained with blood were deep tyre marks; it could be deduced that the vehicle concerned had gone on a little way before turning, then stopped at a spot between where the two bodies had been found. In addition, there was a large oil stain, which Hatherill believed had come either from the vehicle's rear axle or one of the wheels. Plaster casts were made of the tyre tracks, and a sample of the oil-saturated soil was also obtained.

Both girls had lost a large quantity of blood – six pints in Doreen's case and four in Kathleen's – so the area was further searched to determine where the murders had taken place; also to look for Doreen's gas mask, which had not then been found.

Three little girls who were witnesses had provided a description of the driver of the lorry, saying that he wore steel-rimmed spectacles; and two boys – one of whom was 12-year-old Norman George Page – gave an excellent description of the lorry. This was a 15 cwt. Fordson, and on its offside front mudguard were the letters 'JP' in blue, joined together in a red circle. There was a figure '5' on the offside front lamp, and on the nearside front mudguard '43' was painted in white in a red and blue square. To complete this excellent picture, Page remembered that there was a Remembrance Day poppy in the top right-hand corner of the radiator mesh.

Hatherill was told that the Army unit had by now relocated to Yoxford, in Suffolk. He had also discovered that steel-rimmed spectacles were standard Forces issue, as were Army knives which had blades five-eighths of an inch wide. He caused enquiries to be made to determine to whom the handkerchief belonged, and travelled from Haslemere to the murder scene, establishing that the distance was fourteen miles. He discovered, late on the evening of Monday, 24 November, that the laundry mark was allocated to one Harold Hill and, pausing only to get a local surveyor to make two large-scale maps of the area, decided to set out for Yoxford the following day – and about time too, one might think.

Hill, as we know, had already been tentatively identified by one of the witnesses and provisionally questioned on two occasions by local officers, making a rather incriminating statement to one of them. Hatherill must have been aware of this, and yet it appeared that he wanted everything neatly put in place before confronting the person who appeared to be the overpoweringly No. 1 suspect.

This was an error, because during the two days that Hatherill spent on the investigation, Hill, who had two convictions for indecently assaulting children, could have deserted and could have molested or murdered other children; thankfully, he did not.

On the Tuesday, Hatherill saw the Commanding Officer of the unit at Yoxford, and a battery commander confirmed that one of the lorries, garaged in a barn five miles away, had a bad oil leak from the rear axle and that its driver's name was Harold Hill. Hatherill inspected the lorry; it was exactly as young Norman Page had described it. A sample of oil was taken for comparison to that found at the murder scene, and the casts of the tyre marks fitted the tyres on the vehicle exactly. Inside the lorry was a tarpaulin saturated in blood.

Hatherill told Hill he was investigating a murder and that he wished to examine his belongings. In his kitbag was a spare uniform, which Hill said he had worn in the rain; in fact, it had been drenched, and Hatherill had no doubt that it had been immersed in water. On the front, back and sleeves of the tunic were spots of blood – also on the trousers. In fact, they were precisely the type of blood spots that one would expect to find if the man wearing them had carried a bleeding child over his shoulder. There were shirts and handkerchiefs in the kitbag; they too bore the laundry mark 'RA 1019'. There was no knife – Hill said he had lost his four months previously – nor were there the steel-rimmed glasses which the children had described; Hill was now wearing tortoiseshell spectacles.

In the vehicle's logbook, Hill's odometer readings on the day of the murder were 4,420 miles at the start and 4,429 by the end. These were authorized journeys. But the following day, 20 November, he carried out two authorized journeys which totalled 29 miles, but the odometer reading concluded at 4,472 miles. Therefore, the extra fourteen miles – the distance from the camp to the murder site – represented a journey which Hill was unable to account for.

Neither, in his statement to Hatherill, could he account for his handkerchief being found in the woods; he thought it might have been returned in somebody else's laundry. He said he had lost his knife about four months earlier. Shown the stains on the tarpaulin found in his lorry, he said, 'It looks like blood', but immediately added, 'I don't admit that it's [the tarpaulin] mine.'

Hatherill saw that the sleeves of his shirt had been shortened at the elbow, and Hill said that they had been torn off at the laundry two months previously – but given the bloodstains on his sopping-wet tunic, it was evident to Hatherill why they had been ripped off – and not at the laundry, either. Hill stated that about two months previously, he had reported the loss of two handkerchiefs to the quartermaster's stores and that on the day of the murder he had gone into the mess, where he had consumed sausages and mash, although he had seen no one he knew there.

Still, Hill was not detained. The next day, Hatherill returned to London, taking the exhibits with him. Doreen's gas-mask case had been found, and it appeared that the case had been wiped to rid it of fingerprints. But a leaf still adhered to it; lifted, a fingerprint was revealed underneath. It belonged to Hill.

The blood on the lorry's tarpaulin was the same group as the murdered girls', hairs were found which were similar to the girls' head hair and, although it could not be grouped, the blood found on Hill's clothing and in the lorry was human. Hill was now taken to Chesham the following day, where he was charged by Chief Inspector Rawlings of the Buckinghamshire Constabulary with the two murders – but Hatherill's enquiries still continued.

He now set about disproving the claims Hill had made in his statement. Had he reported the loss of Army-issue handkerchiefs to the quartermaster's store? The quartermaster and all of his staff were questioned – and the answer was: no, he hadn't. Up until the morning of 20 November – the day following the murder – all of the men in Hill's battery confirmed that he had been wearing the usual steel-rimmed spectacles; but thereafter, he had worn tortoiseshell ones.

Had the shirt sleeves been torn off in the laundry two months previously? No. They were intact up to the night before the murder, said the men who slept in bunks either side of Hill. In fact, one soldier recalled that it was only on the day after the murder that Hill had shortened them.

The Army-issue knife which Hill had lost four months previously? Not so, said two men from Hill's battery – they had lost theirs, so they had borrowed his knife at the end of October and several times thereafter.

Nobody who went to the mess for tea on the day of the murder (and at the time Hill said he went there) could recall seeing him there – nor could they have eaten sausage and mash, as Hill said he did, because that particular delicacy was not on the menu that day, neither was it served for several days before or after the murder.

After thirty-seven witnesses were called for the prosecution at Chesham police court in January, Hill was committed to the Old Bailey, and the trial commenced at on 2 March 1942 before Mr Justice Humphreys. Norman George Page gave evidence that he had attended an identification parade at the camp, and when asked in court if he could identify the driver of the truck, he pointed at Hill and decisively replied, 'Yes.'

The fingerprint department's expert, Fred Cherrill, described finding the fragment of a fingerprint on Doreen's gasmask case, and when he examined the fingerprints provided by Hill at Oxford Prison, he came to the conclusion that the mark on the case had been made by Hill's left middle finger.

When Sir Bernard Spilsbury was handed an Army-issue knife, he told the jury, 'This is just the sort of knife which might have inflicted the wounds.'

The defence was that, firstly, the long statement of denial which Hill had made to Hatherill was true; then, if it wasn't, that Hill was a schizophrenic and if he had committed the murders, he hadn't known what he was doing. A Harley Street specialist was called to say just that, adding that even if Hill had committed the murders he would not have realized he was doing wrong, and that schizophrenics were often responsible for crimes without motive.

This caused Mr Justice Humphreys to explode. 'Murder without motive!' he roared. 'Have you never heard of sadism?'

After a four-day trial, it took very little time for the jury to find Hill guilty of murder, and he was sentenced to death.

At the Appeal Court on 16 April, before the Lord Chief Justice, the Viscount Caldecote, Richard O'Sullivan KC for the appellant stated that 'The bodies showed no sign of interference and the murder was therefore entirely casual, causeless and apparently motiveless.'

The only point of substance in the appeal, stated the Lord Chief Justice, was based on the submission that Mr Justice

Humphreys had failed to direct the jury properly or clearly on the difference between sadism and schizophrenia, leaving the jury with the impression that if it was a case of sadism, it could not therefore be schizophrenia. In effect, the judge had told the jury that sadism (which was probably the explanation of the crime) was not insanity. However, said the Lord Chief Justice, the jury were entitled to come to the conclusion that Hill was in his right mind at the time, there was no defect in the summing-up and the appeal must be dismissed.

Hill was hanged by Albert Pierrepoint at Oxford prison on 1 May 1942.

The case raises some questions. Hill was known to give children lifts in his lorry. Alan Page, then aged eight, had, together with a little girl, accepted a lift from Hill the day before the murder. Speaking in 2002, he said he believed that something might have happened to disturb Hill and that was why they had survived unmolested. This is a possibility.

Secondly, Hatherill took too long before interviewing Hill. He was collecting important evidence, certainly, but timing the distance between the camp and the murder scene and calling for maps of the area were matters that could have been left in abeyance until Hill had been interviewed. That he cobbled together a case that was absolutely watertight is not in dispute; but by delaying matters he could have put other children's lives in jeopardy.

Hatherill later stated that it was not a particularly difficult case to solve, and that was true. However, that was due in no small way to 12-year-old Norman Page, who had been evacuated from London to Penn during the Blitz and whose keen eyes had put Hatherill on the right track, right from the commencement of the enquiry.

At the conclusion of the case, and complimenting Page on being 'a clever boy', Hatherill suggested, 'When you grow up, you ought to be a detective.'

Instead of offering blushing, stammered thanks for these kind words, the streetwise Master Page crushingly replied, 'What, me? Sit on my arse doing nothing all day? Not bloody likely!'

CHAPTER 5

A Very Imprudent Letter

Suffolk, like Norfolk (as Noël Coward observed), is 'very flat', and therefore it made perfect sense that the last airfield to be built during the Second World War was at Ellough, near Beccles, Suffolk, the most easterly aerodrome in wartime England.

Opened in 1943, RAF Beccles (Ellough) – known locally as Ellough Airfield – was initially intended for use by the American Air Force, but for whatever reason, it was never used by them, and from October 1944 until October 1945 it was the home of three RAF squadrons as an Air-Sea Rescue post. The station personnel were accommodated in eight sites, of which Site 7 was used by the Women's Auxiliary Air Force (WAAF) and included a designated ablutions block.

On the evening of 8 November 1944, Winifred Evans, a 27-year-old member of the London (Harlesden) WAAF attached to the station, had returned with her friend Corporal Margaret Johns from a dance held at an American air base near Norwich. It was now midnight, and Miss Evans changed into uniform since she was to go on duty as a radio operator at the signals office situated in the administrative site in Sandpit Lane. She was late; her shift started at 11.30 pm, but another girl was covering for her. Corporal Johns asked if she would be all right, and Winnie (as she was known to her friends) replied that she would and set off, using the beam from a borrowed bicycle lamp to light her way.

The next person she met – at the spot which locals would later refer to as 'Murder Lane' – would be her killer.

Her body was found by Claud Ernest Fiske, an electrician (and special constable), who was cycling to work at 8 o'clock the following morning. He informed the local police; they in turn lost no time in contacting Scotland Yard. Suffolk Constabulary simply did not have the resources or expertise to interrogate the 2,694 personnel at the base, or the 200 Italian prisoners of war incarcerated nearby. The next officer 'in the frame' at Scotland Yard's Central Office to be sent on a major enquiry was Detective Chief Inspector Ted Greeno.

* * *

As a murder investigator, Greeno was something of an anomaly. Murders then were investigated by officers of the rank of chief inspector; usually, in the rank of detective sergeant, those officers had been bag-carriers to their seniors, learning all the tricks of the trade – but not in Greeno's case. Joining the Metropolitan Police in 1921, this brawny young pugilist, who possessed an excellent knowledge of the denizens of the underworld, was quickly conscripted into the Flying Squad and rose through the ranks, staying there for the next seventeen years.

Having been promoted to chief inspector in 1940, this was Greeno's introduction to the world of murder investigation. With the traditional Flying Squad officer's unconventional flair, Greeno followed his friend Peter Beveridge's lead: he used his own car, pausing only to pick up Professor Keith Simpson from his Marylebone flat in Weymouth Street, and drove the 125 miles to Beccles. Since a cold south-easterly wind, accompanied by snow showers, was cutting across his route along the A12, the trip took ten hours, so possibly it would have been easier (and quicker) to have taken a train, even though they were not noted for their punctuality in wartime.

The reason for conscripting Simpson at such an early stage was that during the 1940s pathologists still dealt with fibres, blood, hair, dust and other items found at the scenes of crime; later, these matters would be dealt with by the police laboratories. Besides, the two men had worked together before, especially in the case which became known as 'The Wigwam Murder', and each admired the other's abilities.

It was close to midnight when they arrived at the scene; the snow had settled, but the body had not been moved and had been covered with a tarpaulin. Life had already been pronounced extinct by the police surgeon, Dr H. Grantham-Hill, who had noted that around the victim's neck was a tie, in a sailor's knot, and it appeared that 'she had been subjected to tremendous violence'. Examination at the scene revealed that Aircraftwoman 1st Class Service No 2143847 Winifred Mary Evans was lying face down in a ditch. Her greatcoat, tunic, shirt and vest had been drawn up over her shoulders; her slacks, knickers, suspender belt and a sanitary towel had been pulled down.

As Greeno set off to interview the commandant of the Italian PoW camp, to establish whether any of his inmates were missing, the body was removed to East Suffolk and Ipswich Hospital, where at 2 o'clock in the morning an autopsy was carried out by Simpson and his old friend, Dr Eric Biddle, the county pathologist.

The initial injuries were bad enough; the rest were frightful. Her lower lip had been split against her teeth, her nose was grazed and there were abrasions on her chin, neck, right breast and the back of her right hand. There were numerous very fine scratches across the right side of her face and hand; Simpson deduced that these could well have been caused by thorn bushes growing by the side of the ditch. There was nothing to suggest a preliminary struggle; it appeared she had fallen on her right-hand side and then either rolled (or been pushed) on to her face and held down with great force; that had caused the split lip. Her attacker had violently knelt on her, under her right shoulder blade, with such force that her liver had ruptured, causing a haemorrhage into the stomach.

She had then been sexually assaulted with great force; her vagina had been torn and she had been anally raped. And yet none of these terrible injuries had been the cause of death. She had suffocated, as a result of being forced face-down in the mud. Simpson concluded that she had died 24–36 hours previously – and no one had heard or seen anything; except, of course, the killer.

But whoever the perpetrator was, he must have been covered in blood, as well as material from the surrounding countryside, plus hair and fibres from the dead woman's clothing. What was of paramount importance was to find the man responsible. Initially, that appeared to be easier than might be thought possible.

*   *   *

As Winifred Evans set off along that dark road, never to reach the signals office nine-tenths of a mile away, so her friend Corporal Johns went to the ablutions hut, turned on the light and was surprised – and probably not a little perturbed – to see an airman there. He had been drinking.

'What are you doing here?' asked Corporal Johns sharply.

'I'm lost', replied the airman. 'Is this No.1 site?'

'No, this is the WAAF site – get out', she replied.

'Will you show me the way out?' asked the airman. 'I'm drunk and I can't see', and with that, he lurched against the door.

Corporal Johns left the ablutions block and pointed out the road to him; the same route that Miss Evans had just taken.

But then the airman moved towards the corporal. 'Can I thank you?'

Clearly, Miss Johns had a shrewd idea of the type of gratitude he had in mind, because she replied, 'No. Get down the road.'

This incident seemed so pertinent that, following the discovery of the body, Corporal Johns immediately informed the police.

Later that morning, a pay parade was being held; it was attended by Detective Constable Bedingfield from Lowestoft police station, Greeno and Corporal Johns, to attempt to identify the airman she had seen several hours previously. This was the fairest type of identification parade imaginable; it was not a case of a witness attempting to identify a suspect from a line-up of a dozen men; here there were several thousand men on parade, all in uniform. The identification was supposed to be a clandestine affair, with the suspect having no prior knowledge that anything of the kind was happening; so perhaps it was slightly surprising that, instead of waiting in the section for personnel whose surname began with the letter 'H', Leading Aircraftsman Arthur Heys slipped out of that queue and joined those whose surnames commenced with the letter 'R'.

Not that it made any difference; he was immediately identified by Corporal Johns, and Detective Constable Bedingfield took him to Beccles police station for an interview with Greeno.

* * *

Whenever his authority was challenged, at a pub, a club or in the street, off would come Greeno's jacket, an impromptu ring made up of spectators would be formed, and Greeno's ill-advised adversary would receive a pasting for his impudence. At racetrack meetings, Greeno would single-handedly confront up to fifty of the worst gangsters and tell them to 'Clear off!' – and generally, they did. On one occasion when a particular gangster demurred, Greeno found himself in a quandary; the next day was the start of his annual leave, and if he now arrested this impudent rascal, the regulations demanded that he would have to take him to court. So Greeno compromised; he simply placed his ham-sized fist under the miscreant's nose. 'Are you getting off this track?' he asked, and the racetrack gangster, the error of his ways having been duly pointed out to him, took Greeno's advice and 'cleared off'.

But whatever may have gone on before his appointment as chief inspector, rough-house tactics could not feature in a murder investigation. The sole purpose, Greeno knew, was to get at the truth, so while two local officers stepped in, Detective Constable Brown taking possession of Miss Evans' clothing from the hospital, and Detective Sergeant Long gathering up Heys' kit from the camp – his tunic was hanging on a line over the bed, his trousers were beneath the mattress – Greeno invited Heys to give an account of his movements the previous night.

At thirty-seven, Heys was probably the oldest of the airmen in Hut 28 on No. 3 Site. He was married, with two sons aged eleven and thirteen and a daughter aged ten. The previous night, he told Greeno, he and his colleagues either walked or cycled into Beccles to go to a dance at the Pavilion. It was also a chance to have a beer; in Heys' case, eight pints of mild and bitter. The dance finished at 10.45 pm and the airmen returned to the camp, but not Heys. He had mislaid his bicycle and he reported its loss at Beccles police station. In fact, in his befuddled state, he had probably forgotten where he had left it, since it was later found in the road where he told the police he had last seen it. He then walked back to the camp; he admitted straying into the women's ablutions block by mistake but, sticking to the main road, he had returned to camp at about 12.30 am. And that was that.

No, it wasn't. Greeno believed that Miss Evans must have been attacked at about 12.20 am, because if she had continued walking, she would have reached the signals office by then. And if Heys had walked the road as he said he did, even though he had had quite a lot to drink, he would have covered the 900 yards to camp by 12.20 am.

Greeno looked him over. There were scratches on the back of his hands which Heys said had been made by a pair of dividers, a day or two before. But scratches made by dividers run in parallel lines; these didn't. They looked fresh and they could have been made by contact with a thorn bush – the sort of scratches sustained by Miss Evans. Greeno later spoke to the police officer who had recorded the details of Heys' lost bicycle an hour before Miss Evans' death; the officer was certain that at that time there were no marks or scratches on Heys' hands.

Inspector William P. Bryant had found a jigger button from a service greatcoat at the scene. Heys' was missing – so was Miss Evans. Did it belong to Heys? If it did, that was an important piece of evidence, but there was no way of checking; all government-issue jigger buttons were identical.

Next, there was a recent tear in Heys' greatcoat; it could have been made by the barbed wire next to the ditch where the body had been found.

On his coat – and on Miss Evans' slacks – were found rabbit hairs.

Under the instep of his shoes was red, brown, beige and yellow brick rubble; just like the debris found on Miss Evans' shoes, and just like the detritus at the bottom of the ditch, where her body had been found.

Was there, asked Greeno, any blood on his clothes? There might have been, responded Heys, just a spot or two from a wound he had sustained twelve months earlier. Next, Greeno made him roll up his trousers; there were bruises on his knee and shins; but they were old bruises, said Heys.

Well, that was what Heys said. What did anybody else say?

Corporal Johns said that in the ablutions block Heys had asked if he was at No. 1 Site. But why would he say that? He was billeted at No. 3 Site.

Therefore, it would be important to know what the other occupants of Hut 28 had to say. Some of them had walked back from the dance in Beccles, some had cycled, although all had returned by 11.00 pm. Heys had told Greeno that he had returned to the hut by 12.30 am – not so, said the other airmen. Leading Aircraftman Victor Redmonds was one of those who said that Heys had returned between 1.00 and 1.30 am and did not switch on the light. Instead, he had undressed by the light of a torch. Several of them noticed that his shoes were unusually muddy; but that would not have been the case if, as Heys had told Greeno, he had remained on the main road. Usually he would have accompanied his colleagues into breakfast; but not that morning. He had stayed in the hut, sponging his clothes with a towel and a wet rag. Because of wartime austerity measures, fires were expressly forbidden until 4.00 pm; and in any case, there seemed no point in lighting one, since Hays was going on duty at 8.30 am. But he obviously thought there was, because at 8 o'clock that morning, Heys did light a fire in order to dry his clothes; and into the fire went that rag.

During the afternoon when Miss Evans' body had been found, Heys cycled past the ditch where her body still lay; but, as LAC Redmonds told Greeno, although the whole topic of conversation in the hut was about the murder, Heys did not participate in it. But, Redmonds added, he did notice fresh scratches on the backs of Heys' hands.

There were a lot of oddities and inconsistencies in Heys' story, but they were not sufficient to detain him, let alone charge him; so Greeno let him go.

What was Professor Simpson up to? He inspected Heys' assiduously cleaned, sponged and pressed tunic and trousers. However, Heys had not been as thorough as he might have wished; there were traces of mud on both sleeves of the tunic and stains on both tunic and trousers which gave a positive reaction for human blood; but these extracts proved too weak for grouping.

Simpson was less impressed than Greeno had been with the debris found on Heys' shoes. 'There are common features of a too everyday character', he told Greeno, adding that in any forthcoming cross-examination he would have to say so. Greeno refused to discard his own pet theories about the brick-dust. He toured the camp and the countryside, looking to find identical debris; he couldn't. Next, he collected Heys from the camp and drove around the area, telling Heys to direct him to every road, pathway or lane that he had visited since arriving in Beccles, to determine if there was any similar brick-dust anywhere; there wasn't. Greeno retrieved Heys' shoes – some dimwit had actually returned them to him – and by now, they had been really cleaned and polished. However, there was still some tell-tale debris in the seams above the heels. It was clear that Greeno was becoming fixated with what still clung to Heys' shoes; it was not damning proof, but it was something which certainly could be added to the melting pot of what would become circumstantial evidence.

*   *   *

Despite Simpson's misgivings regarding the lack of strong evidence surrounding Heys, Greeno thought there was a sufficiency of it; so did the Director of Public Prosecutions. On 5 December 1944, Greeno took Heys to Beccles police station, where he told him, 'I am not satisfied that you have told the truth with regard to your movements on that night. You will be detained in connection with that murder.'

After being cautioned, Heys spent four or five minutes looking at the floor before saying, 'I've been thinking. I can't see what evidence you have to convict me. Can't you tell me?'

'No, not at this stage', replied Greeno. 'You must be detained.'

It was always policy for a local officer to prefer a charge; that was done by Detective Inspector Read, and after being cautioned, Heys replied, 'I didn't do it.'

As in all murder cases, when an accused person charged with murder was detained at the police station overnight, a police officer was always in the vicinity to (a) thwart any possible suicide attempts or (b) to jot down any suddenly blurted-out confessions.

Heys was neither suicidal nor desirous of divulging any incriminating statements; however, he was pensive. At 11.45 pm that evening, he said to Police Constable Harold Squire, 'I wonder what clue they have got? They must have something.' PC Squire replied that he was not in a position to discuss the case and reminded him that he was under caution, but it appeared that Heys wanted to discuss the matter. Ten minutes later, Heys asked, 'What time did the murder take place?'

PC Squire replied, 'I don't know', to which Heys said, 'I have seen by the papers that it was around half past twelve. I was there, round about twenty past twelve.'

It appeared that Heys felt he might have said a tad too much, because he immediately followed this up by saying, 'I didn't ought to have made a statement at all. Let me see: it's one, two, three, four I've made.' He later said, 'Chief Inspector Greeno took six hairs from my head. If any of them are found on her clothing, how am I to prove he didn't put them there? If there is any evidence against me, it's faked by the police.'

Greeno had indeed taken hair samples from Heys. And in addition to the rabbit hair found on the clothing of both him and his victim, Simpson found ten head hairs from Heys' clothing. Four of them could not have come from Heys but four were identical with those found on the body of Miss Evans; a similar hair was found in Heys' hairbrush. Greeno sent Detective Inspector Read of Beccles CID to 22 Harold Street, Colne, Lancashire, which was Heys' home address, with instructions to tell Mrs Heys what was happening in the case, to sympathise with her – and to pat her on the head. 'Make sure you come away with a sample of her hair', was Greeno's unequivocal instruction – which was what Read did. Simpson's analysis revealed that the hair from Mrs Heys' head was identical with the four hairs found on the body of the dead girl; and the one found in Heys' hairbrush.

Following a brief appearance at the Magistrates' Court, Heys was remanded in custody at Norwich Prison.

Greeno had done his best. He had traced all five drivers on the road at the time when Heys had said he had walked on the night of the murder – none had seen him. He had measured the distances from Site 7 to Sandpit Lane, the Administrative Site and to Site 1, and had timed how long it had taken for officers to walk those routes.

Anything else? Not really. Heys had carried out watch repairs for some of the other airmen and had provided hand-written receipts for them – so what? They certainly had no connection with the case – but Greeno hung on to them, anyway. In fact, detectives would often keep hold of items which appeared to be unconnected with their investigation; they could always be returned, or disposed of, after the case was concluded.

However, in this case, it was a prudent move.

★   ★   ★

Committal proceedings to the County Court of Assize were fixed for 10 January 1945, to determine if there was a sufficiency of evidence for the defendant to stand trial. And then, round about 5.00 pm on the evening of 9 January, there was a bombshell. Greeno received an urgent telephone call from the airfield's adjutant that had him racing to the camp. The officer commanding showed him a letter which he had received in the 4.30 pm post. It was dated 7 January and had been posted in Norwich at 8.30 pm the following day.

Both the envelope, addressed to 'Officer Commanding Air-Sea Rescue Squadron, Beccles, Suffolk', and the anonymous letter it contained were written with a blue crayon in block capitals, as follows:

SIR, WILL YOU PLEASE GIVE THIS LETTER TO SOLICITORS FOR THE AIRMAN SO WRONGLY ACCUSED OF THE MURDER OF WINNIE EVANS AT BECCLES RAF STATION.

TO WHOM IT MAY CONCERN: I WISH TO STATE THAT I AM THE PERSON RESPONSIBLE FOR THE ABOVE-MENTIONED GIRL'S DEATH. I HAD ARRANGED TO MEET HER AT THE BOTTOM OF THE ROAD WHERE THE BODY WAS FOUND ON THAT WED. AT MIDNIGHT. WHEN I ARRIVED, SHE WAS NOT THERE. I WAITED SOME TIME AND DECIDED TO WALK DOWN THE ROAD TOWARDS THE WAAF QUARTERS. JUST BEFORE I REACHED THE LATTER I HEARD VOICES AND STOOD CLOSE IN THE HEDGE. ON MY LEFT, I HEARD FOOTSTEPS APPROACHING FROM THAT DIRRECTION [sic]. IT PROVED TO BE AN AIRMAN; I DON'T THINK HE SAW ME. I THEN SAW THE DARK FIGURE OF SOMEONE ELSE COMING THE SAME DIRECTION. AS SHE GOT NEAR, I RECONNISED [sic] IT WAS WINNIE AND I SPOKE TO HER AND WE PROCEEDED TOGETHER TOWARDS THE ROAD, WHERE WE AGREED TO MEET. SHE SAID I SHOULD NOT HAVE COME DOWN THERE TO MEET HER. A WAAF FRIEND ASKED TO COME ALONG WITH HER AS THE AIRMAN AHEAD WAS DRUNK AND LOST HIS WAY.

SHE HAD HER CYCLE LAMP. NO ONE WILL EVER FIND THIS. WE STOPPED AT THE ROAD LEADING TO THE S.S.Q. SHE TOLD ME SHE COULD NOT STAY LONG BEING NEARLY HALF PAST TWELVE.

SHE SHOULD HAVE BEEN ON DUTY. SHE ACCEPTED
MONEY FROM ME WHICH I GOT BACK, FINDING
SHE WAS UNCLEAN. THIS IS THE TYPE OF GIRL
SHE WAS, A GOLD DIGGER. I HAVE KNOWN HER
TO GO WITH THREE YANKS IN ONE NIGHT. I MUST
HAVE GONE MAD. I DON'T REMEMBER EXACTLY
WHAT HAPPENED. I KNOW WE STRUGGLED AND
I TORE HER TUNIC AND SLACKS AND BELIEVE
OTHER THINGS AND I WAS MOST INDECENT. A CAR
CAME UP ALONG THE ROAD GOING TOWARDS THE
AIRFIELD; I THEN LEFT, IT MUST HAVE BEEN AFTER
1 A.M. SINCE THEN I HAVE COVERED UP MY TRACKS
AND GOT RID OF ALL MY CLOTHING WHICH
WERE COVERED WITH BLOOD DOWN THE FRONT
AND WILL BE GOING OVERSEAS SHORTLY. PLEASE
CONVEY MY HUMBLE APOLOGIES TO THE AIRMAN
CONCERNED – R.C.A.E.

Greeno simply smiled. Now, there was absolutely no doubt at all that Heys was the killer, and that it was he who had written this letter. All he had to do was prove it. But not at the committal proceedings the following day, no, not likely. There was quite a bit of work to do before this piece of evidence saw light of day.

★   ★   ★

On 10 January 1945, committal proceedings opened at a special court in Beccles before the magistrate, Mr H. W. Blower. The Director of Public Prosecutions was represented by Mr H. J. Parham, and Mr F. T. Alpe appeared for Heys.

The evidence of thirty-one witnesses was heard, twenty-three of them 'live'. In outlining the case and calling the witnesses, Mr Parham stressed certain points: why had Heys asked Corporal Johns if he was at No. 1 Site, when in fact he was from No. 3 Site and had nothing to do with No. 1?

Leading Aircraftsman Reginald A. E. Hunter stated that some days after the murder, Heys had told him that when the murder took place he must have been at a corner 30 yards away and that visibility was only half that distance; however, he had not heard any screams.

The County Pathologist, Dr Biddle, gave interesting evidence which was slightly at variance than that of his colleague, Professor Simpson, whose evidence was given by statutory declaration.

Dr Biddle stated that he had found no foreign human hairs on any of Miss Evans' clothing. On 13 December, he took a blood sample from Heys which revealed that it was of a group completely different to Miss Evans'. Out of a very large sample of hairs taken from Heys' clothing, four were identical with samples taken from Miss Evans' head; however, he stated they were of a common type and not very distinctive. On one of Heys' clothes brushes he found a hair similar to that of Miss Evans. Dr Biddle noted that Heys' jacket and trousers appeared to have been recently sponged and pressed and that a bloodstain appeared to be of the same group as that of Miss Evans. In addition, material found on the shoes of both victim and accused was similar to that on the ground where the body had been found.

In cross-examination it was put to Dr Biddle that the hairs from Miss Evans' head were similar to those of 'thousands of other women' and the results of the tests were 'suggestive but not conclusive'.

Nevertheless, the Magistrate decided there was enough evidence to commit Heys for trial at the Suffolk Assizes at Bury St Edmunds, to commence on 19 January; Heys pleaded not guilty and reserved his defence.

Greeno had less than two weeks to get his case firmed up.

*   *   *

Now let's take a look at the anonymous letter.

Obviously, it had been written by the man who had committed the murder. There was the reference to the WAAF friend who had offered to accompany Miss Evans – either overheard by Heys in the latrines or told to him by her, prior to the attack. 'The airman ahead was drunk'? Again, only Corporal Johns and Heys knew that, as they did that the airman 'had lost his way'. The fact that the letter was addressed to the O. C. of the Air-Sea Rescue meant that it must have been written by one of the personnel at that base, since its designation was secret – outsiders would refer to it as No. 3 Squadron. Only Corporal Johns, Miss Evans and the killer knew of the existence of the cycle lamp. The killer stated, 'No one will ever find this', and he was right; nobody ever did. He mentioned that 'she was unclean', and again, this was something only the killer would know; Miss Evans had been experiencing her menstrual period and was wearing a sanitary towel, but this detail had not been released to the press.

There was an attempt at justification in the letter: 'I have known her to go with three Yanks in one night.' This was nonsense. The victim's parents, William Henry and Eliza Winifred Evans, were too distraught to attend the court proceedings, but John

Albert Roberts, Winnie's brother-in-law, did and described her as 'rather a reserved type'. In fact, she had been a virgin – until that night when she was brutally raped and her hymen had been ruptured.

Now – back to the letter itself.

Greeno went to the prison, where he found crayons similar to the one used. And although the letter had not been sent via the prison authorities, men from the War Agricultural Committee drove prisoners to work on the farms. Not that Heys was amongst them, of course, but one of the drivers admitted posting letters for prisoners, and Heys was not as sedulously watched as he would have been in a London prison. He exercised in the yard with other inmates and obviously had given one of them the letter to be passed on and posted.

That much was obvious; but now it was of paramount importance to prove that it was Heys who wrote the letter.

Greeno wanted a sample of Heys' handwriting. There were the misspellings: 'dirrection' and 'reconnised' – how would Heys spell those words at Greeno's dictation? He would never find out. On being asked, Heys demanded an urgent telephone call to his solicitor, and it's easy to imagine the gasp of shocked incredulity at the other end of the telephone line: 'Absolutely not!'

The Metropolitan Police's Laboratory set up its Questioned Documents Section in 1968, although like many examples of forensic evidence, these were open to interpretation.

From my experience of them, the Forensic Document Examiners could be evaluated as either brilliant or tragic. An example of the former was when, after examining known writing with a questioned document, the conclusion reached was that the suspect had written the questioned document, 'to the exclusion of anybody else'. It was sufficient for the suspect, who had refused to answer any questions whatsoever, to plead guilty.

On the other hand, another examiner looked at two documents and told the court that whilst there was a very slight possibility that the accused person in the dock had written the questioned document, it was far more likely that I had forged his signature! This brought howls of delight from the prisoner, gasps from the jury and a sharp intake of breath from yours truly. Fortunately, there was other evidence for the jury to consider, and after the prisoner was convicted and sentenced to eight years' imprisonment, his mood was less ebullient than previously.

The point I'm making is that handwriting analysis was still an imprecise science, and at the time of the Heys investigation no experts were marshalled at the Yard's Forensic Science Laboratory to come out and support their detective colleagues. However, Greeno knew someone who might fit the bill.

Fred Cherrill has already been mentioned in this book; it's time for a closer look at him. He joined the Metropolitan Police in 1914 and after six fairly unspectacular years as a police constable, he volunteered for the Yard's Fingerprint Branch. He had always possessed a fascination with fingerprints and he took to the work with great enthusiasm; during the next thirty-three years he rose to the rank of detective chief superintendent and collected many commendations and monetary awards for his work. He was also a complete pain in the arse.

Cherrill was an expert, absolutely no doubt about that, and he was infallible regarding identification. He was also insufferably pompous and condescending; as soon as he reached the rank of detective inspector, he was permitted to wear a bowler hat – it stayed with him for the rest of his career; junior ranks were only permitted to wear trilby hats. An example of his self-importance may be seen in his cameo role as a fingerprint officer in Basil Dearden's 1949 film, *The Blue Lamp*, following his examination of the getaway car used to convey the killers of PC George Dixon. It was not very different to his portentous, magisterial statements in court; his word was law, and the defence lawyers trembled.

So how could Cherrill assist in this case? Even if there had been fingerprints on the anonymous letter, they would not have been of assistance; it was not until 1954 that Swedish investigators discovered that the ninhydrin process of immersing a document into a poisonous-looking purple solution could be used to develop latent fingerprints. However, it was also Cherrill's assertion that he was a handwriting expert.

He examined the letter; he compared it with applications made by Heys for leave; he also compared it with one of the watch-repair receipts retained by Greeno, which at the time were thought to be of no evidential value whatsoever. Now they were.

Heys had written, in block capitals in an instruction to a watch repairer, 'HAIR SPRING STRAITENING' leaving out the 'GH' between the 'I' and the 'T', and Cherrill noted strong similarities between the 'P' in SPRING and the 'P' in the letter – on fifteen occasions. These were also compared with the writing included in Heys' applications for leave, and they were identical.

* * *

The trial commenced at Suffolk Assizes, Bury St Edmunds on 22 January 1945 before Mr Justice Macnaghten, and John Flowers

KC for the prosecution told the jury that although much of the case was circumstantial, its cumulative effect would lead to the conclusion that Heys, and nobody else, was the murderer.

Cherrill told the court that after many years of comparing handwriting samples, he had found that the characteristics of handwriting were even more significant in block letters than in cursive.

Mr Flowers asked him, 'What is your opinion as to whether the anonymous letter was written or not by the same person who printed the letters on the leave forms and tab?'

'It was the same person', replied Cherrill firmly.

'Have you any doubt about it at all?' asked Flowers.

'No, Sir.'

Just to hammer the point home, Flowers asked, 'If the other ones were written by the prisoner, so was the anonymous letter?'

'Yes.'

Mr Alpe for the defence asked at length about the formation of the characters. 'How do you account for the difference in many of the letters?' he asked, to which Cherrill replied, 'That might be due to the speed of the writing or the desire on the part of the writer to write in other than his natural style. While some of the letters are superficially different, basically, they are not. There are certain basic characteristics which the desire for anonymity cannot entirely conceal.'

For someone who was a pain in the arse, Cherrill certainly knew his onions and, what was more, how to give evidence.

Dr Biddle gave evidence of the post mortem and stated that the human bloodstains on Heys' jacket were, in his opinion, the victim's blood; he also mentioned the similarities between the material found on Heys' shoes and those of the girls and the debris in the ditch.

In giving evidence, Heys stated that he had been at the site for four days, having spent ten days' leave with his wife and children. Having drunk three pints of mild and bitter in Beccles, he had consumed five more pints at a pub before mistakenly believing that the WAAFs' ablutions hut was his. He stated he had lost his way. After being directed to his site, he arrived there at 12.30 am and did not put on a light because it was not the custom to do so, unless on duty. 'I believed my pals were asleep.'

'Did you kill Winnie Evans?' asked Mr Alpe, to which Heys replied, 'I did not.'

'And you never wrote this anonymous letter?'

'No, Sir.'

Reading out the relevant passage of the letter, Mr Flowers, in cross-examination, asked, 'Do you see that the writer is purporting to say the poor girl came along and told him that her friend had offered to come along with her, as an airman ahead had lost his way and was drunk?'

Heys replied, 'I should not know anything about that.'

'But *you* were the airman who had lost his way', exclaimed Flowers. 'How could anyone else in the world have the knowledge to put it in this letter, but you?'

For the second time, Heys denied writing the letter.

'How do you account for the blood on the tunic?' asked Flowers.

'The only reason I can give is that on one occasion, I went out with two men and one cut his hand in falling off a cycle and I helped him to get up. It would be last October', replied Heys, but it did not sound particularly convincing, because he had never mentioned it to Greeno.

Summing up to the jury, Mr Flowers referred once more to the part of the letter which referred to the WAAF friend who had suggested accompanying Miss Evans and the drunken airman who was ahead, saying, 'Nobody in the world could have put that in this letter, according to any reasonable view of the evidence, except this man.'

During his summing up, Mr Alpe alluded to the suggestion that the letter had been smuggled out of prison. 'Would a man charged with murder be wandering about the prison?' he asked. 'Letters from prisoners were on official paper – is it suggested he had accomplices in prison?'

With a flair for rhetoric, Mr Alpe quoted a line from Richelieu to the jury: 'Give me a dozen lines written by the hand of the most innocent man and I will find something therein which will cause him to hang.'

It was a very odd quotation to use; it suggested that his client had indeed written the letter.

But not content with that, he backed up Richelieu's quote with another, this one from the Rubáiyát of Omar Khayyám:

> The moving finger writes; and, having writ,
> Moves on: nor all thy piety nor wit
> Shall lure it back to cancel half a line,
> Nor all thy tears wash out a word of it.

It's possible that Mr Alpe was drunk on his own verbosity; this quote from that Persian poet of long ago was even more damning than the one by the French Cardinal.

It suggested that Heys had not only written the anonymous letter but that now he was very sorry for having done so.

Opening his summing up, Mr Justice Macnaghten told the jury that the crime was 'a murder more savage and horrible than any in my experience of crime' and that the victim 'had been treated with such savagery and violence that she was not able to breathe' before adding, 'If you think that the statement made by the accused to the police might be true, he is entitled to be acquitted.'

It took the jury just forty minutes to think otherwise and, asked if there was any reason why sentence of death should not be passed on him, Heys replied, 'God knows I am innocent of this foul crime. I know God will look after me; I am not afraid.'

On 26 February 1945, at the Court of Criminal Appeal, Mr Justice Humphreys, Mr Justice Wrottesley and Mr Justice Croom-Johnson considered the appeal of a man sentenced by Mr Justice Macnaghten, gave the prisoner the benefit of the doubt and quashed the conviction.

Actually, this was John Canny, who had been sentenced to eighteen months' imprisonment for inflicting grievous bodily harm at Winchester Assizes.

Arthur Heys was not so fortunate; his appeal was heard the same day, and Mr Justice Humphreys referred to that 'fatal, anony-mous letter' and said that the victim was 'a perfectly respectable member of that splendid body of women, known as the WAAF', adding, 'The writer of this anonymous letter is the person who killed that girl – he says so.' Giving judgement, he stated that the summing up was 'a fair, full and accurate one and the court saw no grounds for interfering with the verdict; the appeal is dismissed.'

On 12 March 1945, Heys was discharged from the RAF, so that his death would not be recorded on his record as a serving airman. The following day, he was executed at Norwich prison by Thomas Pierrepoint; it was the first execution at the prison since 8 March 1938. He was buried in the prison yard on 17 March.

So that was the end of the man who had been described in court as a Jekyll and Hyde character; a model husband and father when sober, but prone to violence when drunk.

His wife, who attended the police court and Assizes hearings, married twice more; she died aged seventy-nine in 1990.

The case begs the question, if Heys had not sent that letter, would he have been convicted on the other evidence as it stood? Difficult to say; with nobody witnessing the murder and Heys maintaining his innocence, the case for the prosecution was pretty well circumstantial. But Heys, in sending that letter, tried to hedge his bets – with disastrous consequences for him.

There was a macabre twist to this case. Heys was not the only member of his family to hang. The other was his father, Edward Heys who, suffering from depression, had hanged himself in July 1913; at the time of their deaths, father and son were almost exactly the same age.

CHAPTER 6

Murder in the King's House

King George II of Greece had a pretty unsettled reign, what with political unrest in his kingdom during the 1920s and '30s, plus a divorce; during the Second World War, he fled to England and in 1941 set up residence at Brown's Hotel. On 31 March 1946, it appeared that his country's monarchist parties had obtained a clear majority of parliamentary seats, and a referendum was set for 1 September. However, the registers came under Allied supervision, and it appeared that there had been significant fraud during the election, so the King remained in London and purchased the lease of a Georgian mansion at 45 Chester Square, Belgravia, whilst the future constitution of his country remained under consideration.

The services of a housekeeper, 41-year-old Elizabeth McLindon, were engaged on 26 April 1946, and although the house was being thoroughly renovated and redecorated, she moved in.

At 3 o'clock on the afternoon of Sunday, 9 June 1946, King George II arrived at the mansion, where he noted that the milk was still on the doorstep but there was no answer to his repeated knockings, and the premises was locked up. None of his entourage had the keys, and the King, obviously annoyed, left. Three days later, the King's private secretary, Sophocles Papanikolaou, went to Chester Square; no one answered his knock either, so he fetched a set of duplicate keys and let himself in, but found the place deserted. However, whilst he was there, he received a telephone call from a man named Boyce, who anxiously wished to know where Miss McLindon was. However, Mr Papanikolaou didn't know, and neither, it appeared, did anybody else.

On 14 June, the police were called. Divisional Detective Inspector John Ball went to the house and forced the door of the one room that was locked. There he found the body of Miss McLindon. She was seated on a chair in front of a small table on which was a telephone and a directory; she had been shot in the head from behind, from a distance of about two feet. There was no sign of a struggle; the room had not been ransacked. On the floor at the back of the chair was a .32 calibre cartridge case. The pathologist, Keith Simpson, believed that she had been murdered on the last day she had been seen alive, 8 June – which was the day before the King's visit. From the angle of the wound, it was clear to Simpson that she had not seen the pistol.

DDI Ball had been a Flying Squad officer from its early days; as an energetic detective inspector, he had smashed up a dog-doping gang. Tall and immaculately dressed, Ball was a quintessential murder investigator, and now he got to work.

He found two letters addressed to Miss McLindon, both unopened. The first was dated 11 June:

My dear Elizabeth,
     Just a few lines to let you know I 'phoned you but got no answer, nor when I 'phoned on Sunday. Now, Elizabeth dear, let me know where you have been. For your future sake, play the game. All my love is yours forever.
     Arthur xxx

The second was dated a day later:

My dear Elizabeth,
     Will you please let me know what is the trouble? I 'phoned you but got no reply. If you have finished with me, let me know as you promised you would, as we have lived together as man and wife for three months. Have you gone back to live with the other men? If I don't get into touch with you, I am going to get in touch with the King's secretary. I am getting fed up at the way you are treating me.
     All my love, from your loving and true hubby, Arthur

Neither letter showed an address, although they had been posted in Brighton. Ball spoke to Miss McLindon's sister, Veronica, who told him that 'Arthur' was Arthur Robert Boyce, a painter and decorator who lived in Brighton and who was her sister's fiancé. She also told him that her sister had found an old wedding invitation in one of Arthur's pockets on which Arthur was named as the bridegroom and a Miss Whitty of Bournemouth as the bride; he had dismissed this, said Veronica, as 'just one of my affairs, and it's over now'.

Ball carried out a check at Criminal Records Office which revealed that the affair with Miss Whitty had gone rather further than that; the couple had indeed married, and since Boyce was already married at the time, he had been sentenced to eighteen months' imprisonment for bigamy and had only recently been released. That was just one of his peccadilloes; he also had seven previous convictions for breaking and entering and another for leaving his lawful wedded wife unsupported. And as if that were not enough, he was currently circulated as being wanted for a series of cheque frauds, including one allegedly signed by the King's secretary, Mr Papanikolaou.

Neighbours stated that on 8 June they had last seen Miss McLindon hurry out of the Chester Square house at noon, slam the door and run down the street. Shortly afterwards, Boyce appeared from the other end of the square and then was seen to knock loudly on the door. When he received no reply, he ran in the same direction that Miss McLindon had taken; the witness remarked that 'he had looked angry'.

DDI Ball caught the afternoon train to Brighton and chatted with Boyce's landlady at his lodgings in Elder Street while he waited for Boyce to return. She told Ball that Boyce had apparently gone to London to try to find Miss McLindon on 11 June since he was very upset at her failing to make contact with him; he had told his landlady, 'The King has gone off to one of his other places and taken her with him.'

Boyce was forty-five years of age; he had been a regular soldier and had rejoined in 1939 at the commencement of hostilities. After his discharge, he had become a painter; fair-haired, thin and wearing glasses, despite being a serial philanderer Boyce was hardly the picture of love's young dream.

When Boyce arrived back at his lodgings and Ball told him of the reason for his visit, Boyce gave every indication of being considerably upset, telling Ball that he had telephoned Miss McLindon 'sometimes a dozen times a day' and that when he received no reply, he had telephoned her sister, Veronica, in Liverpool, since she was to be a bridesmaid at their wedding on 16 July. 'My mother and I have been trying to find her', he told Ball.

The officer asked Boyce if Miss McLindon had any other male friends, and he agreed that she had and named them. He added that a number of 'queer people' had called at the Chester Square address for an interview with the royal resident, several of whom appeared to be nursing grievances; was it possible that Miss McLindon had encountered a political assassin?

Asked if he owned a gun, Boyce replied that he had possessed a Colt .45 but that at Miss McLindon's request he had thrown it into the sea from the end of Brighton Pier; he denied ever having had a pistol with a .32 calibre.

Leaving Boyce, Ball strolled off to the Palace Pier, where Boyce was employed as a painter, and spoke to some of his workmates. One recalled that Boyce had shown him an automatic pistol; when asked if it was loaded, Boyce had replied, 'Yes, there are five up the spout.'

Ball searched Boyce's lodgings looking for the murder weapon, but without success. There was a luggage label addressed to a Mr John Rowland with a Caernarvon address, and that was one of several items – which on the face of it looked as though they had little or no evidential value – which Ball removed.

During the train journey back to London, Boyce said, 'Look here, you think I shot her. You have made a big mistake. The only gun I had I threw over the pier, weeks ago.' He then named a man, saying, 'That's the bloke you want.'

Boyce was locked up on the cheque fraud charges, and now Ball really got to work.

Elizabeth McLindon has since been described as 'a high class prostitute' which may be rather unfair, although from the number of lovers she possessed, she might well have been styled 'flirty'. Nor was she particularly honest in her dealings with the Greek King and his entourage; the glowing references which had been provided to obtain her position as housekeeper had been forged by Boyce.

Boyce and Miss McLindon had lived together in Brighton, and later, on 1 June, she invited him to move into the Chester Square address. Despite being married with a grown-up family, and although he had been just released from a prison sentence for bigamy, Boyce proposed to Miss McLindon on 3 June and telephoned a West End jewellers, asking for a sample of engagement rings to be sent round. When they arrived, he selected one costing £175, although the jeweller's representative became concerned when Boyce had difficulty in spelling 'hundred' and decided to retain the ring until the cheque had cleared. Since Boyce had £75 in his account, it didn't, and it was returned marked, 'Refer to drawer'. There were several other presents for the housekeeper, who was obviously impressed with the sincerity of her suitor; the same day, she wrote a letter to the local newspaper in Liverpool informing them of her impending marriage, and started to purchase her trousseau.

Although she had given Boyce a key to the premises on 6 June, when the dishonoured cheque was brought to light, cracks in the relationship were beginning to appear, and Miss McLindon wrote to Miss Whitty to find out what exactly had happened regarding the proposed wedding. Perhaps by the afternoon of 8 June she had found out; hence the door slamming and the running off, with Boyce 'looking angry' in pursuit.

All of which was very curious but not proof of murder; however, a very interesting piece of evidence was just around the corner.

Ball set about tracing John Rowland, but he was not at the Caernarvon address; he was serving 'somewhere in the Army', but when Ball caught up with him, he had a remarkable story to tell.

He had shared rooms with Boyce in Fulham in October 1945 and had purchased, quite legitimately, a .32 Browning automatic pistol. Boyce had admired the firearm and asked if he could buy it, but Rowland refused. Several months later, when Rowland returned to Wales, he realized that the pistol was missing. Putting two and two together, he deduced that Boyce had stolen it and wrote to him, sending a box and a label and asking for its return. Boyce did not reply to the letter but kept the label – which had been found by Ball.

On an off chance, Ball asked if he had kept any cartridge cases fired from that gun; and Rowland had. He had fired the gun into a river to test it – and he had kept one cartridge case, using it as a spool for some adhesive tape – 'It should be about my house, somewhere', he said.

Back to Caernarvon went Ball and there, in the pocket of a jacket, he found the cartridge case, wrapped in tape, just as its owner had described. That case, plus the discarded one found at the scene of the murder, was sent to the Metropolitan Police laboratory, where the ballistics expert, Robert Churchill, placed the two items in a comparator microscope. The firing pin depression pattern, the ejector-claw markings and the bolt-head/breech-face markings on the shell base on both were identical. Mr Churchill did not have the pistol – in fact, it would never be found – but it really didn't matter. The shots fired into the river by Mr Rowland and the bullet which ended the life of Miss McLindon were fired from the same weapon, the weapon alleged by Rowland that Boyce had stolen, the one which Boyce stated he had never possessed.

It was circumstantial evidence, but after appearing at Marlborough Street Court on 15 July 1946, Boyce was committed to stand his trial at the Old Bailey, eleven days later.

The trial commenced on 16 September 1946 before Mr Justice Morris, with an impressive array of legal talent. Anthony Hawke and Henry Elam appeared for the prosecution, with Derek Curtis-Bennett KC and Mr R. E. Seaton for Boyce's defence.

There were any number of red herrings: Miss McLindon's name and address were found in possession of a man named Arthur Clegg, when he was arrested on 3 July. An anonymous note, written in block capitals, was found in a cell beneath Maidstone Assize Court on 30 August which had been occupied by Clegg. In part, it read:

> THE MAN CLEGG IS MIXED UP IN A CASE OF MURDER. HE SAYS THEY CAN'T TOUCH HIM NOW AS THEY HAVE A MAN CALLED BOYCE IN BRIXTON PRISON FOR THIS JOB

Ball agreed with Mr Curtis-Bennett that Clegg was at liberty on 8 June and also agreed that in all probability Clegg had written that note, but he added that Clegg was 'an unbalanced man whose sanity had been in question some years ago'.

The waters were further muddied because an Arthur Clegg had been executed for the murder of his 11-day-old granddaughter (although it was said that Clegg was, in fact, the child's father) on 19 March 1946, some three months *prior* to the murder. By the oddest of coincidences, it appeared that there must have been *two* Arthur Cleggs.

When Boyce came to give evidence he painted a very different picture from the testimony he had provided for Ball. He agreed that he and Miss McLindon had lived together in Brighton, that he had owned a .45 Colt pistol and that at her insistence he had thrown it into the sea in April. About one month later, he said, she entered the service of the King of the Hellenes and went to live at Chester Square.

However, he stated that Rowland had earlier offered to sell him a .32 pistol for £9, but he thought the price too high, and when Rowland left the lodgings to join the Army he had left the pistol behind. Later, Rowland wrote to Boyle asking him for the return of the weapon plus some items of laundry, but Boyle kept the gun in his possession until 1 June.

It was on that date that Miss McLindon asked him to throw up his job and come and live with her at Chester Square. The reason for this was because a lot of people had called asking for King George. Some of these people, said Boyce, had become very abusive and threatened her when she refused to disclose His Majesty's whereabouts.

So when he arrived, Boyce handed the pistol to her. Precisely why he did this was unclear because, as he told the court, he did not want to do it and did not agree with her having it, because it was loaded. But, said Boyce, she told him, 'That is just the thing I need', because she wanted it for her own protection, should these shadowy figures persist in calling.

On the morning of 8 June, Boyce went out to see the Victory Air Pageant, then he and Miss McLindon had lunch, after which they went to bed. An hour later, the front doorbell rang, and while Boyce remained in bed, Miss McLindon put on her dressing gown and slippers and went to see who it was. She returned a few moments later to say that the caller had said that the King would be calling at the house that night. Rather illogically, she said that she did not stay in the house while the King was there; in fact, due to the refurbishments, the King had not stayed there at all. But she suggested that Boyce should go back to Brighton and return the following day. Although she seemed apprehensive about him leaving, Boyce did so but telephoned her at 7.45 pm when he arrived at Victoria Station.

'She seemed all right', he told the court.

'Did you murder Miss McLindon?' asked his barrister, Mr Seaton, to which Boyce emphatically replied, 'Certainly not.'

When Anthony Hawke for the Crown asked, 'Were you free to marry her?' Boyce replied just as forcefully, 'No, and Miss McLindon knew it.'

However, this was at variance with the evidence previously given by a William Mutlow, who said that he had known Miss McLindon for about fifteen years and Boyce since the beginning of April that year, and that Boyce had told him that they were going to be married and 'were already virtually married'. It was also at variance with the testimony of Veronica McLindon, who believed she was going to be a bridesmaid at her sister's wedding which, as Boyle had told Ball, was going to be on 16 July. A friend with whom the couple had lived gave evidence that Miss McLindon had said that she did not love Boyce but was afraid to leave him because he had threatened to shoot her if she did.

Summing up for the jury, Derek Curtis-Bennett said:

> Boyce was one of McLindon's lovers. How many others she had, we do not know. One thing is certain, Boyce was the reigning lover. Supposing this woman of many lovers had yet another one? What better way of getting rid of Boyce on the afternoon of June 8th than to say the King of Greece was going to the house that night, telling Boyce to sleep at Brighton and then letting in, not the King of Greece, but the king of her heart at the time?

It didn't work, and after a four-day trial, Boyce was found guilty and asked if he had anything to say before the death sentence was passed. Boyce said to Mr Justice Morris:

I should like to tell your Lordship and the members of the jury I have had a fair trial and I should like to express my sorrow to the family of Miss McLindon but I must also stress, here and now, that I am entirely innocent of this charge.

Sentenced to death, Boyce appealed, but the Home Secretary stated that the offence was aggravated by his effort to put the blame on innocent people and there were no grounds for a reprieve; and so, on 1 November 1946, he was hanged at Pentonville prison by Albert Pierrepoint, assisted by Henry Critchel.

Why was she killed?

Her savings were intact and nothing had been stolen from Chester Square. But at the time of her death, she had just been about to make a telephone call; the receiver was still in her hand. Was she about to make accusations? Demand answers? In some way betray the worthless Boyce?

Only he knew, and it was enough to impose a death sentence on her, five months before one was imposed on him.

CHAPTER 7

The Blackburn Baby Murder

Whenr Detective Chief Inspector Jack Capstick flopped into bed at his home in Norwood, Surrey on the evening of 14 May 1948, he was utterly exhausted. He and his bag-carrier, Detective Sergeant John Stoneman, members of the Yard's Murder Squad, had spent a month in Farnworth, Lancashire, investigating the murder of 11- year-old Jack Quentin Smith. It had happened on 12 April in broad daylight. Jack and his friend, 9-year-old David Lee, were playing after school on a railway embankment where they had lit fires. A man had approached them, telling them he was a railway employee and that the boys would have to go with him. 'You lie over there', the man said to David, whereupon he was attacked with a knife, sustaining stab wounds to his chest and groin. He managed to run the half-mile to his home in Macdonald Avenue, before he collapsed and was taken to hospital, where he remained for ten days. It was only later that he was told that his friend Jack had been bludgeoned to death.

A manhunt was immediately launched, using 110 police officers (including Capstick, brought in from the Yard at the Chief Constable's request), plus bloodhounds, walkie-talkie radios, searchlights and even mine detectors; but although the search for the killer – a tall, thin young man with a rather spotty face and deep-set, staring eyes, wearing what was described as 'a zig-zag pattern' suit – continued unabated, it was unsuccessful.

This was the latest of several attacks on children. As long ago as 18 August 1944, 6-year-old Sheila Fox – who lived in the same street as David Lee – had gone missing. A little girl had been seen riding on the crossbar of a man's cycle. It may or may not have been Sheila; but whatever the case, she has never been found. A year later, in October 1945, Patricia McKeown, aged six, was attacked by a man, again in broad daylight as she walked home from school. He dragged her behind the local chapel and as Patricia put up her hands to protect her chest he stabbed at her, but she managed to run away; a witness later said, 'She looked like a pin cushion.' Patricia ran down a slope into Barton Road and right into the arms of Mr Bath, the local headmaster. He passed the terrified girl to a woman passer-by, telling her to get an ambulance, and chased after the assailant, who ran across some fields; but Mr Bath was disabled and limped badly, and he had to give up the pursuit. Despite a great deal of police activity, the man was not traced. Following that, as the local population linked the two attacks, a rota system was set up, with one deputed parent bringing home anything from twelve to fourteen children from school.

And now, with the murder of Jack Smith and the attempted murder of his friend, the parents of young children were deeply concerned for their welfare, and quite rightly so. The Sunday newspaper, the *News of the World*, initially offered a £500 reward for information leading to the arrest of Jack's murderer; on 2 May 1948, it was increased to £1,000.

The reason for Capstick's return to snatch a night's sleep prior to reporting to the superintendent at C1 regarding his progress – or perhaps, lack of it – in the Jack Smith case, the following day. It was particularly irksome for Capstick; he was not used to failure. During his twenty-three years' service he had enjoyed a series of tremendous successes, first with the Flying Squad (he had been seconded to the Squad with just four years' service), followed by crewing the first of the Met's 'Q' Cars in 1934; he had headed the post-war (and highly secretive) Ghost Squad, and now, in his second year as a chief inspector, he had solved a number of baffling murders.

But Capstick would not be making his report to the Yard that morning. As he drifted off to sleep, 241 miles away to the north a horrifying, bestial murder was being perpetrated, just 33 miles away from where Jack Smith had been killed. And once again – although he was unaware of it – Capstick would be looking for a tall, thin young man with deep-set staring eyes.

The ringing of the telephone awoke Capstick at 4 o'clock in the morning; the caller was Mr C. G. Looms, the Chief Constable of Blackburn, Lancashire, whom Capstick had met several times during the Jack Smith murder investigation. Telling him that a little child had been abducted from her cot in a hospital and foully murdered, Looms requested his presence. Scrambling into his clothes, Capstick telephoned Commander Hugh Young CBE, KPM at home. Young was still grieving over the loss of his wife some months previously but he had lost none of his resolution.

'Get on your way', he said, decisively. 'Take Stoneman. I'll send a couple more good men after you.'

Two Night Provs Flying Squad cars[1] arrived to take Capstick and Stoneman to Euston Station to catch the 6.20 am slow train to

---

[1] These were cars which formed part of 'Night Provincials' to deal with any requests from provincial forces – or anywhere else in the Metro-

Preston; they tried to make up their interrupted sleep on the way. From Preston station a car took them to the police headquarters at Blackburn, where they met Looms, Detective Superintendent John Woodmansey, who was chief of the Lancashire County CID, and other officers, and the horrifying story of what became known, nation- and then world-wide, as 'The Blackburn Baby Murder' was recounted to them.

⋆ ⋆ ⋆

Blackburn had been a boom town of the industrial revolution, a textile manufacturing mill town, but by the middle of the twentieth century it had begun to fall into decline; there was economic deprivation, and the town's 110,000 inhabitants mostly lived in poor and small houses. But situated above the town was the Queen's Park Hospital, which until 1911 had been the Blackburn Union Workhouse and was a model of its kind.

The hospital was situated in 70 acres, its frontage extended over a quarter of a mile and it was surrounded by a high stone wall. At the north-west corner of the grounds there had been subsidence and the result was a deep, disused quarry, known locally as 'The Delph'. The subsidence had claimed a portion of the wall, and there was a temporary erection of six-foot-high chestnut palings, together with barbed wire, although there was a gap in this fence.

The hospital accommodated some 1,200 people, both patients and staff. It had wards for medical, surgical, maternity and psychiatric patients. There was also a juvenile ward and one with nightly accommodation for about ten homeless people.

Entry to the hospital was via the porter's gate, and at a point furthest from the porter's lodge was Ward CH3, known as the 'Babies' Ward' and part of the children's department. It measured forty by eight feet and contained twelve high-sided cots, six on each side of the ward.

On the night of 14/15 May 1948 there were six children in the ward, and one of the patients was June Anne Devaney, aged three years eleven months, the only child of Albert and Emily Devaney, who had been admitted on 5 May suffering from pneumonia. However, she had recovered sufficiently to be recommended for discharge on 15 May. She was big for her age and the only one of the six children who could talk. She occupied the third cot on the porch side of the ward.

---

politan Police Area – to render any assistance needed in London. They provided a 24-hour coverage.

The night duty nurse was Gwendolyn Humphreys, and at about midnight she had gone into an adjoining kitchen to prepare breakfast for the children. She heard crying coming from one of the cots; it was a baby named Michael Tattersall, who was in the cot next to June Anne, and Nurse Humphreys remained with him for about 20 minutes before he settled back to sleep. She looked at June Anne – she was fast asleep – and went back to the kitchen. At about half-past twelve, Nurse Humphreys thought she heard a girl's voice but could not see anything when she went to the porch door, so returned to the kitchen. At 1.20 am she felt a draught from the veranda door. She went and closed it, but then suddenly noticed three things. First, a Winchester bottle of sterile water had been moved from a trolley and was underneath June Anne's cot; next, her cot was empty; and third, there appeared to be footprints around the cot.

Nurse Humphreys raised the alarm, the police arrived at 1.55 am and a systematic search of the hospital grounds began. That search ended at 3.17 am, when June Anne's lifeless body was found next to the hospital's boundary wall, 283ft away from the ward. The child was identified by her father. A bloodhound was brought to the hospital but after being given the scent from the child's cot and the footmark, it followed a trail to the child's body and to nothing else thereafter.

As well as telephoning Capstick at 4 o'clock that morning, at the same time the Chief Constable also contacted Detective Chief Inspector Colin Campbell, the officer in charge of the Lancashire Constabulary's Fingerprint Bureau who went direct to the hospital, arriving there at 5.10 am and immediately getting to work. It's fair to say he did a magnificent job.

Sealing the ward as a crime scene, Campbell walked around the outside of the building looking for signs of a forcible entry; there were none. The six doors, three on either side of the ward, were unlocked as was a door at the south end of the ward. Additionally, the windows in the small room at the north end of the ward were open. He then commenced a search for fingerprints, starting on the exterior of the ward. The walls were made of brick, but all painted surfaces on the doors and windowsills, the windows themselves and the brass door handles were treated with Hydrerg-cum-creta[2] applied with a squirrel hair brush.

---

[2] This rather toxic substance, comprised of one part of mercury to two parts of chalk, was in common use at the time; by the 1970s and '80s, aluminium powder or Bristol Black (a carbon powder) had been substituted.

Several finger and palm prints were found; these were photographed in actual size with a Graflex fingerprint camera, using orthochromatic and panchromatic film.

Next, entering the ward, he could see what initially appeared to be bare footprints on the wax-polished floor. In fact, these prints had been made by someone in stocking feet. That someone had entered the ward by the porch door and gone to the trolley where the Winchester bottle was standing. Having picked up the bottle, the person had walked along by the wall, pausing at three of the cots in turn before finally stopping at June's. The bottle had then been placed on the floor.

These footprints were 10¼ inches long but only fragmentary; the pressure of the feet had made micro-shallow indentations on the waxed floor. Only by Campbell getting down on his hands and knees, a few inches from the floor, could they be seen by specular reflection – the way the light fell upon the marks. Several types of fingerprint powder were used to make those prints more easily visible, but without success, so they were circled with white chalk. A 15-inch ruler was placed alongside the prints, so that after being photographed and when the negative was placed in the enlarger, it was possible to reproduce the footprints at their actual size. One photograph clearly showed the texture of the sock; additionally, a section of the wax polish scraped from the floor revealed fibres from the sock not visible to the naked eye.

Next, the Winchester bottle. On it were at least twenty finger, thumb and palm prints, but being the expert that he was, Campbell was able to accurately deduce that ten had been made recently and were larger than the older prints. These recent prints he labelled 'L', 'M', 'N', 'O', 'P', 'Q', 'R', 'T', 'CC' and 'DD'.

As well as fibres from the waxed floor, David Noel Jones from the Home Office Forensic Science Laboratory at Preston took other fibres from the ward's windowsill, as well as samples of bloodstained grass, hair which had adhered to the grass and hair from the boundary wall, as well as samples of the wall's brickwork. The whole exercise of evidence-gathering took fifteen hours.

It was now time for Capstick to see Julie Anne's body, which had remained in situ. Capstick was a hard man. During a raid in the wartime blackout, he had hit a gangster so hard with his truncheon that the man left the ground and landed in the back of a Flying Squad tender. When a West End ponce thought himself immune from prosecution after razor-slashing one of his girls, Capstick disabused him of the notion after he ran him to ground in a Soho pub, hitting him across the face with his truncheon, left and right, fracturing both cheekbones, before dragging him through the street to Bow Street police station, past cheering prostitutes. It was difficult to square this conduct with Capstick's appearance as an avuncular gentleman farmer, a man whose passions were playing bowls and cultivating the scented roses which habitually adorned the buttonholes of his immaculate suits.

But on that afternoon of 15 May, as he stood in the drizzling rain in the hospital grounds, Capstick looked neither tough nor clean and tidy. He was forty-four years of age, but on that day he looked older and haggard, he was tired, hungry and unshaven; his suit, creased from the train journey, was no longer immaculate, and as the sheet was pulled back to reveal June Anne's body, Capstick wept. It is easy to understand why.

Her body was dirty, as though it had been rolled about in the wet grass; her nightdress was also wet and muddy. Both body and nightdress were bloodstained, and her nightdress was pulled up, exposing her buttocks. There were bruises, one on each of the inner and upper parts of her thighs, consistent with very severe thumb pressure – there was also a bruise across the throat which suggested it had been firmly gripped. Superficial bruising appeared all over the body: left knee, hip, elbow and forearm and both feet.

On her left buttock were two crescent-shaped bruises, consistent with a severe bite. She had been forcibly raped; all the walls of the vagina had been lacerated and the force of the rape had penetrated her rectum. Blood and fluid had exuded from her nose and vagina. All of these horrific injuries had been inflicted prior to death.

That had occurred when June Anne's attacker had gripped her by the ankles, swung her and smashed her head against the boundary wall; small puncture wounds were found on her left ankle which had been the result of fingernails digging into her skin.

It affected Capstick profoundly and would do so until the end of his life. Little wonder that he later wrote, 'I swore, standing there in the rain, that I would bring her murderer to justice if I had to devote the rest of my life to the search.'

In fact, it would take less than three months.

⋆   ⋆   ⋆

Initially, it seemed the case would be resolved far sooner than that.

Some nurses in the nurses' home, which was attached to the hospital and only 100 yards away from Ward CH3, had seen a man, peering in at a window on the night of the murder; when he was challenged he put his finger to his lips and told them,

'Hush – don't tell anyone!' He behaved in a disgusting manner, and then two parties of nurses returning from leave reported that on the same night they had been accosted by the same man in the grounds of the hospital. He had walked with them to the nurses' home, and later they saw him staring at them through a window.

Understandably, he was regarded as a prime suspect, and a manhunt was launched. He was found on 19 May, sitting by the bed of his wife in the maternity ward of the hospital. Arrested, he was questioned and admitted being in the hospital grounds within an hour of the murder but denied any involvement in the death of June Anne. His fingerprints were taken, but they did not match any of those on the Winchester bottle, and once it was established that he was merely a Peeping Tom, he was released; he was, however, kept under surveillance until the murderer was caught.

Finally, Capstick and Stoneman were afforded the luxury of a meal, a shave and some sleep, when reinforcements in the shape of Detective Inspector Wilfred Daws and Detective Sergeant Ernie Millen arrived from the Yard.

Ernie Millen was then aged thirty-six; a former assistant at Boots the Chemists, he had been both a detective constable and sergeant at C1 Department since 1941. He specialized in the patient investigation of long, complicated fraud cases. While Daws and Stoneman merged more into the background of this investigation, Millen moved to the front, to become Capstick's main assistant.

* * *

So far in the investigation, this much was clear. No member of the hospital staff had entered the ward in their stocking feet, and none of the staff had carried the Winchester bottle from the trolley and put it on the floor by June Anne's cot.

Next, it was established that just before midnight on 15 May, Bernard John Regan, a taxi driver, had picked up a man who hailed him at Darwen Street bridge, at the bottom of Lower Audley Street, and driven him to Queen's Road near the quarry on the outskirts of the hospital's grounds. When the man got out of the taxi, the driver saw him run towards the quarry. He was unable to give a precise description of his fare, although he was certain that he spoke with a local accent.

Detective Chief Inspector Bob McCartney of the Lancashire County Force was given a room at the hospital as an office, and he and a team of half a dozen officers got to work. Statements and fingerprints were obtained from doctors, matrons, sisters, nurses, orderlies, ambulance drivers, their boyfriends and girlfriends, the coalman and the milkman, plus patients, former patients and their relatives – anyone who had worked or had any kind of business at all at the hospital during the past two years. They traced 642 people who had actually been in the ward; altogether, 2,017 were fingerprinted, and all of them were eliminated from the enquiry. Therefore the remaining fingerprints on the bottle and the footmarks found in the ward were undoubtedly those of the murderer – and his fingerprints were not on record at the Yard, or anywhere else.

He must have been a local resident, not only from his accent but also because only a man with local knowledge of the area could have negotiated the quarry in the dark.

With feet measuring 10¼ inches, he must also have been reasonably tall. This was borne out by the fact that the cot sides (to prevent a child falling out of bed) were still raised in position on June Anne's cot – and from floor to the top was a distance of four feet.

Lastly, his clothing must have been bloodstained.

Detective Inspector Bill Barton and a team of his men were placed under the direct control of Capstick by the Chief Constable – and he put them straight to work, telling them to visit every lodging house, hotel, pub and doss-house in the area. He told them to check the railway station and all of the dyers, cleaners and laundries, and everybody who was able to walk and lived in the streets around the hospital.

Due to the nature of the crime, 3,600 people who had been discharged from psychiatric hospitals were fingerprinted. The bite marks on June Anne's buttock were the subject of comment; it was comparatively rare for this to occur in England during a sexual attack, but more common on the continent; therefore prisoner of war camps within a 20-mile radius of Blackburn were visited, and 3,000 Germans were fingerprinted. So were people suffering from venereal disease (it being a commonly held, if nonsensical, belief that sexual intercourse with a virgin would cure them), people reported missing from home at that period, persons who had attempted suicide and homeless people who had stayed in the hospital's casual ward and would have knowledge of the hospital's surroundings.

It would have been useful if somehow the search could have been narrowed down, but in fact it only expanded. The team knew that the murderer was a tall man with big hands. It was clear he was also a young man, because the clearness of the ridges revealed none of the cracks and breaks likely to be found in the fingerprints

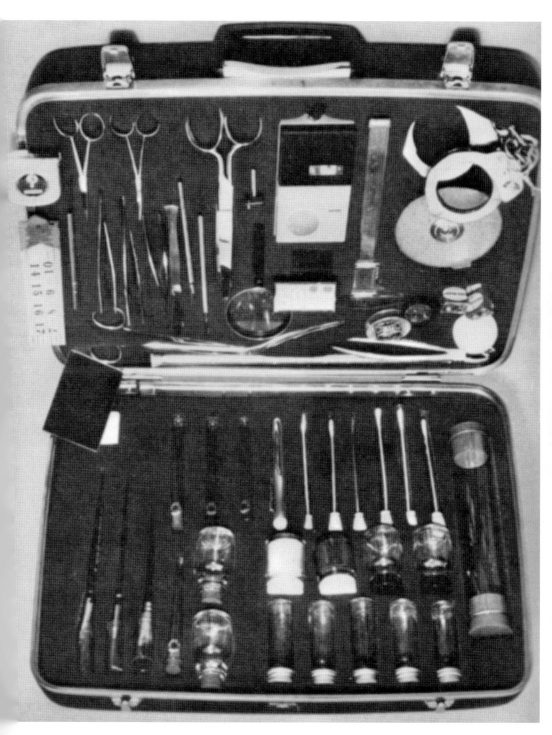

The murder bag, circa 1960.

Above: The old New Scotland Yard . . ..

Below: . . . and the later version.

Above: A very early photograph of fingerprint cabinets at Scotland Yard.

Below: An early photograph of the Yard's photographic studio.

Commissioner Sir Edward
Henry Bt. GCVO, KCB, CSI.

AC(C) Sir Melville
Macnaughton CB, KPM.

Detective Superintendent Charles Stockley Collins.

Sir Richard Muir KC.

The Stratton Brothers.

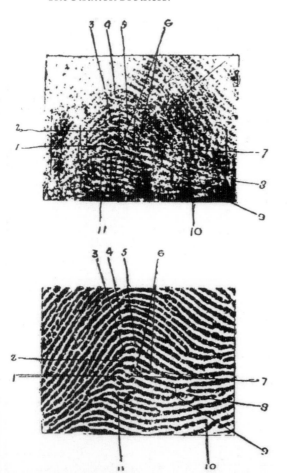

Above: Masks used by the Stratton brothers.

Left: The marks left on the cashbox and Alfred Stratton's fingerprint.

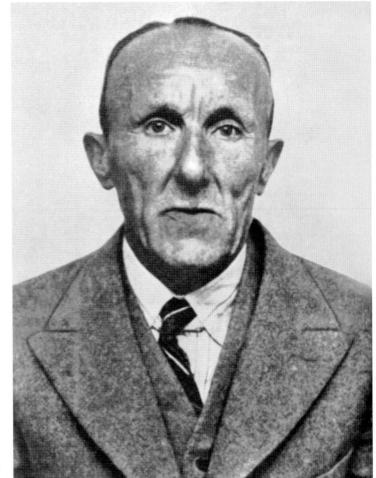

Right: Harold Dorian Trevor – 'The man with the monocle'.

Below left: Detective Superintendent Bill Salisbury.

Below right: DCS Fred Cherrill MBE.

Mrs Florence Ransom.

Mrs Fisher and her
daughter, Freda.

DCS Peter Henderson Beveridge MBE.

Beveridge arrests
Mrs Ransom.

Above left: Commander George Hatherill CBE.

Above right: Murderer Harold Hill.

Below: Hill's Army truck.

DCS Ted Greeno MBE.

Detective
Superintendent
John Ball.

Murderer Arthur Boyce.

Murderer Peter Griffiths.

DCS Jack Capstick.

DAC Ernie Millen CBE.

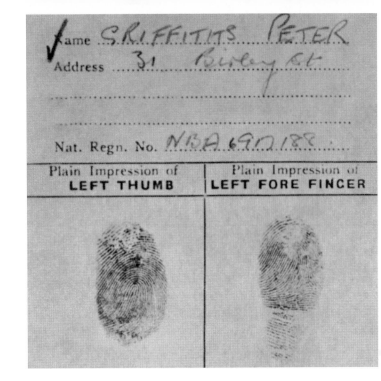

Griffiths'
fingerprint card.

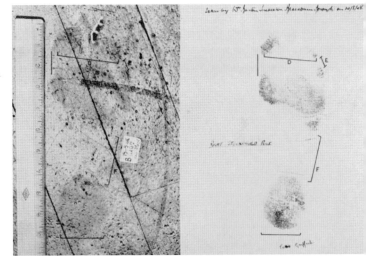

(L) Footprint
impressions found in
Ward CH3, and (R)
Griffiths' footprint
impressions.

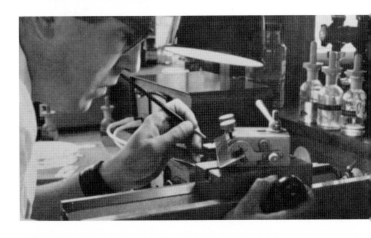

Scientific analysis in
the Griffiths case.

Left: The Winchester bottle, showing fingerprints.

Below: Ward CH3 – June Anne Devaney's cot is 3rd on left.

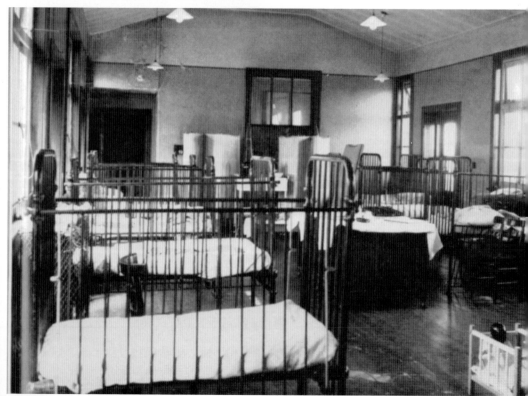

of older men. There was none of the coarseness, calluses or injuries which would appear on the hands of a man engaged in manual work.

But since he was a young man, would he have served in the armed forces? If he had, he might have served overseas, and if he had been arrested, having committed a sex offence, he would have been fingerprinted. Therefore, photographs of the suspect's prints were sent to fingerprint bureaux in all parts of the world where British troops had served, with the request that comparisons be made with their collection – all without success.

Letters were received by the enquiry team offering suggestions of persons responsible for the crime (usually those convicted of sex offences) – all had to be checked out and eliminated. A man was disturbed bending over a child's cot at St John's Hospital, Andover, Hampshire by a nurse who had left the ward for two minutes to get her meal. The man escaped, and although the local police spent the rest of the night, plus all of the following day, searching for him, they were unsuccessful. Since it is 230 miles between the two hospitals, it did seem unlikely that the Andover prowler and the Blackburn murderer were one and the same, but the matter was followed up by Superintendent Woodmansey and Capstick – without success.

One man confessed to killing Jack Quentin Smith, and when an investigation revealed that this could not possibly be the case, he confessed to murdering June Anne Devaney as well. This, too, was positively discounted and, probably tiring of living in a fantasy world, two months later he emerged into the real one and killed his own brother.

On 20 May a decision was reached by the hospital sub-committee of the Blackburn Public Assistance Committee, which ran the hospital, that the hospital staff were quite rightly completely exonerated of any blame for the murder.

On the same day, a conference was held in the Chief Constable's office. Capstick suggested that every male over the age of sixteen who was in Blackburn on the night of 14 May should be fingerprinted. The Chief Constable was astonished; given the number of inhabitants in the town, he believed it would take years; nor was he completely sure that everyone would agree to it.

Besides being a brilliant investigator, Capstick was also an innovative one. In one murder case, he stationed himself outside the prime suspect's house in the dead of night, continually flashing a torch and making strange owl-like sounds. This resulted in the superstitious suspect going to where he had buried his victims to ensure they were still there. Other detectives had solved cases by asking the local schoolchildren to write essays on what they had done and seen on the day of a murder. Now Capstick played the trump cards in his hand.

He was sure, he told Looms, that few people would refuse to give their fingerprints. Feelings in the area were running high about the murderer, and despite the detectives' massive workload, there was no flagging of effort or lack of enthusiasm. As one of the detectives had pointed out to Capstick, 'June Anne was a Blackburn babe.' But to start the ball rolling, Capstick decided to ask Mr Robert Sugden, Blackburn's mayor, to be the first to volunteer and to assure the public that their fingerprints would be used only for the purpose of the murder enquiry and that afterwards they would all be destroyed.

The plan was taken up by the mayor and his council, who gave it unequivocal backing, and with enormous press coverage, on 23 May, the mass fingerprinting exercise got underway.

* * *

A special card was devised: it measured $3^3/_8 \times 3^3/_8$ inches and it had space for the person's name, address, National Registration Number and their left thumb and index finger prints, these being the clearest prints on the bottle.

Blackburn was divided into fourteen voting divisions, sub-divided into three, four or five sections, according to the size of the area. Those sub-sections were arranged in alphabetical order by streets or roads. A team of twenty officers, taken off normal duties and under the control of Inspector Barton, were sent out with their cards and ink pads to visit every house in the borough. Upon their return, the cards were handed over to five male and female officers; they checked the names and addresses against those on the electoral roll. Once that was done, the cards went off to Chief Inspector Campbell for examination.

Those twenty officers worked from 8.00 am to 9.30 pm. Often, the male member of the household would not be in; this would mean a return visit. The month of May came to an end, and the townspeople were anxious to help; a very few people objected, but those that did acquiesced after it was pointed out to them, with typical Lancastrian tactfulness, that if they persisted in their recalcitrance, word would soon get out about the possibility of their being thought to be a murdering, drooling pervert.

The search continued into June and July, and by now over 40,000 sets of fingerprints had been received without a match being found. The people of Blackburn started getting restless. What was going on? Was this some sort of a police bluff, an excuse to gain access to people's homes and try to pick up clues to pin goodness-knows-what on them? The initial spirit of cooperation was now dissipating; it was being replaced by a feeling of resentment. Who were these 'super detectives' from Scotland Yard – what had they done to solve the crime? The police officers engaged on office duties discovered that when they went to a pub or café for a beer or a bite to eat they were looked on askance by the locals. What were these coppers doing in a pub, enjoying themselves, wasting their time, when they ought to be out catching a murderer? From then on, the decision was made to have food sent into the office for the investigating team.

It was just as frustrating for the police officers. What if the suspect wasn't a local man? What if he lived just outside Blackburn? What if he had gone to live in another country – or was dead?

Just when the team thought they had come to a dead end, they suddenly discovered that 900 Blackburn men had still to be fingerprinted. Between 30 June and 18 July the Food Office had prepared new ration documents giving the name, address, date of birth and National Registration Number of every person receiving a new ration book.

But suddenly it was Wakes Week. This was a tradition in Northern towns since the industrial revolution; between June and September, each town would take a weekly holiday on a different week, in order that the cotton mills and factories could be closed for maintenance. Now it was the second week in July, when the vast majority of Blackburn townspeople packed their suitcases and headed for Blackpool.

But not all. Twenty police officers went to the Food Office and checked the names on the new ration books against the electoral rolls. New name, road and street lists were made up of those men who, for whatever reason, were not on the electoral rolls. With the townspeople returned rested from their holiday, on Monday 9 August the team restarted their door-knocking and fingerprinting.

In the meantime, with Blackburn like a ghost town, Capstick and Millen were told by the Yard to take their own summer holiday. But no sooner had Capstick arrived at the house which he had rented at Pevensey Bay for his wife and family when the telephone rang; it was Chief Constable Looms telling him to return immediately. 'We've got him at last', Capstick was told.

He paused only to telephone Millen at his home at Westgate, then both men raced north for a briefing with the rest of the team.

On 11 August Police Constable Joseph Calvert of the Blackburn Borough Police Force had knocked on the door of 31 Birley Street, Blackburn. It was one of a long row of terraced houses in one of the poorest parts of Blackburn; even nowadays, prices for such a property are in the region of £80,000.

There, he saw Peter Griffiths, a 22-year-old flour mill packer. Calvert asked if he had any objection to having his fingerprints taken. He made no reply, but neither did he protest. He supplied his fingerprints, and his name, address and National Registration Number (NBA 6917-188) were added to the card, which was duly handed to Inspector Barton. An examination revealed that the prints on card No. 46253 were identical with those on the bottle.

It was discovered that Griffiths worked night-shift at a nearby flour mill, and by 9 o'clock on the evening of Friday, 13 August, the plan to arrest him had been set up. The officers would wait until Griffiths left the house; there was one long continuous loft space running straight through the terrace, and it was feared that if he managed to get into this, any of the neighbours or police officers could be injured. The local police thought it possible (incorrectly, as it happened) that Griffiths might be in possession of a firearm, since many wartime servicemen returning from overseas brought with them a captured weapon as a souvenir. Capstick was secreted in a building opposite, and a few minutes after 9.00 pm, Griffiths left the house. He walked down Birley Street and into Moss Street, where a police car was waiting. Capstick, Barton and Millen stopped him, and Barton said, 'We're police officers. I'm going to arrest you for the murder of June Anne Devaney at Queen's Park Hospital on the 14th/15th May this year.' He then cautioned him.

'What's it to do with me?' replied Griffiths. 'I've never been near the place.'

He was then put in the back of the police car next to Capstick, and the car drove off to Blackburn police station. During the journey, Griffiths said, 'I've never been in any ward at Queen's Park Hospital, but as a lad I used to play in the Delph there.'

Capstick cautioned him for a second time.

Shortly afterwards, Griffiths said, 'Is it my fingerprints why you came to me?' and Capstick replied, 'Yes' and cautioned him again.

As they arrived at the police station, Barton was waiting on the pavement. Griffiths got out of the car and said, 'Well, if they're about my fingerprints on the bottle, I'll tell you all about it.'

Nobody had mentioned anything about the bottle, so that was an interesting admission; and Griffiths was cautioned for a fourth time.

Ernie Millen then took down Griffith's statement which read as follows:

I want to say that on the night the little girl was killed at the Queen's Park Hospital, it was on a Friday night, the Friday before Whitsun. I left home that night on my own about six o'clock. I went out to spend a quiet night on my own. I went to the Dun Horse pub or hotel and bought myself about five pints of bitter beer, then I went to Yates Wine Lodge and had a glass of Guinness and two double rums. I then had another glass of Guinness and then went back to the Dun Horse again. I then had about six more pints of bitter, I was on my own and came out of there at closing time. I walked down to Jubilee Street off Darwin Street, and I saw a man smoking a cigarette sitting in a small closed car with the hood on, with wire wheels, they were painted silver. I did not know him, I had never seen him before, I asked the man for a light as I had no matches to light my cigarette. I stayed gabbing to him for about fifteen minutes, he said to me, 'Are you going home?' I said, 'No, I'm going to walk round a bit and sober up first.' He asked me where I lived and I told him. He said, 'Well get in, open the window and I'll give you a spin.' He took me to the front of the Queen's Park Hospital and I got out opposite the iron railings. I don't know what happened to him. I never saw him again. I must have got over the railings, but the next thing I remember was being outside the ward where there was some children. I left my shoes outside a door which had a brass knob, I tried the door and it opened to my touch and I went just in and I heard a nurse humming and banging things as if she was washing something so I came out again and waited a few minutes. Then I went back in again and went straight in the ward like, I think I went in one or two small rooms like, like a kitchen, and then came back into the ward again. I then picked up a biggish bottle off a shelf. I went halfway down the ward with it and then put it down on the floor, I then thought I heard the nurse coming, I turned round sharply, over-balanced and fell against a bed. I remember the child woke up and started to cry and I hushed her, she then opened her eyes, saw me and the child in the next bed started whimpering. I picked up the girl out of the cot and took her outside by the same door. I carried her in my right arm and she put her arms around my neck and I walked with her down the hospital field. I put her down on the grass. She started crying again and I tried to stop her from crying but she wouldn't do like, she wouldn't stop crying. I just lost my temper then and you know what happened then. I banged her head against the wall. I then went back to the veranda outside the ward, sat down and put my shoes on. I then went back to where the child was. I like just glanced at her but did not go right up to her but went straight on down to the field to the Delph. I crossed over the path alongside the Delph leading into Queen's Park. I walked through the park and came out on Audley. I went down Cherry Street into Furthergate, then I went down Eanam to Birley Street and got home somewhere around two o'clock on Saturday morning. It would be somewhere about that time, I went in my house, took me collar and tie off and slept in my suit on the couch downstairs. Mother and father were in bed and did not know what time I came in. I woke up about nine o'clock, got up, washed and shaved, then pressed me suit because I was going out again after I had had my breakfast. I went out then down the town, had a walk round then went to the Royal cinema afternoon, came out of the pictures at five o'clock, went home and had my tea. I looked at the papers and read about the murder. It didn't shake me so that I just carried on normally after that. My mother and father asked me where I had been that night and what time I came home and I told them I had been out boozing and had got home at twelve o'clock. This is all I can say and I'm sorry for both parents' sake and I hope I get what I deserve.

Now that a full set of fingerprints was obtained from Griffiths, it was discovered that the ten other sets of fingerprints on the bottle – 'L' through to 'DD' - were identified as his. His footprints in stocking feet matched those found in the ward precisely. The blue and red woollen fibres which had been found in the waxed floor of the ward matched the wool of the socks found in Griffiths' bedroom. He had pawned the suit he had worn on the night of the murder on 31 May for £1 10s 8d and he left the pawn ticket with his mother, who handed it to the police; laboratory tests revealed that fibres from the suit were identical to those found at the ward's window. Additionally, the suit's woollen fibres, ranging in colour between blue and violet, were identical to those found on the body of June Anne, as they were on her nightdress.

There was more. There were traces of Group 'A' blood – the same as June Anne's – on the suit: at the bottom of the trouser fly, the lining of both side pockets, the lining of both sleeves, on the right front above the top button on the jacket and on the lapels – these last were blood splashes, rather than smears.

Griffiths wanted to distance himself from the rape of the child; in his statement, he contented himself by saying simply, 'You know what happened then.' An adult pubic hair was found on the little girl's genital area, and in the presence of his solicitor, Griffiths was asked for a sample of his pubic hair; he replied, 'I would not care to.'

When he was charged with murder by Inspector Barton, he replied, 'I do not wish to say anything.'

He appeared at Blackburn Borough Police Court on 16 August; public feeling ran high, and it was necessary to request a squad of mounted police officers from Liverpool to keep order. After a series of remands, on 2 September Griffiths was committed in custody for trial at Lancashire Assizes. Capstick's enquiries continued, to ensure that he had a watertight case and also to ponder the background of the murderer who, like Jack Quentin Smith's killer, was 5 feet 10½ inches tall, thin, young and possessed of deep-set, staring eyes.

★   ★   ★

The background enquiry started with Griffiths' father, also named Peter. In July 1918 he was admitted to Prestwich Mental Hospital as 'a dangerous lunatic soldier' suffering from what was then described as 'delusional insanity' and later as schizophrenia. There he remained until 25 March 1919, when he was discharged as 'recovered'. Following his release, his behaviour was regarded as 'queer'; he was only able to obtain employment as a loom sweeper in a cotton mill, about the least skilled form of work in that industry, and he was delusional. In 1931 a murder had been committed in Yorkshire, and four men were circulated as being wanted for the offence. Peter Griffiths Sr. had gone to the Central Police Office in Blackburn saying that he had seen the four men, plus the car in which they were travelling, during the early hours of the morning; it was a complete fabrication. The illness of Griffiths' father is mentioned because it is a commonly held medical belief that schizophrenia can be hereditary.

Griffiths Sr. married Elizabeth Alice on 28 June 1923 – she was unaware of his stay in hospital – and there were three children: James Joseph Brennan (Elizabeth's son from a previous relationship), Mary Ellen and Peter Griffiths, who was born in 1926. They were raised in a household of grinding poverty. When he was six years of age, Peter Griffiths fell from a milk float, landing on his head. His mother was not aware of the incident until a week later, and he did not receive medical attention for it. Two years later, he was admitted to Queen's Park Hospital due to incontinence of urine, and there, perhaps surprisingly, he stayed for two years. No records existed, nor were any explanations given for the prolonged stay.

In the same way that the police referred to Griffiths Sr. as 'queer', the epithet was used by Peter Griffiths' mother to describe her offspring. He was solitary, had no friends, was not interested in sport and was forgetful. Much of his time was spent in his room, playing with matches and cutting out pictures from magazines. As he grew older, he was a loafer, sponging off his parents, and between the ages of fifteen and sixteen he was arrested on three occasions for breaking into premises; but as a juvenile, he would have been dealt with by means of summons, and consequently his fingerprints were not taken. Between December 1939 and February 1944 he had twelve different jobs, interspersed with periods of unemployment. On 17 February 1944 he was called up for military service as a private in the Welsh Guards. He served in Africa and North-West Europe and was slightly wounded. He went absent without leave or deserted on two occasions, but each time he was recaptured, he refused to say where he had been or what he had done. When he was discharged from the Army in February 1948, his military character was described as 'indifferent' – or in more prosaic terms, utterly useless.

He worked for approximately six weeks until 21 May 1948 – this employment commenced round about the time that Jack Quentin Smith was murdered – and had no other employment until 10 August, when he worked for one day.

Perhaps surprisingly for such a solitary person, Griffiths had a girlfriend, named Rene Edge. She was a mill worker and also a cub mistress and a member of the chapel choir; they had kept company on and off for five or six years. He appeared very attached to her; they would go for country walks and visits to the cinema. Griffiths was prone to bouts of heavy drinking, and this resulted in squabbles between the couple. During his Army service, Griffiths wrote frequently to Miss Edge, and following his demobilization, they resumed their relationship.

There were two further disagreements about Griffiths' excessive drinking; perhaps, with her strong moral background, Miss Edge thought she could curtail her boyfriend's bibulous habits. The first row was round about the time of Jack Quentin Smith's murder, when their relationship was broken off; but it was after the second of these upsets, which occurred on 10 May, that Griffiths committed June Anne's murder.

The day after the murder, Sunday, 16 May, she and Griffiths, who was wearing his freshly-pressed suit, went for a walk. Jokingly, she asked him what he was doing on the night of the murder; he replied that he had gone to town, had a few drinks, come home at about 10.45 pm and gone to bed. Nothing that he said, or his conduct – from the time of the murder to his arrest – suggested anything that would draw attention to his dark secret.

There was another incident just prior to the murder. The half-brother, James Brennan, had been estranged for three months from his wife, Elizabeth Ellen Brennan, with whom he had five children. He had returned to live at 31 Birley Street, and on 8 May there was a disagreement at that address between the couple, with James Brennan demanding custody of the children. Mrs Brennan was particularly vexed with her husband because their daughter, Pauline, who was aged two years, nine months, was in hospital and he had not been to see her. He replied that he did not know where she was; she informed him that it was Queen's Park Hospital – Ward CH3 – and said this in the presence of Peter Griffiths.

Several witnesses would testify that Griffiths loved children, especially his nieces and nephews, but when he was told that his niece Pauline was in Ward CH3 – she was in fact there on the night of the murder – he was unaware that she was not in the same room as June Anne Devaney. Did this explain why he went from cot to cot in that ward – this was borne out by his footprints – and was he looking for Pauline? Why had he picked up the Winchester bottle? The general consensus of opinion was that he intended to use it as a weapon in the event that he was interrupted during his depredations.

A chilling indication of Griffiths' mental state may be gleaned from the results of a search of his bedroom at Birley Street. Among a bundle of old letters there were five sheets of notepaper. On them, in Griffiths own unformed handwriting, was a misspelt old Arabic proverb that was used in the opening scenes of Merian C. Cooper and Ernest B. Schoedsack's 1933 film about the giant ape, *King Kong*:

> WARNING
> For lo and behold, when the beast
> Look down upon the face of beuty
> It staids its hand from Killing
> And from that day on
> It were as one dead.
>   The Terror

In the meantime, the investigation continued. On 25 August, an identification parade was held at Walton prison. Griffiths was one of nine men on the parade and was identified by the taxi driver, Bernard Regan, as the man he had taken to the hospital on the night of the murder.

David Lee, who had been seriously wounded when Jack Smith was murdered, also attended a parade. He was unable to identify anybody, saying that Griffiths was 'too tall'.

Ernie Millen had played a large part in gathering and collating the evidence, and it would be fair to say that he had no sympathy for Griffiths, probably because like the Devaney family, he had just the one daughter, who was then aged nine. During a previous murder investigation, as Millen was about to go into the witness box, the accused said to Millen's senior officer, 'If Ernie Millen gives evidence that hangs me, I'll come back and haunt him.'

To this, the officer replied, 'You'll have to get in the fucking queue!'

Griffiths once asked him how much of a chance Millen thought he had. Holding his outstretched thumb and forefinger close together, Millen replied, 'About so much' and obviously said it with such conviction that Griffiths replied, 'I thought as much.'

This may have played on Griffiths' mind. During a journey by police van from the prison to court, he asked for some water. The van stopped at a garage, and Inspector Barton got an earthenware jug of water, which he poured into a glass. Millen saw – or perhaps thought he saw – a certain expression on Griffiths' face and knocked the glass to the ground, where it smashed.

'What have you done that for?' exclaimed Barton.

'It's taken us this long to catch him . . .' muttered Millen. 'Let him drink out of the jug.'

Griffiths later admitted that it was his intention to crush the glass in his mouth, 'in order to do the job myself'.

The trial commenced on 15 October 1948 at the Castle, the autumn Lancashire Assizes, before Mr Justice Oliver. Mr W. Gorman KC and Mr D. Brabin appeared for the prosecution, with Mr Basil Nield KC, MP and Mr J. V. Nahum for the defence. Griffiths pleaded not guilty to the murder.

Very little of the evidence was in dispute, until it came to the state of Griffiths' mind. Doctors Gilbert Bailey and Geoffrey Talbot thought he was not responsible for his actions; Dr Alistair Robertson Grant thought that he was; and then Dr Francis Herbert Brisby, who had been the principal medical officer at Walton Gaol for twenty-two years and had kept Griffiths under constant observation, was called by the prosecution to rebut the evidence of the first two doctors.

The photographs of the dead child (which Millen described as being 'the most horrifying I have ever seen in my experience of police work') were never shown to the jury.

There was an impassioned plea from the defence for the jury to find Griffiths, 'guilty of the act but insane at the time'. Summing up, the judge told the jury:

> You are not bound by any of the doctors' opinions in this matter – you are not bound at all. You will ask yourselves before you return your verdict: when this man did this act – I am assuming that he did it – when he did this act, did he know that what he was doing was wrong? – and if he did, then your verdict will be, guilty of murder. Will you please consider your verdict.

This was the second day of the trial; the jury retired at 4.40 pm, only to return 25 minutes later and find Griffiths guilty of murder.

Before passing the sentence of death, Mr Justice Oliver told Griffiths, 'This jury has found you guilty of a crime of the most brutal ferocity. I entirely agree with their verdict.'

On 11 November, the Home Secretary, Mr Chuter Ede, stated that the death sentence would stand. On the day before the execution, Griffith was visited by Capstick and Superintendent Lindsay of Lancashire CID. Once more, Griffiths was asked if he had murdered Jack Quentin Smith; the answer, as before, was 'No.' Was he responsible? It seems highly likely that he was.

Griffiths was hanged on 19 November 1948 at Walton Gaol.

Sixteen days previously, 46,500 fingerprint cards were publicly pulped at a Blackburn paper mill in the presence of the mayor, the Chief Constable and many other luminaries; the event was given immense publicity. Not all of the printed cards were destroyed; about 500 were kept at the request of their owners, who wanted a memento of the biggest fingerprint hunt in criminal history.

CHAPTER 8

The Deadly Doctor

Eastbourne is a pretty town on the south coast of England. Not too large, at just over 17 square miles, it boasted a pier, Victorian hotels and smart, expensive houses, mainly occupied by those who could well afford them: retired, prosperous businessmen and their wives.

But matters changed during the Second World War; initially thought a safe haven for evacuees from London, it was in fact directly on the line of Hitler's proposed invasion of England. But although 'Operation Sealion' never materialized, bombing did: during May 1942 and June 1943, German bombers struck havoc in the town, prompting the Home Office to state that Eastbourne was 'the most bombed town in South-East England'.

During the mid-1920s, when the population of the town was 62,030, a new general practitioner arrived, and some of the town's inhabitants – wealthy ones – began to depart this life rather sooner than was strictly necessary. It seemed Hitler had a competitor. The Luftwaffe claimed the lives of 187 residents; according to the pathologist, Professor Francis Camps, Dr John Bodkin Adams was responsible for 163 deaths.

★   ★   ★

Adams was born in Co. Antrim, Ireland in 1899; his father was a member of the Plymouth Brethren and believed that his son's mistakes and/or slovenliness should be beaten out of him. Perhaps understandably, young Adams discovered that the best way to avoid corporal punishment was to lie and cheat, and this would mean that God would absolve him – in his father's eyes, at least – from his sins. His mendacity would stand him in good stead. Eventually, he passed his medical examinations and qualified as a doctor; with his mother and cousin he arrived in Eastbourne and bought into a practice.

In 1929, he borrowed £2,900 from William Mawhood, who was one of his patients, and purchased a three-storey house called Kent Lodge at 6 Trinity Trees. He then got into the habit of charging items to the Mawhoods' accounts at local stores without their permission. Prior to Mr Mawhood's death in 1949, his wife caught Adams telling her husband to leave him all of his money and assuring him that 'she would be well cared for', and she chased him out of the house. Adams received nothing from the will; instead, he helped himself to a 22ct gold pen and put in a bill for his services to the amount of £1,102. Mrs Mawhood described Adams as 'a real scrounger' and never saw him again.

Some questions were raised regarding Florence Emily Chessum, a 72-year-old widow who died in May 1936 without leaving a will, but from whom Adams received £689. A spinster left a sum to Adams when she died – she had witnessed the wills of three other women (each of whom named Adams as the beneficiary) – but she hardly knew him and she died thirteen days after one of the three. But this was mere speculative chatter.

A matter that was more than idle gossip centred on Mrs Matilda Whitton, who died at the Kenilworth Court Hotel on 11 May 1935. She left £11,465 12s 3d, of which Adams received £7,385; but although the will was contested by Mrs Whitton's relatives, it was upheld in court. Adams also helped himself to Mrs Whitton's gold watch, which he took off her dead wrist.

There was a nasty rumour that when Adams visited a blind patient, he had helped himself to her chocolates; and solicitors representing Agnes Pike were concerned by the amount of hypnotic drugs being administered to their client in August 1939, especially since Adams had banned her relatives from seeing her. The solicitors called in another doctor, who could find no trace of disease, but Mrs Pike was incoherent, delirious and gave her age as being two hundred. During the other doctor's examination, Adams suddenly administered a morphine injection 'in case she becomes violent', and his medication (and his services) was immediately withdrawn. Two months later, after being in the care of the second doctor, Mrs Pike had completely regained her faculties, knew her correct age and was able to do her own shopping.

Ada Harris was another survivor; she permitted Adams to arrange the sale of her house and he promptly pocketed the £1,901 proceeds. It was only the threat of legal action by Mrs Harris' solicitors that produced repayment in full.

Another who slipped through Adams' net was wealthy widow Mrs Margaret Pilling; Adams had been called when she succumbed to influenza. Within two weeks, due to heavy drugging, she was described as being 'practically in a coma', her condition was deteriorating rapidly and she was unable to recognize members of her family. They were so concerned that they spirited her away from Eastbourne (and, of course, from Adams) and took a house for her at Ascot. Two more weeks passed, and at the end of that time, not only had Mrs Pilling fully recovered, she was able to attend the races and a friend's wedding.

In 1941, Adams gained a diploma in anaesthetics and worked one day a week at the Princess Alice Hospital. He was described as 'a bungler', often falling asleep during operations, eating cakes, counting money and mixing up the anaesthetic tubes, which resulted in the unfortunate patients either waking up or turning blue.

But notwithstanding these deficiencies, by the time thirty years had gone by, Adams was the wealthiest GP in the area and possibly in the whole of England. It was not that he was a brilliant doctor – he most certainly was not – but his patients included some of the most affluent people in the town. He often eschewed presenting a bill at the time of their treatment, requesting instead that they remember him in their wills. He often went one step further, assisting them to prepare their wills, which would some-times name him as the sole executor. A case in question was when Adams took over the finances of Irene Herbert and helped her make a new will; when she died at the early age of fifty in 1944, Adams found himself £1,000 the richer.

He would usually encourage cremation to be specified in the will. And when others were named as executors, they would often be astonished to receive a staggeringly large bill from Adams, even though he had previously airily dismissed the idea of such a payment, since he had been named as a beneficiary. This happened when Emily Mortimer died in 1946; not only did Adams benefit by £3,600 in her will, he also slipped in an invoice for his services to the tune of £234.

Adams was an unprepossessing sight at 5 feet 5 inches and 17 stone (fuelled by his obsession with chocolates), bald, his grey/green eyes blinking behind steel-rimmed spectacles; but he fawned on his usually elderly patients, turning out at all hours of the day and night for them, and the vast majority adored him, with his quiet, comforting Irish brogue and his injections. Sometimes there was a variation on the theme. Annie Norton-Dowling had what turned out to be cancer of the stomach; one doctor advised an early X-ray – Adams said not. He carried on with his injections, and when she was finally operated on, it was too late, and she died in November 1952. Under her new will, made three months before she died, Adams benefited to the tune of £500.

Often, Adams' syringes contained heroin or morphine. Some-times, the patients received a dose of both drugs. And more often than not, there was no earthly reason why these patients should have been administered such drugs at all.

These pampered individuals were unaware of the contents of those deadly syringes; all they knew was that the portly, balding, bespectacled Irishman, who held their hands so comfortingly and told them precisely what they wanted to hear, was the finest doctor they had ever met.

So the GP who had initially used a 2½hp Velocette motorcycle on his rounds now had a Rolls-Royce (plus another in the garage) and was chauffeur-driven to his appointments. As well as receiving a host of bequests, he had a whole range of adoring patients. But not everybody loved Dr Bodkin Adams. Most of the other GPs in the area detested him, not only because they thought him incompetent but because he had cornered the market in prosperous patients. Many of the nurses employed by his patients were not too keen on him, either. He was often as rude and brusque to them as he was obsequious towards their employers; and it was certainly not unknown for the nurse to be sent out of the room whilst he tended to a patient.

Adams had now established himself as a pillar of local society; he was prominent in the local YMCA, he was a member of both the Bisley Rifle Club and André Simon's Wine and Food Society, as well as being the founder of a local camera club. He was certainly the darling of many of the wealthier residents of Eastbourne. It was inevitable that petty jealousies would arise, but there was more than that; rumour was sweeping the town, and when the highly suspicious deaths of two of Adams' patients – Mr and Mrs Hullett – were brought to the notice of the town's Chief Constable, Robert Wallace, action had to be taken. But those enquiries would have to be circumspect. The Chief Constable and his wife were Adams' patients, and when Detective Inspector Brynley Pugh was deputed to investigate he found it embarrassing, because Adams had delivered two of Pugh's children. Then there was Adams' friendship with Sir Roland Vaughan Gwynne DSO, previously the mayor and now chairman of the Magistrates' Court. Sir Roland was a noted and flamboyant homosexual, who frequently went on holidays with Adams; it was rumoured that Adams was also gay and that he attended louche parties, at which the crowd included Alexander Seekings, the deputy to the Chief Constable. Although homosexual acts were then a criminal offence, nobody made detailed enquiries of that particular clique to discover who did what to whom; but it was clear that in respect of enquiries into the deaths in the town, the resources of the local police would be insufficient, and it was inevitable that the Yard would be called in.

Two detectives from C1 Murder Squad were sent, and it is interesting to take a close look at both of them.

★　★　★

The senior man was Detective Superintendent Herbert Wheeler Walter Hannam, who had joined the Met on 12 December 1927. His first commissioner's commendation was awarded five years later, when he was a police constable on 'V' Division, for 'skill and ability in the arrest of a suspected person'; by the end of his career, he would be awarded fifteen more commendations. Bert Hannam could not be described as the 'bull in a china shop' type of cop; he was patient and methodical, gathering in every available piece of information in an investigation before he pounced. He was also immaculately dressed, known to his contemporaries as 'Suits' Hannam and to the press as 'The Count'. He smoked expensive cigars, spoke with a cultured (or perhaps cultivated) accent, and he had bags of charisma. But more than anything else, he was not cowed by lawyers in court. When police were accused of impropriety in the witness box, it was the norm for purple-faced officers to splutter, 'No, Sir!' and nothing more. Hannam, however, not only impressively denied allegations of misconduct, he would also fence with the barrister concerned and, in so doing, score impressive points in the eyes of the jury.

One such case was that of Alfred Charles Whiteway, who was on trial at the Old Bailey in 1953; he had raped, then murdered two teenagers with an axe on a towpath near Teddington, and had also raped a third girl, who had survived. It was whilst Whiteway was on remand in Brixton prison in respect of the latter rape that he was again interviewed by Hannam regarding the murders.

Whiteway had already made a 16-page statement denying murder. Now, twenty-four days after obtaining that statement, during which time Hannam had intensified his enquiries, he told Whiteway that he had one or two points which needed clearing up and produced the offending axe from his briefcase.

'Blimey, that's it!' exclaimed Whiteway. He then made a further statement, still repudiating the murders and denying that one of his shoes was covered in blood.

When the statement was completed, Whiteway said, 'Were you kidding about the blood on my shoe?' to which Hannam replied, 'One of your shoes had heavy bloodstains on it.'

Whiteway paled and trembled before exclaiming, 'You know bloody well it was me. I didn't mean to kill 'em. I never wanted to hurt anyone.'

Hannam then invited Whiteway to make a further statement, which he did. In part, it read:

> It's all up. You know fucking well I done it, eh? That shoe's fucked me. What a fucking mess. I'm mental. Me head must be wrong. I must have a woman, I cannot stop myself . . . Put that bloody chopper away, it haunts yer.

If the statement could be relied upon, it was a complete confession, but it came in for devastating criticism from the defence barrister, Peter Rawlinson, after the judge said that the suggestion by the defence was that the statement – exhibit 24 – was a completely manufactured piece of fiction written by Hannam, who calmly stated, 'That is completely untrue.'

Rawlinson riposted with: 'I suggest that no such words were ever used by Whiteway on July 30 or at any other time when you saw him?'

'If you are referring to exhibit 24, my answer is that they are in his own words, from his own lips.'

'I repeat the suggestion that that statement was invented by you.'

'I repeat it is a shocking suggestion and I am pleased to deny it.'

In his summing up, the judge told the jury, 'Look at the statement . . . do you think that an experienced novelist, a writer of fiction could have done much better than that?' Rather dismissively, and with a strong note of disbelief in his voice, he then remarked, 'It is *said* to have been done by a police officer!'

Whiteway was convicted; his appeal was smartly kicked into touch by the Lord Chief Justice, and he was duly hanged.

There was absolutely no doubt that Whiteway was guilty; the statement had gone into such minute detail that only the murderer could have written it. The only way to discredit the statement was to discredit Hannam, hence the all-out attack on his character by Rawlinson. This would be one of several attacks on Hannam's veracity; the next came when he investigated corruption, after a Maltese pimp named Joseph Grech was sentenced to three years' imprisonment for housebreaking. He had tried the rather clever defence of saying that the key which fitted the front door of the burgled premises and which had been found in his possession was, in fact, the key to his own front door and that the locks were therefore identical. To assist with this ingenious theory, he bribed Detective Sergeant Robert 'Jock' Robertson to try to get a locksmith to manufacture a lock to his own front door that would be opened by the same key. When the duplicate lock was not forthcoming and Grech was convicted, he complained to the Yard, and the matter was investigated by Hannam.

Astonishing admissions were made, with one of the gang telling Hannam, 'Don't hold it against Jock Robertson; he is a decent bloke and he only loaned us the key – "Spider" fixed the rest . . . Grech had a monkey out of the peter and some groins but they were tripe.'

After Hannam had explained to the bemused jury that 'a monkey' was £500, 'a peter' was a safe, 'groins' were rings and the fact that they were 'tripe' meant that they were worthless, the sergeant, a solicitor and a go-between were convicted and sentenced to various terms of imprisonment.[1]

Matters went further than that; Hannam thoroughly investigated the whole cloud of corruption that surrounded West End Central police station, and an inspector was sacked and others transferred. It was during the trial that Hannam brought the completed file into court which, with every indication of reluctance, he handed to the Lord Chief Justice, telling him, 'I do not want to let it out of my hands', adding, 'It is highly confidential.' It was a piece of inspired Hannam showmanship, giving the impression to the jury that the file would be seen at cabinet level, and that if that was the case, the prisoners in the dock must be guilty.

But despite the bravura, the showmanship and the charismatic persona, Hannam was a straight cop and a hardworking and dedicated one. It was a great pity that his efforts in the bribery case irked some senior officers – including the Commissioner, Sir John Nott-Bower – as well as not a few junior ones, seeing that he had worked so thoroughly to expose the corruption at West End Central.

The second of the Yard's officers was Hannam's bag-carrier, Detective Sergeant Charles Ernest Hewett. After ten years service in the Met, Hewett was promoted to detective sergeant (second class) and on 5 July 1948 he was posted to the Flying Squad. It was the rule in those days – indeed, it continued to be for many years afterwards – that a newcomer to the Flying Squad was not really accepted by his contemporaries until he had proved himself

---

[1] For further details of this case, see *Scotland Yard's Ghost Squad: The Secret War Against Post-War Crime*, Pen & Sword Books, 2011

in some way. It took Charlie Hewett just three weeks to do so. On 28 July, he was part of a Flying Squad team who set up an ambush in a warehouse at Heathrow Airport. They had received information that a gang was going to steal goods worth £237,900, having drugged the coffee of three security guards, and the guards were replaced by three Squad officers, of whom Hewett was one. Feigning unconsciousness, the three 'guards' were slumped over a table when the gang entered the warehouse; Hewett was slapped across the face and kicked in the stomach by one of the gang, Alfred Roome, before the safe keys were taken from his pocket. As the keys were inserted in the safe, the 'attack' was given, Squad officers rushed out from behind the packing cases where they had been secreted and a battle royal commenced. Severe injuries were inflicted on both sides, and Hewett dished out some of the most severe to Roome; he later said, 'I didn't feel guilty about what I did to "Big Alfie".'

In fact, 'Big Alfie' was not among the eight prisoners who appeared at Uxbridge Magistrates' Court later that morning; his injuries were so severe that he was hospitalized. He was able to later join the others in the dock at the Old Bailey, where they all pleaded guilty to robbery with violence. The Recorder of London bemoaned the fact that an Act of Parliament had recently abolished corporal punishment but told them, 'You went prepared for punishment and you got it. You got the worst of it and you can hardly complain about that,' and sentenced them to a total of 71 years' penal servitude.[2]

Hewett's bona fides were certainly established with his contemporaries and not only with them; the ultra-secret Ghost Squad, tasked with tackling the post-war warehouse-breakers, hijackers and receivers, were not supposed to carry out arrests themselves, so needed resolute officers to make arrests from the information gleaned from their snouts and decided that Hewett fitted the bill admirably. They chose wisely; Hewett was responsible for carrying out twenty-two arrests and recovered stolen quantities of timber, cloth, nylons and lorries with their contents, valued at over £23,000.

Hewett spent six years with the Squad and during that time he was commended by the Commissioner for his courage and excellent detective ability on twelve occasions. Promoted to

---

2 For further details of this case, see *The Sweeney: The First Sixty Years of Scotland Yard's Crimebusting Flying Squad 1919–1978*, Pen & Sword Books, 2011

detective sergeant (first class), he was posted to C1 Department – and Bert Hannam.

They couldn't have been more unalike. Hannam, forty-eight years of age, grey-haired, dignified, 'an officer of the old school, a very private man', as Hewett's son described him to me, had cut his teeth on murder investigations as the bag-carrying detective sergeant to such luminaries as Detective Chief Inspector Peter Beveridge. Hannam possessed an almost photographic memory; he could memorize whole passages of script without having to resort to his notes. Hewett was six years younger, an inch and half shorter, balding, cheerful and a detective brought up in the rough and tumble, hit and run tactics of the Flying Squad. But together they made a formidable team.

'I remember Dad once joking that he thought Bert must have descended to earth a fully fledged DI', David Hewett told me, 'as he couldn't picture him getting up to the sort of things that DCs and DSs did!'

* * *

The press coverage of the Adams case was sensational. 'Yard Probe Mass Poisonings', claimed the *Daily Mail*, whilst the *Evening Standard* treated its readers to 'Mystery of 300 Women' under the banner headline, 'Yard Probing Hypnotic Killer Theory. Ten Years of Murder'.

Under the editorship of Michael Foot MP, *Tribune* hit back, stating, 'Not a scrap of evidence has been discovered to support any theory of a maniac killer.' Certainly with one eye on a possible slump in the tourist trade, this was backed up by Brighton's mayor, Alderman Sydney Caffeyn, who said, 'I am extremely distressed at the unfortunate publicity the resort is receiving.'

However, those fears were offset (certainly for the time being) by the reporters, over a hundred of them from London, Europe and the USA, who set up camp in the town's hotels, pubs, bed and breakfasts and boarding houses.

Hannam (who during the towpath murder investigation had held two press conferences a day), like most senior detectives of that era, was an ace manipulator of the press. In fact, Reggie Spooner, the head of the Flying Squad, would hold court with reporters in the snug bar of the Red Lion, by Cannon Row police station, telling them which stories they should publish and which they should put on hold. So now, Hannam held court with the reporters who had thronged to the seaside resort.

However, the chief crime reporter of the *Daily Express*, Percy Hoskins, was not among them. He disliked Hannam, especially after Peter Rawlinson, who had been the defence barrister in the towpath case, was employed by Hoskins' paper as a legal advisor. It had been suggested that Hannam had manufactured evidence in that case, and although that was nonsense, Hoskins now not only started a campaign in the paper to clear Adams, he also befriended him. It was an odd situation: a well-respected crime reporter, with many contacts among the senior figures at the Yard, taking sides with an alleged murderer; and it was dangerous for the newspaper, too. If Adams fell, so would Hoskins, and the credibility of the paper would take a nosedive. Was it part of an inventive plan to discredit Hannam? It certainly looked that way.

★ ★ ★

Charlie Hewett was one of the team who discovered that Adams had, in the previous ten years, been mentioned in 132 wills. The death certificates of those people (and others) were also scrutinized; Adams had signed 301 of them, of which 163 were considered suspicious.

Of immediate interest to Hannam was the death of 50-year-old Mrs Gertrude 'Bobbie' Hullett on 23 July 1956; on the death of her husband, Jack, four months earlier, she had been left £107,647 in his will. The death certificates of both husband and wife had been signed by Adams. In Mrs Hullett's case, the cause of death was shown as bronchopneumonia and respiratory failure. That conclusion was also reached by the noted pathologist, Professor Francis Camps, who carried out a post mortem on the body. However, he also found that barbiturate poisoning was a contributory factor. Perhaps there was a mystery attached to Mrs Hullett's death, and if so, it would be flushed out at the inquest. And perhaps not.

On 21 August 1956 the inquest, which had already been opened and adjourned, now recommenced at Eastbourne with a jury of six men and two women, under the direction of the coroner, Dr A. C. Sommerville. The jury heard that Mrs Hullett had been depressed since the death of her husband and that on 19 July she went to bed, complaining of a headache. There she remained, unconscious, until the morning of 23 July, when she died. On Saturday 21 July, Dr Ronald Vincent Harris had gone to Mrs Hullett's cliff-top house at Holywell Mount, King Edward Parade. He was in partnership with Dr Adams, who was temporarily unavailable. In the bedroom there was no evidence of a container or empty bottle which suggested that tablets might have been taken. Later the same day, Dr Adams arrived, spent the night at the house and told Mrs Hullett's daughter, Patricia Tomlinson, that there had been 'some sort of pressure on the brain'. This was the conclusion reached by a joint consultation with Harris, but they decided to call Dr Arthur Geoffrey Shera, a consultant pathologist. When Dr Shera examined Mrs Hullett he felt that her condition might well be due to narcotic poisoning and suggested that her stomach contents should be examined, but both Adams and Harris were opposed to this. Nevertheless, specimens were taken and sent to the local hospital.

Dr Adams – he was represented by a barrister, Mr J. R. Cumming-Bruce – told the court that he had prescribed sleeping tablets – two, each containing 7½ grains of barbitone, to be taken each night. However, before he had gone on holiday in May, he had supplied her with thirty-six more tablets 'to keep her going', and twenty-four more since then, plus some phenol-barbitone tablets.

'Then in eighty days she had taken 1,512 grains of barbitone?' asked the coroner, to which Adams shrugged and replied, 'I'm not a mathematician.' He added that he believed that Mrs Hullett was suffering from a cerebral haemorrhage and did not suspect anything else until later.

'Surely, with this woman in a depressed state', asked the coroner, 'it would have been reasonable to wonder if she had taken an overdose of barbitone?' but Adams was ready for that one, saying he had expected that the hospital would have given the results of the tests more promptly than they had. Since the specimens had not been submitted to the hospital until Saturday evening, and the results arrived on the Monday when Mrs Hullett died, it is difficult to know how much prompter they could have been.

In a letter written on 17 July, Mrs Hullett had asked her executor to ensure that Adams' blue MG Sports car (a bequest from her late husband) was paid for, and a cheque for £1,000 was taken by Adams to his bank, the Westminster, which was paid in on 18 July. Normally, it would have been credited to Adams' account two days later, but Adams asked the manager, John Robert Oliver, for 'special clearance' which, Mr Oliver told the court, was 'highly unusual'. Special clearance usually meant either that the recipient was in urgent need of funds or it was thought that the provider might not have sufficient funds in their account to meet the payment. In this particular transaction, these notions were nonsensical; both parties were wealthy. The cheque was cleared the following day, but had Mrs Hullett died prior to the cheque being cleared, it would have been dishonoured. What was more, in addition to the £1,000, Adams had also received a Rolls-Royce from Mrs Hullett.

Had prompt action been taken, Mrs Hullett might possibly have lived. Following his post mortem on 23 July, Professor Camps' report stated, 'In my opinion, the clinical picture was such as inevitably to lead to a suspicion of barbiturate (or other hypnotic) poisoning.' He discovered twenty barbitone tablets in her stomach, the majority of which had been taken after 10.00 pm on 19 July; they were superimposed on previously taken tablets.

Telling the jury there was no doubt that Mrs Hullett had died from barbiturate poisoning, the coroner said:

> You may consider it most extraordinary that a doctor know-ing the past history of the patient did not at once expect barbiturate poisoning.
>
> If he had . . . then possibly the circumstances might have been otherwise. We do not know. An unreasonable attitude which might be considered by you, as reasonable members of the community, is that a patient was left unconscious all day long and is not attended by anybody until the doctor came in – from 9.00 am to 9.00 pm.

Since the normal, acceptable dose of barbitone tablets was just two, who had administered the extra eighteen?

After thirty-six minutes of deliberation, the jury unanimously decided that Mrs Hullett was responsible and a verdict of suicide was duly recorded. Fourteen witnesses had been heard, the last of whom was Hannam, who agreed with the coroner when he asked if he had been called in to investigate 'certain deaths in this neighbourhood'.

After Adams drove off in his MG sports car, he was interviewed at home by the press. 'I am glad my name has been cleared', he said. 'What started all the rumours, I don't know . . . As for the Rolls-Royce, that was the first time I heard of it today. And I never wanted it; I have a car already.'

But the result of the inquest did not quieten the rumours; they intensified. And while Adams unctuously stated that his name had been cleared, he was one of the few who said – or thought – so.

Enquiries at Somerset House in London continued, and Hannam's team now occupied a large room opposite to the CID office at Eastbourne police station. Along the length of one wall were trestle tables containing files on the dead persons.

On 23 August, for the first time, the word 'exhumation' was mentioned. The following day, the grave of 85-year-old Mrs Julia Bradnum in the Ocklynge Cemetery, Eastbourne was inspected. Her house at Goodwood Bank, Cooper's Hill, Willingdon was now occupied by three elderly spinsters. One of them, Miss Grace Hine, said, 'Mrs Bradnum died very suddenly; there was not even time to call in a nurse. I never knew what she died of.' She had complained of pains in her stomach; Adams was called, gave her an injection and said, 'I'm afraid she's going.' And he was right; she was. Mrs Bradnum changed the contents of her £4,600 will shortly before she died. Her house was sold and the proceeds were split six ways; Adams was a beneficiary.

On the same day, Adams returned to Eastbourne having spent two hours in the company of legal experts from the Medical Defence Union in London, who had provided the barrister for his attendance at the Hullett inquest. 'I can say nothing' he told reporters. It was not only Adams who was given cogent advice; by the following Tuesday the Eastbourne branch of the British Medical Association informed all doctors in the town that they were not to talk about their relationships with patients to anyone without the consent of those patients or, in the event that the patient in question had died, without the consent of the relatives. Asked about a deceased former member of the Upperton Congregational Church, the minister, Dr H. Ingham, told his flock, 'If anybody asks you, say your minister knows no more about it that you do.'

It appeared that certain members of Eastbourne's community – including some police officers – were closing ranks in an effort to frustrate Hannam's enquiries. The Attorney General wrote to the secretary of the British Medical Association (BMA), Dr MacRae, in an effort to get him to lift the ban, but without success. On 8 November, the Attorney met Dr MacRae and, astonishingly, handed him a copy of Hannam's 187-page report to try to convince him of the importance of the enquiry. Dr MacRae took the file to the president of the BMA and returned it the next day. Was a further copy made? Possibly. But not only did it fail to produce a cohort of GPs ready and willing to give evidence against Adams, it rebounded badly on the Attorney, when questions were raised in the House by two Labour members.

Hannam now dealt with the case of Mrs Edith Alice Morrell, who had died aged eighty-one in 1950 at her ten-bedroom home, Marden Ash, on Beachy Head Road. She had changed her will on several occasions (ultimately leaving £77,990), and Hannam interviewed her nurse, Mrs Helen Mason-Ellis.

Mrs Morrell had come to Eastbourne in 1948 and after being attended by Adams had suffered hardening of the blood vessels which supply blood to the brain; in addition, she suffered a slight stroke, which caused her difficulty in walking.

She was a cantankerous old woman who often changed her will. In April 1949, Mrs Morrell's solicitor, Mr Hubert Sogno, received an urgent message from Adams saying that Mrs Morrell was anxious about the contents of her will and wanted to see him that day. A new will was drawn up on 9 June 1949. On 8 March 1950, Sogno received a call from Adams saying that he wished to see him 'very, very urgently'. He said that many months before, Mrs Morrell had promised to leave him her Rolls-Royce Silver Ghost in her will but had forgotten to include it, as well as a locked box at her bank that contained items of jewellery. Adams then made the incredible suggestion that the solicitor should prepare a codicil, that it should be executed and, if it did not meet with the approval of the executor, Mrs Morrell's son, it could be destroyed. The solicitor had no hesitation in telling Adams that this was impossible. Her final will was drawn up on 24 August 1950, and Adams was bequeathed the Rolls-Royce, a chest of silver and an Elizabethan court cupboard.

Although Mrs Morrell did not suffer any appreciable pain from her illness, Adams had prescribed morphine and heroin. There were two aspects to this: first, Mrs Morrell soon developed a dependency on these drugs – in other words, Adams had turned her into an addict; and second, in the two weeks prior to her death, the dosage was increased substantially, to three times as much as in the preceding months. In November it was six times as much as in July and sixteen and a half times as much as in October. On 12 November, she was in a coma. There was no need for an injection, since she was having spasms which one witness said, 'nearly jerked her out of bed' – a common sign of heroin overdose – but Adams gave her a substantial dose and told the nurse to provide another if she failed to quieten down. The nurse did so, and Mrs Morrell died a few hours later on 13 November. The cause of death given by Adams was cerebral thrombosis, and she was cremated. Adams frequently refused to discuss with nurses the nature of injections, but one important point was this: he was qualified as an anaesthetist and therefore knew perfectly well the effect that morphine and heroin would have on a patient. It is likely that Adams visited Mrs Morrell on 321 occasions; he later sent in an invoice claiming fees totalling £1,674.

On 29 August, Hannam spent the day with George Hatherill, the Commander of the CID, to bring him up to date with his enquiries, and Hatherill told him to press right on with them. A little light humour was introduced into the proceedings when a local hypnotist was asked if he could shed any light on the investigation; not only was he unable to do so, but he volunteered to cure Charlie Hewett's catarrh and abysmally failed to do so.

Whilst nurses and relatives of the deceased women continued to be interviewed, on 12 September Professor Camps drove to Eastbourne for a conference with Hannam which lasted two hours. The subject: exhumation. It was a matter that was deferred – for the time being.

On 1 October, Hannam saw Adams at the back of his house as he was putting his car away in the garage following a holiday in Scotland. They spoke in generalities until Adams said, 'You are finding all these rumours untrue, aren't you?'

Hannam replied, 'I am sorry to say that is not my experience, doctor.'

After some more conversation, Adams asked, 'What have you been told about me?'

Hannam mentioned that he knew that Adams had forged prescriptions in the name of another doctor for some of his other National Health patients, to which Adams replied, 'That was very wrong. I've had God's forgiveness for it. All of them were only to help the poor National patients. I love helping these National patients for I gave a vow to God that I would. The health people can afford it . . . You haven't found anything else?'

'Doctor, I have been anxious about some of the gifts you have received under wills from your patients', said Hannam.

'A lot of those were instead of fees. I don't want money; what use is it? I paid £1,100 supertax last year', replied Adams, and when Hannam mentioned the chest of silver, Adams said, 'Mrs Morrell was a very dear patient. She insisted a long time before she died that I should have that in her memory and I didn't want it . . . I knew she was going to leave them to me and her Rolls-Royce car . . . oh yes, and another cabinet.'

Switching his line of questioning, Hannam stated, 'Mr Hullett left you £500.'

'Now, now, he was a lifelong friend', replied Adams. 'He was a very ostentatious man about his wealth; he liked to talk about it. There is no mystery about him; he told me long before his death that he had left me money in his will; I even thought it would have been more than it was . . . Every one of those dear patients I have done my best for. I have one thing in life and God knows I have vowed to Him I would – that is, to relieve pain and try to let these dear people to live as long as possible.'

'Doctor, I have examined the cremation certificate forms you filled in, in your own handwriting, for Jack Hullett and Mrs Morrell', said Hannam, 'and you have said on them that you were not aware that you were a beneficiary under their wills. That is quite a serious offence.'

'Oh, that wasn't done wickedly, God knows it wasn't', protested Adams. 'We always want cremations to go off smoothly for the dear relatives. If I said I knew I was getting money under the will, they might get suspicious, and I like cremations and burials to go off smoothly. There was nothing suspicious, really. It wasn't deceitful.'

'I hope I shall finish these enquiries soon', said Hannam, 'and we will probably have another talk.'

Although those words sounded as ominous as Julius Caesar's warning, 'Thou shalt meet me at Philippi', Adams was unfazed.

'Don't hurry', he replied. 'Please be thorough. It is in my interests. Good night and thank you very much for your kindness.'

Gathering together all of the information he had accrued, on 16 October Hannam sent a report to Alex Findlay, the detective chief superintendent of C1 Branch.

The next meeting was at 8.30 pm on 24 November, when Hannam, Hewett and DI Brynley Pugh arrived at Adams' surgery. Adams, resplendent in black tie, was descending the stairs, about to depart for a dinner engagement. What follows was taken from Hannam's notebook.

'Good evening, doctor. You know who I am?'

'Uh, yeah. Hannam.'

'May we go in to a private room? I have something to say to you.'

'There is no question of a statement, for I have been told not to make one.'

They then went into the surgery, where after some conversation, Hannam said, 'I must tell you immediately I have here a warrant, signed by a magistrate, directing DI Pugh to search the house under the Dangerous Drugs Act; I will read it.'

He did so and cautioned Adams, who replied, 'There are no dangerous drugs here. What do you mean by dangerous drugs?' As he said this, he walked to a built-in cupboard in a right-hand recess with three compartments and three keys in locks and opened the middle one (here Hannam made a small sketch of the cupboard in his notebook).

'I have quite a bit of barbiturates here; is that what you mean?'

'DI Pugh's quest is for dangerous drugs', replied Hannam.

'What do you mean by dangerous drugs? Poisons?'

'Morphine, heroin, pethidine and the like.'

'Uh! That group. You will find none here. I haven't any. I very, very seldom ever use them. I think I have perhaps one little phial of tablets in my bag, but no more.'

At 8.40 pm Hannam made a note that he sent DI Pugh to check the blinds in the front of the house because of the press who had gathered there, and to see what the staff were up to; there were press cameras outside.

'May I have your Dangerous Drugs Register please, or your daybook in which drugs are dealt with?' asked Hannam.

'I don't know what you mean', replied Adams. 'I keep no register.'

'Whenever you obtain for your use a dangerous drug, your acquisition of such must be entered in a proper Dangerous Drugs Register', said Hannam. 'It is that I want.'

'I never knew that', replied Adams. 'I don't keep any record. I am quite at a loss. I have no register and never keep any record of these things.'

Telling Adams, 'We will wait until Mr Pugh returns, for he is the officer directed to make a search', Hannam took from his briefcase the list of medication for Mrs Morrell and said, 'Doctor, look at this list of your prescriptions for Mrs Morrell. There are a lot of dangerous drugs here.'

Adams raised his hands, stopping Hannam. 'Now, all these I left prescriptions for, either at the chemists or at the house. She had nurses day and night.'

'Who administered the drugs?'

'I did, nearly all, perhaps the nurses gave some, but mostly me.'

'Were any left over when she died?'

'No, none. All was given to the patient.'

Hannam then showed Adams the statement which showed details of the last days of the prescribed drugs for Mrs Morrell and said, 'Doctor, you prescribed for her $75\frac{1}{6}$ grains of heroin tablets the day before she died.'

'Poor soul, she was in terrible agony', replied Adams. 'It was all used. I used them myself.'

'I have no medical training myself', said Hannam, 'but surely the quantity of dangerous drugs obtained for Mrs Morrell during the last week of her life alone would be fatal – and is pain usual with a cerebral vascular accident?'

'Let me look at that list,' said Adams, and Hannam showed him the list, running his finger over prescription numbers 87 to 91.

'There might have been a couple of those final tablets over, but I cannot remember', said Adams. 'If there were, I would take them and destroy them. I am not dishonest with drugs. Mrs Morrell had all those because I gave the injections.' Then, perhaps astonishingly, he added, 'Do you think it was too much?'

'That is not a matter for me, Doctor', replied Hannam. 'I simply want to get at the truth. Were those drugs taken to the house by you?'

'The chauffeur collected them and I got them from the nurses', replied Adams.

There was some further conversation, during which Adams stated he did not keep records of what he prescribed to patients and only made a record of visits which was destroyed a year after a patient had died.

What then followed was a series of questions and answers; they appeared on Hannam's police statement but they were never heard in court, being thought to be 'too prejudicial'.

'Many of your patients' deaths, particularly those from whom you received some pecuniary advantage, appear suspicious', said Hannam. 'Can you tell me, what was the injection you gave to Mrs Bradnum?'

'She was a cerebral haemorrhage case, so it would have been a stimulant, quite likely caffeine', replied Adams, adding, 'She was dying when I got there.'

This appeared not to have been the case because, as Hannam said, 'A few minutes before you arrived at her house, she got out of bed, walked across the room and unlocked her bedroom door to admit a member of the household, then got back into bed again.'

'I am not certain what it was I gave her, but it would be a stimulant.'

Changing tack, Hannam asked, 'What was the final injection you gave Mrs Kilgour?' and received the astonishing answer, 'Do you think I killed her, too? This is terrible. I've got no dangerous drugs. I haven't bought any for years and years.'

Adams was now visibly upset; his face was flushed and he wiped away a tear. He had every reason to. Annabella Kilgour had suffered a stroke in July 1950 and had been regularly attended by Adams; on 23 December he administered a hypodermic injection and on Christmas Eve, State Registered Nurse Grace Osgood discovered that she could not be roused, and Adams was again called. He apparently gave her an injection of morphine; she suffered spasms and when she died on 28 December 1950 and Adams certified the death as being due to cerebral thrombosis, the nurse said, 'You realize, Doctor, that you have killed her?' She later said, 'I've never seen a man look so frightened in my life' and told the police that she was most concerned about Mrs Kilgour's death. She was right to be concerned; there was no reason to administer morphine, a pain-killing injection, when Mrs Kilgour was in a coma and therefore not experiencing pain. Her estate was valued at £47,600; there were a number of bequests, including one to Adams, who received a clock and £200.

Hannam's questions now came thick and fast.

'When Miss Hilda Neil-Miller died, what articles did you take from her room?'

'I never took anything.'

'Mrs Sharpe was present and a nurse saw you.'

'What did they say I took?'

'I thought you didn't take anything!'

'I only take what the patient has wished me to have.'

In fact, 86-year-old Miss Neil-Miller, who lived with her sister Clara, aged eighty-seven, had not received any post for months, and Adams had cut off all communication with the two old ladies' relatives.

'What about Miss Clara Neil-Miller? Eleven days before her death, when she was only semi-conscious from sedatives, you got her to sign a cheque for £500 in your favour and one for £200 to Mrs Sharpe, and you knew you were already to receive £500 when she died under her will and you were her sole residuary legatee.'

'A dear lady. She insisted I must have the £500 and said Mrs Sharpe must have a present, and I arranged it to give her peace of mind only.'

'Miss Clara was not in a condition to will you money, was she?'

'She would not have been happy if I had not taken it.'

'Why did she die?'

'She was very weak.'

Hannam said that Adams began to cry for a moment or two and then asked, 'Wasn't her death natural?'

'I made no reply to this', recorded Hannam.

And that was the end of the conversation which was never heard in court; however, the matter of Clara Neil-Miller would resurface several weeks later, and that, too, would never be mentioned in court. At that moment, as DI Pugh returned, Adams flopped into a chair holding his head in his hands, and Pugh began the search, with Hewett meticulously recording the details of the drugs in his notebook. The interior of the right-hand cupboard in the alcove was in a disgusting state: large bottles were piled on top of one another, there were slabs of chocolate, sugar, butter and margarine. As Adams called out, 'There are a number of barbiturates there, but no drugs', Hannam took out a bottle containing twelve cachets bearing a label: 'Mrs Hullett'. There were seven empty bottles, each bearing the same name, as well as a further bottle, similarly labelled, containing twenty-two tablets. There were several jars – not very many – which appeared to contain phenobarbitone. As Hannam examined those items, he saw Adams walk slowly to another cabinet, and Pugh nodded to Hannam, catching his eye. They saw Adams unlock a centre compartment with a key on a chain, put his left hand inside and from the centre shelf take two objects which he placed in his left-hand jacket pocket.

'What did you take from that cupboard, doctor?' asked Hannam, and Adams replied, 'Nothing. I only opened it for you.'

'You put something into your pocket', said Hannam, but Adams replied, 'No, I've got nothing.'

Hannam moved towards him and in his notebook recorded that he said 'sternly', 'What was it, doctor?'

Adams took from his pocket a small, intact bottle of morphine and also a carton containing the same. Hannam initialled them, handed them to Hewett and said, 'Doctor, do not do silly things like that, it is against your own interests.'

'I know it was silly', replied Adams. 'I didn't want you to find it in there.'

'What is it and where did it come from?' asked Hannam.

'One of those I got for Mr Soden, who died at the Grand Hotel, and the other was for Mrs Sharpe, who died before I used it.'

After searching Adams' pocket, Hannam told him to sit on a chair in the middle of the surgery, and at 9.10 pm, Adam's solicitor, Herbert James, arrived.

Hannam told the solicitor what had happened, and after discovering that Adams had a bag containing drugs in his car, Hewett brought it in. Showing it to Adams, Hannam said, 'Doctor, please pick out for the inspector all the dangerous drugs. You know what to find rather better than he does.'

'There are a few old ones in there, and there is no more.'

And then, before they left for the police station, Hannam asked once more if Adams had any record cards or records of any kind in respect of Mrs Morrell or any of the other patients, and this was Adams' answer: 'No. I do not appear to have. I expect I destroyed them, after they died.'

He was then taken to Eastbourne police station, where he was charged with thirteen offences, including four charges under the Cremation Act alleging that to procure the burning of the bodies of two men and two women, he had falsely represented that he had no pecuniary interest in their deaths. Other charges alleged forgery and false pretences. Adams was then released on bail and returned to his surgery. His solicitor was hard at work looking for records of treatment given to patients. He found eight interesting exercise books.

Not that those exercise books were produced or mentioned when, on 25 November at the request of both solicitor and client, Hannam visited the surgery once more. Adams handed over two old Dangerous Drugs registers, declaring that nothing had been entered in them since 1949 and saying, 'Mr James told me to say nothing more to you.'

On the following day, Adams appeared at Eastbourne Magistrates' Court facing the thirteen charges and was remanded until 20 December on £1,000 bail, with a surety in the same sum.

At 10.45 am, a local officer, Detective Sergeant Leslie Sellors, told Adams he needed to take a police photograph. Adams agreed and then turned to Hannam and said, 'I would like to have one word with you.'

'I will see you in a moment or two', replied Hannam and at 11.00 am he entered the second-floor photographic room at the police station. DS Sellors waited outside, and then Adams said, 'You told Mr James there might be other charges. I am very worried; what are they?'

'That is not quite accurate', replied Hannam. 'I told him he must not automatically assume the charges preferred were final.'

'Well, what else is there?' asked Adams.

'Hiding that morphine on Saturday night is a serious offence, and I am still enquiring into the deaths of some of your rich patients. I do not think they were all natural.'

'Which?' asked Adams.

'Mrs Morrell is certainly one', said Hannam, which brought forth this astonishing reply: 'Easing the passing of a dying person isn't all that wicked. She wanted to die. That can't be murder. It is impossible to accuse a doctor.'

Hannam had submitted an extremely comprehensive report, which had been presented through the Director of Public Prosecutions to the Attorney General, Sir Reginald Manningham-Buller, who was going to lead the prosecution. These included details of Miss Florence Emily Cavill, aged eighty-two, who died on 9 May 1954; her death was said to be the result of a cerebral haemorrhage, and she left £6,853 and bequests totalling £2,000. Her friend, Mrs Ada Pearson, said, 'Two days before she was found dead, Miss Cavill came to see me. She looked fit and well. I had the shock of my life when the police told me of her death.'

Another cerebral haemorrhage sufferer was Miss Evelyn Richard, who died aged seventy-six in October 1949. She, too, had been in good health when she had been seen by her chauffeur the previous day; she left £31,758 and a number of bequests.

On 19 November 1952, 72-year-old Julia Thomas, who was treated by Adams for depression, was given tablets 'to make you feel better in the morning'. The next day, after more tablets, she lapsed into a coma. The day following that, Adams took possession of her typewriter, telling a servant that Mrs Thomas had promised it to him, and the next day, she died. The cause? Cerebral thrombosis.

On 18 December, a conference was held in the Attorney's chambers; present were his junior, Melford Stevenson QC, the Director, Hannam and Hewett, as well as Francis Camps and Dr Arthur Henry Douthwaite, senior physician at Guy's Hospital. When these last two assured the Attorney that Mrs Morrell's final prescriptions were fatal, he directed Hannam to charge Adams with Mrs Morrell's murder.

Hannam and Hewett were both shocked. There were other cases – the Hulletts, Mrs Bradnum and Clara Neil-Miller in particular – whom they would have nominated to be the subject of a murder charge; not a woman who had died six years previously and whose body had been cremated. But Hannam had already stated in his report that he believed that once he was cross-examined in the witness box at the Old Bailey, Adams would talk himself into a confession, and this appealed to the Attorney, who was known as 'Sir Reginald Bullying-Manner'. He was a political animal and undoubtedly believed that a conviction in the Adams case would lead him to be appointed Lord Chief Justice.

But before Adams could attend the remand hearing at court, Hannam and Hewett, together with DI Pugh, went to the surgery at 11.45 am on 19 December. Several patients were in the waiting room as well as reporters and a photographer from *Paris Match* magazine. Adams had been giving a conference to the reporters, one of whom would later mention that 'a quarter of an hour before the police, a telephone call had made the doctor grow pale'. His composure suffered a further setback when his nurse whispered in his ear, and then the three officers entered. Hannam said, 'We will go into your surgery to talk', told the reporters to leave and shut the door.

'Doctor Adams, on 13 November 1950, a patient of yours, Mrs Edith Alice Morrell, died at Marden Ash, Beachy Head Road, and you certified the cause of death to be cerebral thrombosis', said Hannam. 'I am now going to arrest you and take you to the local police headquarters, where you will be charged with the murder of Mrs Morrell.'

He then cautioned Adams who replied, 'Murder . . . murder . . . Can you prove it was murder?'

Hannam told him, 'You are now charged with murdering her.'

'I didn't think you could prove murder', said Adam, adding, 'She was dying, in any event.'

Then – and what followed was excluded from court proceedings – Adams asked, 'Will there be any more charges of murder?' to which Hannam replied, 'I cannot discuss that with you now.'

However, there was further conversation, recorded in Hewett's pocket book but also not heard in evidence. Adams said, 'The last time you mentioned other names and said some were suspicious.'

'Yes, Julia Bradnum and Clara Neil-Miller I mentioned. I have information that a few days before Clara Neil-Miller died, you were in her room, in the month of February, for about forty minutes and that the bedclothes were off her and over the rail at the foot of her bed. Her nightdress was up over her chest and the window of the room was open top and bottom. That case we are now considering.'

Adams replied, 'The person telling you that did not know why I did that.'

The person in question was a Miss Welsh, but not only was she now dead, the testimony would have been inadmissible in any event, since it had been relayed to a doctor, who had told Hannam. This had occurred in a boarding house, 'Barton' at 30 St John's Road, run by Mrs Annie Sharpe, who had unsuccessfully tried to get the Neil-Miller sisters to invest £5,000 in her business. Hannam felt that she was the key to the whole matter, certainly in the case of Clara Neil-Miller. Having interviewed her once, he and Hewett were all set to question her again – she was involved with many of the victims – but she, like Miss Welsh, would not tell anybody anything ever again. Mrs Sharpe had died on 13 November, eleven days prior to the search of Adams' surgery; she had been Adams' patient and she was cremated. Once more, Hannam was without a body.

After discussing informing Adams' solicitor, Adams and the policemen left the surgery. In the hallway, Adams gripped his receptionist's hand and told her, 'I will see you in heaven.'

'All right, Pugh', he then said, before being ushered out in the street, where the French photographer snapped away to his heart's content.

Charged at 12.30 pm at Eastbourne police station with the murder of Edith Morrell and with three further charges under the Dangerous Drugs Act, namely that he had attempted to conceal two bottles of morphine, that he wilfully obstructed Brynley Pugh in the exercise of his powers under the Act and that he failed to keep a register of dangerous drugs, he replied, 'It is better to say nothing.'

The day following Adams' court appearance, on 20 December, when he was remanded in custody to Brixton Prison, the bodies of Julia Bradnum at Ocklynge Cemetery and Miss Clara Neil-Miller at Langney Cemetery were exhumed; Professor Camps was present, but the condition of the bodies was poor and the results of the autopsies were inconclusive.

★   ★   ★

The committal proceedings commenced at Eastbourne Magistrates' Court on 14 January 1957, and the prosecution was led by Mr Melford Stevenson QC. Adams had additionally been charged with the murders of Jack and Gertrude Hullett. Two hours after the hearing started, Adams' defence barrister, Geoffrey Lawrence QC, asked the bench for the press and the public be excluded, saying, 'A report of these proceedings in the press may affect the minds of those who may have to try him'; and late the same afternoon, the court was still sitting in camera, before it was adjourned for another week.

But before proceedings were resumed, a handwritten note dated 18 January 1957 was delivered in an envelope headed 'Adams' Case' and addressed to Mr A. Melford Stevenson QC. It had never been mentioned before, and it was written by the widow of a solicitor. The woman knew Mr and Mrs Hullett well, and although she did not wish to be called as a witness, she stated that she had taken tea with the Hulletts four days before his death and had been very pleased to see that Mr Hullett 'had apparently made such an excellent recovery from his serious operation and illness'. She had then left for a three-week holiday and was shocked to receive a letter from a friend informing her that Jack Hullett had died suddenly. The announcement in the newspaper said, 'No letters', so it was not until the writer returned from holiday that she was able to express her sympathies to Mrs Hullett and tell her what a great shock it had been to hear of Jack's death. She then went on to write:

> This is the important part.
> She [Mrs Hullett] said it had been a terrible blow to her but that Adams had warned her that Jack could not possibly make a complete recovery and, in fact, that he did not think he would last more than about three months after his operation.

He was operated on, on the previous Nov. 19th. I particularly remember the date because it was my daughter's wedding day and of course, the Hulletts were not able to come.

At the time she told me I naturally thought that Jack's death was caused in some way by the operation he had had & did not ask for any details. However, when I saw Inspector Pugh – some time ago when enquiries were being made – he told me that cerebral haemorrhage had been given as the cause of death by Dr Adams on the certificate.

Might Dr Adams' warning to Mrs Hullett be evidence of premeditation of the crime? I cannot believe that the date of death by cerebral haemorrhage of a patient could possibly be foreseen, almost to a month, by any doctor, however clever!

Not only that, but Melford Stevenson also mentioned that when Adams obtained special clearance for Mrs Hullett's £1,000 cheque, it was obvious that he knew she was going to die that weekend. This was because Adams had telephoned the coroner, Dr Sommerville, at 8.30 in the morning of 22 July, when he was still in bed. Adams told him that he was not satisfied with the cause of death of one of his patients and asked if he could arrange a private post mortem.

'Certainly not!' replied the coroner. 'You should report it to me officially and I will deal with the matter', then added, 'When did the patient die?'

When Adams replied, 'The patient isn't dead yet', Dr Sommerville was so surprised that he not unnaturally sat straight up in bed. Asking why Adams was reporting the matter, he was told he was not certain what she was going to die from, and the extraordinary request was once more refused.

The case continued, with more live witnesses being called. Geoffrey Lawrence demanded that Hannam's notebook be made an exhibit.

'The defence is entitled to look at that part of the note about which the superintendent has given evidence', said Melford Stevenson, but added, 'If that notebook as it stands is made an exhibit, then during and thereafter, a jury could read all of it, and I am not sure whether Mr Lawrence would really wish that to happen.'

He suggested that a photostat copy could be made of that part of the book to which Hannam had referred in evidence, but Lawrence replied that as Hannam had stated that they were records made by him of important conversations, he thought it better if the document were to be made an exhibit and remain in the custody of the court.

To this, Hannam said, 'There are many matters in that book, it is required for further investigations and that I must have it in my possession to have constant access to it.'

'I am entitled to see that book', said Lawrence. 'It would be a manifest denial of justice, if I am not. It is a vital document. But how vital, I do not know.'

'If it is decided to retain the book in the custody of the court', said Hannam, 'I ask that it should not be examined except in my presence.'

'Might I enquire', asked Lawrence, 'what the objection is of seeking to prevent the examination of the book except in your presence?'

'I want to see exactly what happens to that book whenever it is examined by anybody connected with the defence. Never before in my experience has a book been retained as an exhibit', said Hannam. 'On many occasions courts have decided that a book should be examined only in my presence.'

'I am not sure we are very interested in your experience', sneered Lawrence, only to receive the snappy reply, 'It affects me very much in the answers I give to you.'

'It would follow reciprocally that the defence should be present whenever you want to examine the book during the same period, would it not?'

'If you made that request, of course the court would consider it.'

Tempers were rising.

'I am asking *you*!'

'That is for the court, not for me.'

'Is that the best answer you can give?'

'I think it is the proper answer for me to give.'

It was the first of several acrimonious clashes between the two, and now Melford Stevenson joined in the fray. 'The defence are not entitled to a roving commission through a police record which might contain references to many matters to which he had not referred in evidence', he told the Bench.

'I have never heard such a proposition in any criminal court', spluttered Lawrence, to which Melford Stevenson crushingly replied, 'Well, you've heard it now.'

But eventually, Hannam's Stationery Office Book 136 became exhibit No. 34 at the Magistrates' Court in the case. Malcolm Morris, Stevenson's junior, examined the next witness, Dr Douthwaite – a heavyweight witness for the prosecution, or so it was thought.

Shown the list of drugs prescribed for Mrs Morrell for the last 10½ months of her life, Dr Douthwaite stated that the total quantities were barbiturates 2,194 grains, sedormid 1,400 grains, morphine and omnopon 171$^{2}/_{3}$ grains and heroin 145$^{1}/_{3}$ grains. He said:

> The points of importance in my opinion are that the dosage of barbiturates in the last thirteen days of Mrs Morrell's life rose very considerably in comparison with the doses administered over the previous months.
>
> Furthermore, in November 1950, the dose of barbiturates was double that prescribed in October.
>
> Bearing in mind that the last thirteen days of November during which Mrs Morrell was alive represented less than half the month, the rate of morphine administration was over three times higher than in any of the three preceding months.
>
> On the same basis, the rate of administration was over seven times greater than the administration in any one of the previous four months, and at a rate of over fourteen times higher than the administration in October.

When Morris asked, 'If the drugs prescribed in those 13 days of November 1950 were used on the patient, what would have been the result?' the answer was, 'Death.'

Dr Douthwaite then said:

> I would like to comment upon prescription numbers 84 to 93 inclusive, the first dated November 8, 1950, the last being November 12, 1950. These show morphine prescribed: on the 8th, ten grains, on the 9th, 12½ grains, on the 11th, 18½ grains. The figures for heroin: on the 8th, 6$^{2}/_{3}$ grains, on the 9th, 6¼ grains, on the 10th, 6¼ grains, on the 11th, 6¼ grains and on the 12th, 12½ grains. If these quantities were all administered, either of morphine or heroin, death would have ensued. It follows, therefore, that if both drugs were administered in these quantities, death was the inevitable outcome.

If that were not enough, he was asked about two prescriptions, both dated 12 November, the first being for four ounces of paraldehyde and the second for heroin tablets, grain $^{1}/_{6}$, three tubes each containing 25 tablets. Dr Douthwaite stated that paraldehyde was a sleeping draught and the normal dose was two fluid grammes, adding that a dose of one ounce had caused death in an adult. There could be no justification for administering paraldehyde to a patient already in a coma – its use would only deepen the coma. Regarding the administration of 75 heroin tablets as 'an enormous dose', he stated that the maximum official dose set out in the 1948 pharmacopoeia was $^1/_6$ of a grain, whereas the last prescription was one of 12½ grains.

That seemed pretty well cut and dried. However, Dr Douthwaite did not fare so well in discussing the death of Jack Hullett.

Evidence had been given by a nurse, who said that Jack Hullett had collapsed downstairs, and Dr Douthwaite gave his opinion that Adams should not have taken Hullett upstairs but should have laid him down, since ascending the stairs could have increased the danger of a heart attack. But when Lawrence asked if an injection of hyperduric morphia might forestall an early morning attack and ensure a good night's rest, Douthwaite was obliged to agree. And when Hullett had woken the following morning, having asked the time, he was asked if he wanted anything and replied 'No', being then told to go back to sleep. When Douthwaite was therefore asked if the previous night's injection was likely to have been the fatal dose, or one intended to kill, he was obliged to reply, 'I agree it is not likely to have been a fatal dose.'

Nevertheless, after the committal, which had lasted nine days, and after a five-minute adjournment by the Magistrates, Adams was sent in custody to stand his trial at the Old Bailey.

★   ★   ★

In the meantime, rumour and speculation regarding Adams' activities had not died down; in fact, they intensified, and a piece of anonymous doggerel entitled 'Adams and Eves' was read at several meetings, including at the Cavendish hotel:

> In Eastbourne it is healthy
> And the residents are wealthy.
> It's a miracle that anybody dies.
> Yet this pearl of English lidos
> Is a slaughterhouse of widows –
> If their bank rolls are above the normal size.

> If they're lucky in addition
> In their choice of a physician
> And remember him when making out their wills,
> And bequeath their Rolls-Royces
> Then they soon hear angel voices
> And are quickly freed from all their earthly ills.

> If they're nervous or afraid of
> What a heroine is made of
> Their mentality will soon be reconditioned.

So they needn't feel neglected
They will shortly be infected
With the heroin in which they are deficient.

As we witnessed the deceased borne
From the stately homes of Eastbourne,
We are calm, for it may safely be assumed
That each lady that we bury
In the local cemetery
Will resurface – when the body is exhumed.

In the mortuary's chapel
If they touch an Adam's apple
After parting with a Bentley as a fee,
So to liquidate your odd kin
By the needle of the bodkin
Send them down to sunny Eastbourne by the sea.

Adams' solicitor was furious, and the matter was reported to the Director of Public Prosecutions, who directed Detective Superintendent Dick Lewis from C1 Department to carry out an immediate investigation. But as Charlie Hewett's son, David, told me, 'The investigation hit a brick wall, and Dad always denied rumours that he, Owen Summers and Norman Lucas co-authored it. Obviously, the fact that both reporters stayed at the Cavendish and were oft to be seen in the company of Dad in the bar of an evening was mere coincidence!'

However, this was not the only piece of jiggery-pokery. Hannam had suspected some sort of duplicity, hence not wishing to let go of his pocket book. But now a vital exhibit, Mrs Hullett's cheque for £1,000, went missing, and a further police enquiry was launched. Hannam suspected the Deputy Chief Constable, Seekings, who had taken holidays with Adams, as had Sir Roland Gwynne, the Chairman of the Magistrates, who had stepped down when Adams' case was heard; but the cheque was never found.

It had always been 'an ancient rule of practice' to deal with only one murder at a time in an indictment. However, there was no debarment to introducing a 'system' to show that the offence alleged was not an isolated one. This had been first introduced as long ago as 1925 during the trial of George Joseph Smith. In what became known as 'The Brides in the Bath Murders', it was shown that Smith had been responsible for the murders of three of his spouses whom he had married bigamously. Each of them had drowned in bathtubs which were too small for them to have accidentally slipped under the water; it was established that Smith had suddenly jerked their ankles upwards, causing their demise. Additionally, all of them were wealthy, either due to inheritances or because Smith had taken out sizeable life insurances policies one day before their deaths.

Similarly, all the prosecution had to do in the present case was to introduce evidence of other deaths to show that the patients were wealthy, they had left legacies for Adams, that Adams had prescribed heavy drugging for their treatment (especially when it was not needed), that they were under the influence of the doctor (for example in his excluding their relatives) and that Adams was anxious to obtain the rewards, as shown by his haste in clearing Mrs Hullett's cheque – and goodness knows, there were enough contenders! But the Attorney decided not to rely upon the introduction of a system; in fact, he went further.

One month before the trial commenced at the Old Bailey, the Attorney also decided not to refer to the evidence obtained during the committal proceedings with regard to Jack and Gertrude Hullett. This should have pleased Geoffrey Lawrence, who had unsuccessfully done his best to have that evidence excluded at the Magistrates' Court. But the Attorney also decided to file a second indictment, alleging the murder of Jack Hullett, and this did not please Lawrence. The Attorney's reasoning was this: at that time, the Homicide Bill was going through Parliament which stated that in a single murder case, such as that of Mrs Morrell, if the accused was found guilty of that murder, he would not hang. But if he was convicted of a second murder, he would. And what concerned Lawrence was that all of the evidence regarding the Hulletts had already been aired, some two months previously; it would still be in everybody's minds – particularly, the jurors'.

The trial commenced in No. 1 Court at the Old Bailey on 18 March 1957 before Mr Justice Devlin; it was not without incident.

*   *   *

After Adams climbed the stairs from Cell No 23 to plead not guilty to Mrs Morrell's murder, the case got underway, and the battle between Hannam and Lawrence had a foregone conclusion. When Lawrence asked about the coincidence of Hannam meeting Adams as he put his car away, Hannam asked what he meant by 'coincidence'.

'Do you mean you don't understand my question?' asked Lawrence.

'It is impossible to understand what the coincidences were, sir, unless you help me to help you', responded Hannam.

When Hannam asked to refer to his notes, and the judge asked if there was any objection, Lawrence replied, 'No, I want to be quite fair. If the superintendent cannot answer my question without his notes, by all means, let him have them.'

To this, Hannam replied, 'That is quite improper. I want to be accurate.'

Unfortunately, Hannam's words cut across the judge's answer, who rebuked him; then Lawrence wanted to know, 'Was that observation addressed to me?'

Hannam replied, 'No. It was an answer, I thought, to something you were saying to me.'

And when Hannam repeated Adams' words to the receptionist – 'I will see you in heaven' – and Lawrence suggested that those words were never uttered, Hannam replied, 'They were very staggering words to me. I recall them quite plainly.'

Lawrence had even less luck with Charlie Hewett. When he was asked if he had made an independent note of the conversations, Hewett replied that he had not; he had been present when Hannam had made up his notes, had agreed with them and countersigned them. Lawrence was fully aware of this. He had sedulously studied the notebook over a period of weeks and he had seen that Hewett had written in red ink:

> I was present when Det. Supt. Hannam made these notes, I watched him write them and agree with them in their entirety.
> C. Hewett D/S COC1.

This was a perfectly proper practice, as Lawrence well knew from the 1953 Court of Appeal decision in R v Bass; but since the jury did not know it, he decided that this was a perfect time for some near-hysterical histrionics, suggesting massive impropriety between police officers.

The novelist Eric Ambler, who was following the trial, described Lawrence 'leaning forward across his desk, his neck outstretched like an indignant, outraged ostrich' as he gasped, 'Am I really hearing what you are saying?'

Hewett, with the experience of almost twenty years of similar unfounded allegations under his belt, cheerfully replied, 'Yes, you are.'

Incredulously (purely for the sake of the jury), Lawrence said, 'That accounts for the fact that what you said was word for word the same?'

'I should hope it would be', imperturbably replied Hewett.

And so it went on, with anything recorded by the officers as said by Adams to be even slightly incriminating being challenged, and Lawrence getting no change out of either of them.

But it was a different matter with the nurses who had attended Mrs Morrell: Brenda Hughes, Annie Mason-Ellis, Helen Stronach and Caroline Randall. When they had made their statements to police, they had relied on the chemists' prescriptions and their own memories of seven years previously.

Lawrence dropped a bombshell when he suddenly produced the eight exercise books found by Adams' solicitor which were written in the nurses' own hand detailing what injections had been given and when – many of them did not record Adams giving the injections. It was one thing for the prosecution to detail the amount of drugs which had been prescribed; that was indisputable. What was in question was: had Adams actually carried out the injections? The proper course of action would have been for Manningham-Buller and Melford Stevenson to have asked the judge for an adjournment so that they might study the books, since it was the first time they had heard of them, let alone seen them, and such an adjournment would certainly have been granted. But they didn't. They scrabbled through them during a luncheon adjournment, with little success.

And after a weasel defence solicitor had surreptitiously sat in the same train carriage as the witnesses from London to Eastbourne and back again the following morning, he was able to recount their unwise conversations to Lawrence, who in turn used them to devastating effect in cross-examination. None of the nurses disputed that they had discussed the case, which obviated the necessity for the solicitor to tell the court what he had heard; in fact, the solicitor was never mentioned at all. In his memoirs, Lord Devlin suggested that it was a public-spirited businessman on his way to and from his London office who had informed the defence team of these revelations, rather than an officer of the court – which was, of course, complete and consummate bollocks.

In fact, Nurse Randall was obliged to admit that she had administered the last injection to Mrs Morrell, an hour before she died – albeit at Adams' direction – and she also admitted that she received £300 as a legatee under Mrs Morrell's will.

Dr Ronald Vincent Harris, who was one of Adams' partners in the surgery and had also visited Mrs Morrell, did not want to be called by the prosecution at all; then again, neither did he want to be cross-examined by the defence. And therefore, in answers to questions from both sides, he managed to sit quite nobly on the fence. The same applied when he was questioned quite strenuously by the judge.

When Dr Douthwaite was called, he gave the strong, uncompromising evidence he had given in the Magistrates' Court. But spending over twelve hours in the witness box, being questioned by both Lawrence and the judge, then Lawrence again, his testimony was not as strong as had been previously thought. And when Dr Ashby was called as the last witness for the prosecution, he, too, admitted that he had based his evidence on the belief that all the drugs which had been prescribed had been administered.

At the close of the prosecution's case, the Attorney called Hannam and Hewett into his room at the Old Bailey and in the presence of Mr Melford Stevenson and the Director of Public Prosecutions, shook hands with both officers and commended them on 'an excellent investigation and particularly on the exemplary manner in which evidence was given and their conduct displayed under very rigorous cross-examination'. The congratulations were a tad premature.

Lawrence now made an application to the judge that there was no case to answer; that the case was so weak it should not go to the jury and should be stopped, there and then. He argued the point for two hours, but the judge opposed the application. And then Lawrence dropped his last bombshell. He stated that he would not call Adams to the witness box. It was an earth-shattering revelation; the Attorney had been patiently waiting his turn to show to the world, by the use of scintillating cross-examination, that not only was Adams a murderer but also, with a little luck on the second indictment, a double-murderer. And in those days, as every judge would tell every jury, nothing sinister should be read into the decision of a defendant not to give evidence. The Crown brought the charges, and it was up to them to prove their case; the accused, innocent in the eyes of the law until proven guilty, need prove nothing.

Dr John Bishop Harman was called for the defence. Not only did he agree with the dosages given, he stated he had often given similar ones himself. In fact, when cross-examined by the Attorney and asked if those fatal injections would have done Mrs Morrell any good, he replied, 'They might have done.'

After the final speeches from the prosecution and defence, plus the judge's four-hour summing-up, on the seventeenth day of the trial – the longest running in Britain at that time – on 9 April 1957, after deliberating for forty-four minutes, the jury of ten men and two women returned a verdict of not guilty.

When Mr Justice Devlin asked, 'Mr Attorney, there is another indictment, is there not?' the Attorney dropped a bombshell of his own. He replied:

> Yes, my Lord. I have most anxiously considered what course the Crown should pursue in relation to the further indictment charging Doctor Adams with the murder of Mr Hullett. My learned friend has referred more than once to the difficulty, owing to the reports and rumours that were current, of securing a fair trial of the case which has now terminated. As one of my distinguished predecessors said, the Attorney General, when deciding whether a particular prosecution is to be carried on, has regard to a variety of considerations and all of them lead to the final question: would a prosecution be in the public interest, including in that phrase, in the interests of justice?
>
> One of the considerations I have felt it my duty to consider is that the publicity which has attended this trial would make it even more difficult to secure a fair trial of this further indictment. I have also taken into account the length of this trial, the ordeal Doctor Adams has already undergone, the fact that the case for the prosecution on this further indictment based on evidence given before the Eastbourne Magistrates depends in part on the evidence of Dr Ashby, and very greatly upon the inference not supported as in Mrs Morrell's case, of any admissions. Having given the matter the best consideration I can, I have reached the conclusion that in all the circumstances the public interest does not require that Doctor Adams should undergo the ordeal of a further trial on a charge of murder, and I therefore enter a *nolle prosequi* in relation to that indictment.

A *nolle prosequi*. Throwing in the towel. The dismissal or termination of criminal proceedings, only by leave of the Attorney General. It was hardly if ever done, as demonstrated by the official shorthand writer misspelling the term on the court transcript. So why was it used on this occasion? Adams not giving evidence, then being acquitted, had been a shattering left and right for Manningham-Buller. If he had progressed with the second indictment, might not Adams' defence team suddenly produce notebooks in respect of Jack Hullett? Who knows? Anything was possible, but the overriding factor was this: if he had gone ahead and there had been a further humiliating acquittal, he could wave goodbye to ever being appointed Lord Chief Justice – in fact, he never did receive that appointment.

Neither did Mr Justice Devlin, who was angling after the same position and who now simply said, 'Then, Mr Attorney, all further proceedings on the indictment are stayed and no further action is taken in this court. Accordingly, John Bodkin Adams, you are now discharged.'

It was a devastating blow for Hannam; his investigation had been a model of what any major enquiry should be. Of course, the jury had seen just a fraction of the evidence.

Adams sold his story to the *Daily Express* for £10,000 and successfully sued thirteen newspapers for libel; later, on 19 May 1961, he received apologies, damages and costs.

But now, six weeks after his acquittal, on 20 May Adams appeared at Eastbourne Magistrates' Court in respect of the outstanding fifteen charges. The prosecution had dropped the charge that he had benefited from the fee for Mrs Morrell's cremation, but the others remained: that Adams had forged the signatures of other doctors to provide medicines and other items by purporting that his private patients were National Health patients, as well committing offences under the Dangerous Drugs Act.

With regard to the other cremation matters, Amy Ware died on 23 February 1950 leaving an estate of £8,993. Adams was left a legacy of £1,000 (it had been increased twice, the second time being one week before her death); when Mrs Ware's niece telephoned Adams to find out about the funeral arrangements, to her surprise he told her that her aunt did not wish anybody to attend her funeral, but 'Not to worry, because you and your husband are both mentioned in her will.' And they were; with £250 each. It was clear that Adams knew the contents of the will, yet when he answered the question on the cremation form as to whether he would receive any pecuniary advantage, he replied, 'Not to my knowledge'.

Mrs Ware's brother-in-law, James Priestly Downs, also Adams' patient, died five years later, on 30 May 1955. About three to four weeks before he died, Adams told Sister Gladys Miller, who was nursing Mr Downs, that an unsigned will had been found in Mr Downs' home by his housekeeper and that she (the housekeeper) was a beneficiary; Sister Miller believed that the housekeeper had shown the will to Adams.

One morning, the Sister had heard the following conversation between Adams and Downs: 'Now look here, Jimmy, you promised me on the day Lily (Mrs Ware) was buried, on the return journey in the car, that you would look after me. I see that you have not even mentioned me in your will.'

Sister Miller said that Mr Downs was confused and sleepy and could not remember what had happened.

Adams continued, 'You have not signed your will; the nieces will get the lot. You do not want them to have it, do you? They have never done anything for you. I have looked after you all these years and never charged you a fee.'

On 7 April, Adams told Sister Miller a solicitor was coming to the house and gave Downs a tablet to render him more alert for the visit. Upon the solicitor's arrival, Downs instructed him that Adams should be a legatee in the sum of £1,000. But when Downs died, Adams wrote, in answer to the pecuniary interest section of the cremation form, 'Of this, I do not know.'

Regarding Jack Hullett, Adams had answered 'No' to that pertinent question on the cremation form; yet Hullett left Adams £500, and he certainly knew he was a beneficiary because he told Hannam, 'I thought it would be more than it was.'

There was some of Hannam's evidence which Edward Clarke QC for Adams wanted excluded, and he also asked if Hannam knew why the Hullett case had not been proceeded with at the Old Bailey. Hannam replied that he did not know the grounds on which the Director of Public Prosecutions had come to his decision. But Clarke went a bit too far when he asked if Hannam had any evidence to suggest that Adams had ever forged more National Health prescriptions than the four with which he was currently charged. This was a big mistake, because Hannam replied that he had further evidence of two definite cases of forgery and about eighteen cases of false pretences in the preparation of prescription forms, of which the earliest was in 1952; and with that, Adams was committed to stand his trial at Lewes Assizes.

On 26 July, before Mr Justice Pilcher, Adams pleaded guilty to fourteen out of the sixteen charges against him, and now the extent of his gains could be made clear. He owned an 18-room house and employed a housekeeper, chauffeur, receptionist and secretary. At the time of his arrest he had a Rolls-Royce, two MG Magnettes and a new Morris Minor, as well as a total of £25,623 18s 1d in various bank accounts. Those accounts provided him with £665 in interest in 1956, and he had additional income from investments which amounted to £2,000 a year. In addition, over the past ten years, the bequests he had received from his patients amounted to approximately £3,000 per annum.

Adams' counsel, Edward Clarke, told the judge his client had dissolved his partnership, relinquished his hospital appointments and abandoned his National Health practice; in fact, on 1 July, letters were sent by the Eastbourne Executive Council of the National Health to all of Adams' patients, informing them of his removal from the local medical list and advising them to find another General Practitioner. Nothing was said about his private patients, however.

Telling him, 'There was a time when I felt I should not be doing my duty unless I sent you to prison on this indictment', the judge fined him a total of £2,400 and ordered him to pay the costs of the prosecution, which amounted to £457.

That was followed, on 10 September, by the Home Secretary withdrawing Adams' authorization to possess or supply dangerous drugs.

Adams was rapidly being transformed into a victim. The Disciplinary Committee of the General Medical Council heard from Noel Leigh Taylor for Adams that since his arrest, 'He had never been free from trials of some kind.' With staggering duplicity, Leigh Taylor informed the committee that prior to the inquest on Mrs Hullett, the Chief Constable of Eastbourne had called in Scotland Yard 'for reasons we will never know'. But after a 10-minute recess on 27 November 1957, the chairman, Sir David Campbell, informed Adams that his name would be struck from the medical register.

The committee took just thirteen minutes longer when they were asked to reconsider restoring Adams' name to the medical register two years later, on 25 November 1959; but even though he was represented by a Queen's Counsel, the result was just the same.

Adams eventually returned to practice on 22 November 1961. He became a founder member of the Clay Pigeon Shooting Association (he owned a formidable array of weaponry) and later its Senior Honorary Life Vice-President. He died aged eighty-four on 4 July 1983 after breaking his hip and then developing a chest infection. He left an estate worth £402,970, having been receiving legacies from his patients until his death.

* * *

Melford Stevenson was by now knighted and a retired High Court Judge; his opinion was, 'If I had been allowed, I could have successfully prosecuted Bodkin Adams for the murders of six people.'

Now Baron Devlin, the former judge, criticised Hannam for 'his flamboyancies and his cultivation of the press, apparently for his own glorification rather than for any assistance which it could give to the investigation'. Manningham-Buller also came in for a mauling for poor preparation of the case and, especially, his use of *nolle prosequi*, which Devlin claimed was 'an abuse of process'; in turn, Manningham-Buller (later 1st Viscount Dilhorne) criticised Devlin for 'judicial misdirection'.

Percy Hoskins (who was left £1,000 in Adams' will) maintained Adams' innocence. It is difficult to accept that such a hard-headed journalist, who since 1924 had been the leading crime reporter for the right-wing *Daily Express*, could have been taken in by that impious, bible-preaching little psychopath; and in all likelihood, he wasn't. But having gone so far with his reporting at the time, and then having written a book about those experiences twenty-seven years later, he could hardly recant and still maintain his credibility. He could (and did) maintain his contempt for Hannam, describing how when he was in the witness box, 'his conceit was never in short ration'. It begs the question, what's worse: conceit in one man or hypocrisy in another? Hoskins was appointed CBE in 1976 and died, like his chum Adams aged 84, in 1989.

If one accepts that Adams was a serial killer, it must mean that before killing his patients he was exerting control over them. Yes, he knew many of them had named him as a beneficiary in their wills, and he was certainly not dependent on getting that money immediately, because he was already wealthy. But he wanted to control precisely when he was going to get it, not merely when that patient chose to die. He would often prevent his patients from seeing their relatives, seizing their letters and informing family that the patient had forbidden them to attend the funeral; or not informing them at all until the funeral service – preferably a cremation – had been carried out. In the same way that the serial killer of 10 Rillington Place, John Reginald Christie, secreted the pubic hair from his eight victims in a tobacco tin, or the killer dubbed 'Jack the Stripper' would take his victims' clothes, jewellery and teeth,[3] so Adams would help himself to tokens from his victims: a pen, an infra red lamp, a typewriter, items that he never used but which he now controlled. And all the time Adams unctuously referred to 'those poor patients', 'those dear relatives' and especially 'God', implying that he had a private telephone line to Him; he spent his time on remand in Brixton prison singing hymns, reading the Bible or loudly praying to his confidant.

Hoskins once referred to Hannam as being like 'a big chocolate Easter Egg; beautiful on the outside but fuck-all inside.'

Coincidentally, a noted psychiatrist, referring to Adams, said, 'There was nothing inside him at all.'

Of course, the difference between the two men was, Adams was a psychopathic murderer.

---

[3] For full details into this investigation, see *Laid Bare: The Nude Murders and the Hunt for 'Jack the Stripper'*, The History Press, 2016

CHAPTER 9

The Body in the Trunk

Edward Coleman – also known as John Thompson – was a thoroughly nasty piece of work. His criminal career commenced in 1957, and at the time of his murder he was thirty-one years of age and had accrued seven serious convictions, which included robbery, possessing firearms, theft and assault. He was described by the police officers who had dealings with him as being 'a very strong and violent individual'. Born in Kirkintilloch, Scotland, his National Service was interrupted by a period of Borstal detention, and although he married in 1960 he left his wife and two children in 1963, and it was only three months prior to his demise that he provided them with any financial support. Released from prison in February 1969, he came to London, where he lived with a number of women, spending the best part of one year with a woman who possessed a conviction for receiving stolen property. Coleman was thought to be living on the proceeds of crime (possibly carried out with his murderer), and if so, he appeared to be doing quite well at it, since at the time of his death he was living in a furnished flat at 202 Kensington Church Street, London, W8, paying a (then) princely rental of £20 per week; by comparison, the present-day owners of these flats demand (and get) a monthly rental of £1,700. So all in all, when his life expired on 25 March 1970, it was possibly only Coleman's landlord who expressed concern; few other people did.

★ ★ ★

It's time to take a look at the characters who were, one way or another, involved in Coleman's demise. All were known to one another and to Coleman. First, David Edward Woods, who was born in 1947 and who, at the time of his arrest, was living with his parents and sister at a council property in what was referred to as a respectable area of Shepherd's Bush. After leaving school aged fifteen, he had various jobs, including in the building trade, where he was described as a willing and capable worker. He had no previous convictions.

Stephen Patrick Raymond's criminal career commenced in 1959, when he was fourteen. In the years that followed Coleman's murder, Raymond's career would become really interesting, but let's not get ahead of ourselves. For now, while Raymond was serving a six-year sentence for robbery he struck up a friendship with the MP for Barking, Tom Driberg, who was a deeply unpleasant homosexual and, as a chum of the Kray twins, anti-authority. Raymond was released from Chelmsford Prison on 29 August 1969 and by 10 November he was circulated as being wanted for dishonestly handling stolen property, going equipped for theft, assault on police and possessing a firearm with intent to commit an arrestable offence. One week later, he obtained a sheepskin coat by fraud in Glasgow, purporting to be Tom Driberg, whose credit card he had used; a sheriff's warrant for his arrest was issued. Raymond was on parole, but with all this criminality going on, it was hardly surprising that he failed to maintain contact with his probation officer, and on 1 January 1970, the Home Secretary signed a Parole Recall Order. As well as being a prolific offender who at the time of the murder was wanted by three different agencies, Raymond was also sly, manipulative and willing to sell his associates right down the river.

Norman Charles Parker was born in 1944 and lived with his divorced mother and his sister at a flat in Brook Green, Hammersmith W14. His first serious brush with the law came in 1963, when he was charged with the murder of his girlfriend, an 18-year-old shop assistant named Susan Fitzgerald. The prosecution's case was that Parker had killed her because he was jealous of her association with another boy and thought she was two-timing him. By any stretch of the imagination, Miss Fitzgerald was an extremely odd person who kept books on concentration camps and admired Adolf Hitler; it was said that her family were affiliated to Mosley's British Union of Fascists. In this strange world she had developed a fascination with violence and violent people, and slept with a gun under her pillow. It was an especially peculiar alliance because Parker was a Jew.

Parker's defence at the Old Bailey was that he intended to inform her boyfriend, John, about her past, to which she replied, 'You won't do that' and pointed her .45 revolver at him. Parker believed he was about to be shot but providentially was carrying a firearm of his own, a Luger, which he used to shoot her fatally in the head.

The jury cleared him of murder, which was just as well since at that time it was a capital offence and Parker was just old enough to hang, but they convicted him of manslaughter.

'I do not think this is a case for a minor sentence', said Mr Justice Winn. 'It is very important that it should be realized how grave a matter it is for anyone to carry such a deadly weapon with him', and on 28 October 1963 he sentenced Parker to six years' imprisonment.

He was released from prison on 6 October 1967 and worked in the antiques trade; at the time of his arrest, he was the manager of Antique Building Components Ltd., 11 Bruce Grove, Tottenham, N17. This building became central to the whole story, because it proved to be the case that Coleman's death had occurred in the small 14ft by 7ft 6in office at that antiques premises in Tottenham.

* * *

A visitor to that office on 23 and 24 March 1970 saw Parker looking at two detective books; one of them dealt with the disposal of dead bodies. Additionally, the visitor saw a map of the New Forest on Parker's desk. Also at that time, Stephen Raymond purchased a trunk from a shop in High Road, Tottenham and handed it to Parker. On the same day, a large polythene sheet was purchased from a shop, also in Tottenham's High Road, and the receipt for it was found in Parker's office. Parker, in his statement to police, would say that he had purchased a polythene dust cover to carry out decorating at his mother's flat; instead, it became Coleman's shroud. Thus, two important items connected with Coleman's death had been purchased on the day immediately preceding it, from shops very adjacent to Bruce Grove; but there was more, and that will be dealt with a little later.

* * *

On the day of the murder, Wednesday, 25 March, Parker asked a member of the Old Grammarians Rugby Club, who used the basement of 11 Bruce Grove as a meeting place, if they would be using it on a Wednesday; he was told they would not, and at 5.00 pm that day, Parker told a visitor that he intended to 'hang on for a bit'.

He was still there at 7.10 pm; the upper part of the building was leased to a dentist, who left the premises at that time, saw Parker and remarked that he (Parker) was working late that night.

Between 8.00 and 8.30 pm, Parker, his girlfriend and Woods were in a flat belonging to the wife of a man – a close associate of Parker's – who was then serving a life sentence for murder.

Parker's girlfriend later admitted that she had looked after a rifle for him early in March and had returned it to him later in the month.

At about 8.30 pm, Woods, who seemed nervous, jumped up from the settee, saying, 'Come on, let's go', and he and Parker left.

★ ★ ★

Meanwhile, Coleman and a woman friend had gone to a pub, where they met another man and, driving their respective cars – Coleman's a red Morris 1100 – they went to The Favourite public house, N19. The other man was one Thomas George Blackmore, whose criminal career had commenced in 1934. While they were having a drink, Blackmore passed Coleman a solid gold snuff box measuring 4″ x 2½″ x 2½″ with a miniature of a grey-haired man in a red robe on the lid. Around the portrait were a large number of diamonds, and engraved on the inside of the lid was 'From King Charles, presented to the Archbishop of Canterbury' and the date '17--'.[1]

It was obviously a very valuable artefact; equally, it was certainly stolen property. Coleman left the pub with the precious item, saying that he would return some twenty minutes later.

But he didn't; he left his car where he had parked it and walked to The Shaftesbury public house, approximately 100 yards away, where at 9 o'clock he met Parker and Woods; the three men had known each other since October 1969.

Coleman passed the snuff box to Parker, the three men were served drinks and they were observed by the barmaid to leave the pub at about 9.10 pm. It would be the last time Coleman was seen alive.

Parker's Ford Transit open truck, used by him in connection with his business, had been seen outside The Shaftesbury; and Parker would later say that Coleman followed them to Bruce Grove in his 1100. This was untrue; Coleman left his car near The Favourite, the pub he had visited earlier that evening, and it was still there two days later.

★ ★ ★

---

[1] The archbishop referred to may have been William Laud who, despite being granted a royal pardon, was executed for treason in 1645 – Charles I himself passed on four years later. Equally, the archbishop could have been William Juxon, who officiated at King Charles II's coronation, but Juxon died in 1663 and the King in 1685. So the date doesn't equate with either king, and therefore '17--' is undoubtedly inaccurate and the witness's memory was at fault.

Early the following morning, at 1 o'clock, Parker and Woods were in Parker's truck when they stopped at traffic lights in Winchester and asked a police cadet where they could obtain petrol. They were directed to a petrol station in the town, where they filled up; however, the cadet had noted the registration number of the truck – NOY 226E – and also a tarpaulin covering something in the rear of the vehicle. The men continued on their way until 2.07 am, when they were stopped by Police Constable John Royston Turk on the B3347 Ringwood to Christchurch Road in Ringwood, Hampshire. He questioned the two men and recorded their details in his police pocket book; additionally, because he had no other form of identification, Parker handed him his business card. But then the officer climbed on to the rear of the truck and lifted the tarpaulin. Underneath he saw a dark blue cabin trunk – it was the same trunk that Stephen Raymond had purchased – and this, Turk told Parker to open. As he did so, Parker called out to Woods, who was returning to the truck, 'Don't leave me now', and PC Turk was then savagely attacked by both men, who knocked him unconscious. As he came to, both were bending over him and removing his pocket book, although they missed the business card, which was in a different pocket of his tunic. PC Turk managed to get to his feet, staggered to nearby 'Jasmine Cottage' and hammered on the door, whereupon Parker and Woods decamped in their truck.

With the alarm raised, an immediate search was made of the area by Hampshire police, but neither the men nor the truck could be found. Ensuing enquiries were made at the home addresses of both men, their haunts and places of work, without success. The reason for this was because Parker and Woods had hidden in the New Forest for two days, before getting a lift from a lorry driver who drove them to Southampton railway station, whereupon they returned to London.

The following day, Friday, 27 March, the truck was discovered in a sandpit in the Bisterne Common area of Sandford, about two miles from where PC Turk had been attacked. It was blood-stained, as was a tarpaulin sheet in the rear of the truck, but there was no trace of the cabin trunk. The vehicle was subjected to fingerprint and forensic examination; the fingerprints of both men were on the vehicle, and in Woods' case, his finger mark was found on the peak of PC Turk's cap. Turk's pocket book was also found.

The search continued, and at 12 noon on 1 April, a spade, a fork, a Pifco lantern and a cufflink box containing .22 ammunition were found. One hour later, the search was cancelled, due to other police commitments. On the same day, Parker and Woods returned to the scene, where they had left a handkerchief tied to a tree as a marker; they then reburied Coleman's body, before returning to London.

Although an extensive search of the area recommenced, it was not until the afternoon of Friday, 3 April that first, the blue cabin trunk was found, concealed under foliage and tree branches, and then the body of Coleman was discovered, wrapped in a polythene sheet and approximately one quarter of a mile from where the truck had been abandoned. The body had been buried in a shallow grave eighteen inches deep. Nearby, newspapers which were subsequently identified as having been delivered to the address of Parker's mother were found.

The following day, a .22 rifle fitted with a silencer was found and later the same day, another spade; it is possible that this was used to rebury Coleman's body, since one spade and the fork had already been recovered.

A post mortem examination carried out at Christchurch Mortuary revealed that Coleman had been shot four times in the head, once in the abdomen and once in the left lower forearm; there were also two fractures of the skull, apparently caused by blows from a hammer.

*　*　*

On 28 March, Parker and Woods called at the flat of one Benjamin Sirett, whom Parker had met in prison whilst Sirett was serving a four-year sentence for receiving stolen property. Parker told Sirett that he wanted to borrow £100 since he needed to leave the country, having hit a policeman; and because, as Sirett told police, he was scared of Parker, he gave him the money. Sirett – an authority on antiques – then stated that Parker left the gold snuff box, which had previously been in Coleman's possession, and Sirett disposed of it, although he declined to say how. The provenance of this item has never been established.

Parker and Woods then took refuge in the London flat of Stephen Raymond at Kendal Parade, N17. The day after the murder, Raymond travelled back and forth to Scotland, finally returning to his flat on Tuesday, 31 March. There the three men remained until Saturday, 4 April, when they read in the newspapers of the discovery of Coleman's body, whereupon they fled to Scotland in a car hired by Raymond. Woods and Parker initially took shelter in a forest near Inchnacardoch, Inverness-shire, under some corrugated iron sheeting, while Raymond returned to London. There he purchased camping equipment and food and then, using trains, aeroplanes and various hired cars obtained by deception, he travelled to and from Scotland on several occasions, assisting the two men and moving them from one location to another.

* * *

On 5 April, a fingerprint and forensic examination was carried out at Parker's office premises in Tottenham. There were a few minute bloodstains on the walls and an ejected .22 cartridge was found there; ballistic tests revealed that the .22 rifle which had been found had been used to kill Coleman – the ejected cartridge found at Bruce Grove had been fired from the same rifle. In addition, there was the receipt for a large polythene sheet. Bloodstains were also found on Wellington boots (which Raymond later stated he had purchased and had lent to Parker).

* * *

The Chief Constable of Hampshire now requested that the Metropolitan Police take over the investigation. Detective Chief Superintendent David Clarence Dilley was, at that time, attached to C11 – or Criminal Intelligence Department – at the Yard. Following wartime service with the Royal Navy, Dilley had served with the Flying Squad, but much of his service was spent in C11 – he had never been attached to C1 Department. However, Geoff Parratt had – he was a detective sergeant there – but as he told me, 'There'd been an influx of murders, it was a Bank Holiday weekend, so due to the shortage of officers at C1, Dave was called in.' They opened a murder enquiry office at Shepherd's Bush and got to work.

Dilley caused a further forensic examination to be carried out at Bruce Grove, and in a storeroom was found a spent cartridge and a live round of .22 ammunition. Additionally, a cardboard box and a hardboard partition, both with bullet holes in them, were found, together with the remains of spent cartridges. It all pointed to a little target practice being carried out prior to Coleman's killing; it would hardly have been necessary after his death.

Traces of blood were found on cupboard doors, also on curtains, but although the office carpet was carefully examined for blood, none could be found.

The evidence was now coming together. One of the spades found in the vicinity of the body had been purchased from a shop in Bruce Grove sometime after 8 March; and a fork, found at the same time, had been purchased from a shop in High Road, Tottenham, sometime after 9 February 1970.

⋆   ⋆   ⋆

On Saturday, 11 April, Raymond was arrested in Scotland and two days later, he appeared at Glasgow Sheriff's Court in respect of the offence for which he was wanted on warrant. Fined £25, he was detained, pending his transfer to London on the other offences for which he was circulated as being wanted, and upon his arrival at Highbury on 14 April, where he was charged, he was spoken to by Dilley.

Raymond was terrified of Parker, whom he referred to as 'a killer', and refused to commit himself to paper since he feared that he, too, would be murdered; nevertheless, he indicated the area where he had last seen the two wanted men. Having informed the officers that Parker was armed, Raymond was locked up, and Dilley and Parratt, in possession of warrants for the duo's arrest for the assault on PC Turk, set off for Scotland to liaise with the local police.

Woods was arrested in the village of Lochinver at 2.10 pm on Friday, 17 April. 'I played the part of a tourist in a broken-down car', Parratt told me. 'Woods came into town to get the newspapers and, as he came alongside, I banged the driver's door open and knocked him over.'

Woods stated that Parker was in possession of an automatic pistol, although he said he had no ammunition for it. 'I think Parker treated him as a gofer', Parratt said. 'Woods was frightened of him.' But the question was, was he telling the truth regarding Parker's lack of ammunition for the pistol? And if Parker had told Woods that he had no ammunition, was he telling him the truth? Bearing in mind that Parker had shot two people dead, no risks could be taken.

Therefore, it appeared the height of foolhardiness when, half an hour after Woods' arrest, the officers found themselves on the mountainside just 15 yards away from the tent which contained Parker, and one of the Scots officers shouted suddenly, 'Come out, Parker, with your hands up!'

'I must admit, my bottle went', said Parratt. 'But he came out and slowly put his hands up.' Parratt was not the only person to be apprehensive, because he added, 'I remember, Parker's Adam's apple was bouncing up and down like a yo-yo.' In the tent the automatic pistol (minus ammunition) was found inside a briefcase and seized.

At Lochinver police station, the warrants for the attack on the Hampshire officer were read to both men, who both verbally admitted the offence.

Woods replied, 'How is the officer? I feel terrible about it, but it was panic and it was all we could do in the circumstances. How is my mother? I'm terribly worried about her.'

In response to the warrant, Parker replied, 'I understand. It's something I've done. I suppose I lost my head.'

Dilley then questioned the prisoners regarding Coleman's death. Woods elected to make a written statement under caution, whereas Parker said, 'I want to see a solicitor before I speak to you, Mr Dilley. I shall not be disputing any of the facts and as soon as I see my solicitor, I will make a full and frank statement as to motivation.'

⋆   ⋆   ⋆

The Scots police officers had looked after their English counterparts very well, and on the last night of their stay, Dilley said, 'Let's put a drink on for them.'

This was nothing out of the norm. 'Every evening', Parratt told me, 'Dave would say, "Geoffrey, it's 5 o'clock – time for a beer!".'

On this occasion it was time for whisky, and with their Scottish counterparts they had some at the inn where the Met officers had been staying.

'One of the officers said to me, "Do you like salmon?"' said Parratt, 'and I replied, "Yes", although the only salmon I'd tasted came courtesy of John West, out of a can. The following morning, the innkeeper said, "There's a wee present for you", and I was given a whole salmon – it must have been three feet long! – and we took it back to Tottenham nick and cut it up in the inspector's office; he wasn't there!'

But on that morning of Monday, 20 April, there were rather more pressing matters to deal with at Tottenham police station than dividing a salmon into acceptable portions for a number of hungry coppers.

Parker, in the presence of his solicitor, wrote his statement himself, and then both men were charged with Coleman's murder, plus the assault on PC Turk, and appeared the same day at Tottenham Magistrates' Court, where they were remanded.

In their statements, both men stated that they had acted in self-defence; Dilley thought differently. He believed that what had happened was a cold-blooded, well thought-out plan to execute Coleman; but could it be proved? Already information was received that there was a move afoot to induce many of the known criminals involved in this case to fabricate evidence for the defence.

Driberg – already on extremely friendly terms with both Parker and Raymond – was most anxious to visit both of them and in fact, had already seen Raymond in prison. When Dilley wrote, 'There is no doubt that Driberg is intensely worried and apprehensive about something concerning these men', he wasn't far wrong.

Since Raymond had purchased the trunk prior to the murder, had there been a plot between the three men to kill Coleman? This, Raymond emphatically denied. In fact, on the evening of the murder, Raymond was quite impressively alibied. In company with his girlfriend, he had dined with no lesser personages than Tom Driberg, his fellow MP Michael Foot and his brother, Sir Dingle Foot, the Attorney General at the appropriately named Gay Hussar, Greek Street, W1 – and that was confirmed by the director of the restaurant.

*   *   *

Raymond had been the manager of a company named Superbuy in Green Lanes, N4 – he had obtained this position by producing a reference on House of Commons notepaper apparently signed by Tom Driberg, but in fact written by Raymond himself. This was before the warehouse used by Superbuy mysteriously burned down, three days before the murder; it became the subject of an investigation as part of a long-firm fraud, in which the owner alleged that Raymond had appropriated money and goods, although that's neither here nor there. What is important is that Raymond had previously employed Parker's girlfriend at his premises, and it was there that she had seen a gun in a briefcase. That was a Hungarian Walam 9mm automatic pistol, which Raymond took with him to Scotland and which was found in Parker's possession when he was arrested; another automatic pistol, a Colt .25, was found in Parker's car.

Raymond appeared at North London Magistrates' Court on 23 April 1970, and in respect of the rather serious offences for which he had been circulated he was given the surprisingly lenient sentence of a two-year conditional discharge. There was no evading the recall to prison, however, and Raymond was sent off to Wormwood Scrubs. Although due consideration was given to using him as a witness against the other two, the Director of Public Prosecutions decided that the best place for Raymond was in the dock.

*   *   *

What the prisoners had to say was as follows.

There had been a disagreement between them and Coleman at Bruce Grove, due to Coleman's incompetence over the proposed theft of a lorry containing silk thread. Coleman, they said, produced a rifle from a cricket-type bag which failed to fire, and then Woods hit him on the head with a hammer, twice, and Parker seized the rifle. Coleman came towards him with a bayonet-style knife which he produced from beneath his coat, and in self defence Parker jumped back and fired the rifle at him. This brought up two matters. First, the shot that was fired into Coleman's abdomen caused powder burns to his waistcoat and shirt, which meant that it was fired at point-blank range. Next, the pathologist was of the opinion that in view of the severity of the blows to Coleman's head and skull, he was extremely unlikely to be in any position to make an attacking movement. No trace of a cricket-style bag or a bayonet was ever found.

Next, the rifle measured 46½ inches in length, and Coleman's girlfriend, who was with him all day, said she saw nothing resembling that or a cricket bag in his car. Despite the fact that Parker said that Coleman followed him and Woods from The Shaftesbury public house to Bruce Grove in his car, he didn't. He must have accompanied Parker and Woods in the truck; it is inconceivable that a criminal of Coleman's calibre would have walked the 3½ miles between the two venues at 9 o'clock at night carrying a bag containing a rifle.

If what the prisoners said was true, blood would certainly have been found on the office carpet, but not if the polythene sheeting had already been laid out; the size of it was sufficient to have covered the whole of that small area. So the evidence for the planned execution was already in place at the time of Coleman's death. As well as the polythene sheeting, there was the trunk, the spade, the fork and the rifle – not Coleman's, but something which had already been seen in Parker's possession. It was the same rifle which ballistic tests had proved had been used to murder Coleman, as well as for target practice in Bruce Grove. And the reason for Coleman's death? Not necessarily Coleman's inability to organize a lorry hi-jacking – more likely, a dispute of the ownership of the solid gold snuffbox.

* * *

On 30 November 1970, Parker, Wood and Raymond appeared at the Old Bailey, before the Recorder of London, Sir Carl Aarvold OBE, TD. They were all charged with murdering Coleman, and Parker and Woods were additionally charged with wounding PC Turk. Raymond was charged with impeding the arrest of Parker and Woods. To these charges, all three pleaded not guilty.

Giving evidence, Parker said, 'I was responsible for his death, but I never at any time planned to do it.' Asked by his barrister if he was frightened about what had happened, Woods replied, 'Ever so much, yes.'

The eleven jurors – one had applied to be discharged at the beginning of the trial due to illness – retired for five hours on 16 December before finding Parker guilty of murder by a majority of 10–1. Woods was found not guilty of murder but by a majority of 10–1 guilty of impeding Parker's apprehension. Both men were found guilty, again by a majority verdict, of wounding PC Turk. Raymond was found not guilty of the murder or manslaughter of Coleman on the directions of the judge, but guilty, by a unanimous verdict, of impeding the arrest of Woods and Parker in respect of (a) Coleman's murder and (b) PC Turk's assault.

Sentence was due to be passed the following day, when who should appear in the witness box but Tom Driberg, who said that Raymond had written to him from prison five years previously.

'As a constituent of mine', Driberg said, 'he was asking me to take up certain matters with the Home Office regarding his transfer to another prison. I tried to help him. The police asked me last November if I knew of his whereabouts, and when I saw him, some months later, I tried to persuade him to give himself up voluntarily in the hope that he would get a lighter sentence. This has always been my practice when constituents were on the run and I have personally taken them to the police station.'

'Did you not conceive it to be your duty to get in touch with the police and tell them you knew where he was?' asked the counsel for the prosecution and received this jaw-droppingly smug, pompous reply: 'No. I do not think it is the duty of a Member of Parliament to act as a police informer against one of his own constituents, any more than it is the duty of a clergyman, a priest or a solicitor to do so. When Raymond wrote to me from prison, he said he was a constituent of mine and we try to look after our constituents.'

Of course, Raymond wasn't Driberg's constituent, any more than Raymond had been Driberg when he forged his signature for a reference or obtained a sheepskin coat with his credit card. Still, he was free of the murder charge, that was the main thing, so he went off to prison for two and three years concurrently. Whilst serving this sentence he escaped, was recaptured and after being involved in a £2 million theft at Heathrow airport, was sentenced to ten years' imprisonment. He attended bankruptcy proceedings, and when an attempt was made to claw back some of the proceeds of the theft, he barefacedly stated that he had given £25,000 of the stolen money to his friend Tom Driberg who, after being elevated to the peerage, had fortuitously dropped dead, three months after the theft. He then provided so-called evidence against so-called crooked police officers during the ill-fated 'Operation Countryman' enquiry, in which simple-minded county officers believed every word he said – although luckily, nobody else did.

Following his release from prison, he defrauded Granada TV of £500,000 and for this (and other peccadilloes) he was jailed for eight years. In 1989, he escaped from prison once more and when he was arrested in 1994 he was charged with conspiracy to manufacture and supply ecstasy worth, it was said, £20 million. He screamed across the courtroom that he had bribed the arresting officer, although after he was acquitted he later admitted to journalists that he had made that story up.

By 2000 Raymond was resident in France, but when he attempted to smuggle 693kg of cocaine worth £35 million into the UK, he came badly unstuck – and found that his excuse, that he was only trying to smuggle in cannabis, didn't wash. Nemesis, in the form of Judge Martyn Zeidman caught up with him in July 2005 at Snaresbrook Crown Court, when he was sentenced to a total of twenty-eight years' imprisonment.[2]

*　*　*

Woods was sentenced to concurrent terms of three years' imprisonment and thereafter disappeared from this scenario.

*　*　*

Parker was sentenced to life imprisonment and five years' imprisonment, concurrently, for the attack on PC Turk. He was released in 1994, having gained an Open University honours degree and a masters degree in criminology. He wrote several successful books about life behind bars and, referring to the murder of Edward

---

[2] For further details of Raymond's criminality, see *Operation Countryman: The Flawed Enquiry into Police Corruption*, Pen & Sword Books, 2018

Coleman, with the usual ex-offender's desire to disassociate himself from the offences for which he's been convicted, remarked dismissively, 'At worst, it was manslaughter.'

Not when the victim's been shot six times at point-blank range, it isn't.

Dr John Bodkin Adams.

Mr Justice Devlin.

Sir Geoffrey Lawrence QC.

Attorney General Sir Reginald Manningham-Buller.

(L) Melford Stevenson QC, and (R) Malcolm Morris, his junior at Eastbourne.

Above: L to R: DI Brynley Pugh, DS Charlie Hewett, DCS Herbert Hannam.

Below left: Hannam's notebook and the letter to Melford Stevenson.

Below right: Adams' surgery.

Above: Adams' arrest.

Below: Charlie Hewett cracks a joke; Hannam is less than amused.

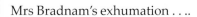
Mrs Bradnam's exhumation . . ..

. . . followed by Miss Neil-Miller's.

Above: DS Geoff Parratt (L) and a colleague arrest Norman Parker for murder.

Below left: Commander David Dilley QPM.

Below right: A C1 Murder Squad tie – the 'C' covers the surface of the globe, the '1' is behind it.

Above: 'Ginger' Hensley's (in bow tie) retirement function in the Murder Squad office; Bernie Davies is at the extreme right and the ship's bell from SS *Rosewood* is on the cabinet at the extreme left.

Above: Murderer Mustapha Bassaine.

Left: Lord Bernstein.

Above: (L) DS Maurice Marshall, (R) DCS Don Saunders in Acapulco.

Below left: Partially opened grave at Las Cruces Cemetery, Acapulco.

Below right: DCS Saunders with sealed coffin, Acapulco.

Left: DCS Saunders with coffin pensively awaiting a post mortem at Uxbridge mortuary . . ..

Below: . . . while DS Marshall relaxes after an exhausting exhumation.

Above: John Basil Cartland.

Below: Jeremy Cartland.

L-R: Jeremy Cartland, Michael Relton, DS John Troon.

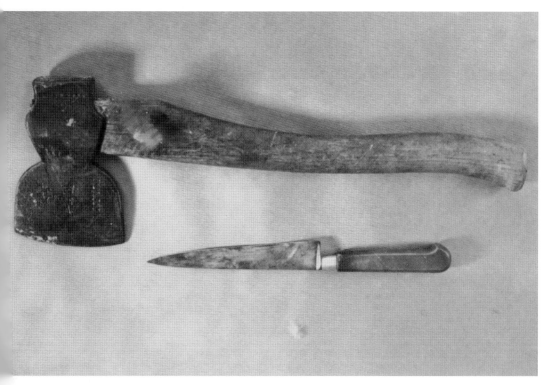

Above: Murder weapons in the Cartland case.

Below: John Cartland's car and burnt-out caravan, following his murder.

DCS Alex Ross.

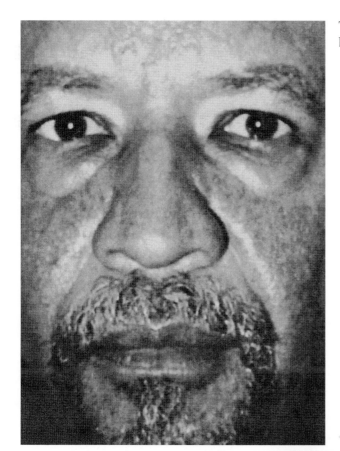

The missing
Dr Herbert.

Charles 'Little Nut' Miller.

The Old Bailey – where so many of the murder trials ended up.

CHAPTER 10

The Peer's Butler

Wilton Crescent in the London borough of Kensington and Chelsea contains beautiful, multi-storey terraced houses which, at the time of writing, command prices of anything from £2½ to £30 million. In 1970, No. 32 was the five-bedroom London home of the chairman of Granada TV, Sidney Lewis Bernstein, who had been elevated to the peerage the previous year.

The basement of the property housed Lord Bernstein's butler, Julian Louis Georges Sessé, who was sixty-five years of age and considered by the household to be very good at his work, kind and reliable. He was also tall, distinguished and as gay as a fruit bat.

Although the Sexual Offences Act 1967 had, to a certain extent, decriminalized relationships between gay men, in 1970 there was still a certain antipathy towards homosexual behaviour, and whether Sessé's employer was aware of his sexual proclivities is not known. However, what is known is that Lord Bernstein (motto: 'If I rest, I rust') was passionately anti-fascist and during the 1930s had assisted many German/Jewish actors and directors to escape from Hitler's repressive regime. Since homosexuals merited the same amount of disfavour as Jews in Nazi Germany, if Lord Bernstein was aware of his butler's inclinations it is quite possible that he would have regarded them in a tolerant vein. What he most certainly would not have approved of was Sessé inviting men to his quarters at Wilton Crescent.

But when Lord and Lady Bernstein left to holiday in Bermuda on Friday, 18 December 1970, that was precisely what happened the following day.

The first intimation that something was amiss was two days later, on Monday, 21 December, when a delivery driver was unable to get a reply at the house. Next, the cleaner and Lord Bernstein's private secretary entered the house and, upon descending the stairs to Sessé's private quarters, discovered blood splattered on the walls of several of the rooms and the bathroom door locked. They telephoned the police.

The nearest police station was Chelsea, and two constables from there arrived and forced the bathroom door. There was the butler's body; his throat had been cut, he had sustained what appeared to be frenzied knife wounds to his head and chest, and his stomach had been ripped open. That last wound had been the result of a meat cleaver being used; that weapon, plus the knife, was found in the lavatory bowl.

The post mortem carried out by the Home Office pathologist, Professor Keith Simpson, revealed that Sessé's cause of death (which probably occurred either late on the Saturday night or early the following morning) had been shock and loss of blood; also, he had engaged in anal intercourse prior to his demise. The local police already had two high-profile murders to investigate, so it was time to call in the Yard.

★   ★   ★

John 'Ginger' Hensley had been promoted to the rank of Detective Chief Superintendent and had just been posted to C1 Department in May 1970. Joining the police as soon as he was demobilized after spending the war years with the Royal Armoured Corps (where he gained a Mention in Dispatches), he had spent over ten years with the Flying Squad. He had taken a decisive part in the investigation into the murder of three police officers, the crew of a 'Q'-Car, in Shepherd's Bush in 1966. Now fifty years of age, Hensley was a terrific all-round investigator, commended time and again for arresting armed robbers, safe-blowers, receivers, fraudsters and drug dealers; he was much admired. Joining him on the Reserve Squad was Detective Sergeant Bernie Davis; they would work together for five years, and one of their first investigations was the murder of Lord Bernstein's butler.

Bit by bit, they pieced together what had happened. There was no sign of forced entry; therefore it was highly likely that Sessé had allowed access to the killer, quite possibly somebody he knew. Initially, he had been attacked in his kitchen with the knife, and the assault had continued into the living room as the unfortunate butler attempted to escape. It was there that his throat had been cut, and after he had been dragged into the bathroom, the butchery continued with the meat cleaver. The killer's bloodstained trousers had been put into the washing machine, and a pair of Sessé's trousers were missing from his wardrobe.

The scene was photographed, forensically examined and dusted for fingerprints; approximately £80 was missing from Lady Bernstein's desk. Elimination fingerprints had to be obtained from all people having legitimate access to the property.

Detective Sergeant Geoff Cameron was a member of C1's 8 Squad, which was colloquially known as 'the odds and sods squad'. He was drawn into Hensley's investigation, and it was his job to obtain Lord Bernstein's fingerprints for elimination purposes, once he returned from holiday. This was his memory of the incident:

> Now His Lordship was a man who was very tall, 6 feet 6–7 inches. Because I was only 5 feet 9 inches on a good day, I found it impossible to take his elims because of the difference in our respective heights. I tried every piece of furniture of varying heights in his palatial lounge, but it was no good. Then His Lordship suggested that it might help if he got on his knees, which he did in front of a writing bureau, and the elims were obtained quite easily, but not before Ginger Hensley quipped, 'I wish I had a camera to photograph Sergeant Cameron of Scotland Yard, bringing a peer of the realm to his knees!' His Lordship, being a good Jewish boy, born in Ilford, took the remark in good humour, commenting that he would have liked a copy.

But there was little else to amuse the officers; it looked as though this case was going to become what in police parlance is known as 'a sticker'.

A witness had seen what was described as 'a foreign-looking man' in the vicinity at the time of the murder; he needed to be traced and interviewed, if only for elimination purposes. Sessé had kept details – names, addresses, telephone numbers – of men with whom he had presumably had sexual relationships; they, too, would have to be seen and interviewed, obviously very tactfully, especially if they were married. Or had this been a chance encounter with a stranger? The possibilities were endless. And then, this happened.

On Wednesday, 23 December, the crew of 'Q'-Car 'November One-One' responded to a telephone call from a girl living in a North London bedsit, in Tufnell Park. What she had to say about the murder was electrifying; and the 'Q'-Car detectives lost no time in contacting the Murder Squad.

Jean Fitzgerald, a 22-year-old waitress, told Hensley and Davis that she had met the murdered butler through her boyfriend, a 26-year-old Moroccan national named Mustapha Bassaine, who had lived with her for several months. Although Bassaine had distinguished family connections – his father was a high ranking official in the Moroccan Foreign Office – he was a sponger and unemployed. He had given Miss Fitzgerald money which, he said, had been given to him by homosexuals with whom he associated. She was aware of Sessé and disapproved of her bisexual boyfriend's liaison with him.

On Saturday, 19 December, she and Bassaine had been drinking in the West End; he telephoned Sessé and, telling her that he was going to meet the butler 'to try and get some money off him', Bassaine left her at 11 o'clock that night.

And that was the last that she heard from Bassaine until almost 24 hours later, when he telephoned her at her bedsit, demanding that she go at once to Lord Bernstein's mansion and threatening to kill her if she refused. Prudently, she refused, but before she put the phone down, Bassaine told her to pack his clothes. He arrived at the bedsit later, drunk, with blood on his shoes, scratches on his neck and wearing a pair of trousers which were far too big for him but would have fitted the unfortunate Julian Sessé perfectly.

The following day – Monday, 21 December – the couple went to a travel agency and, telling Miss Fitzgerald that his mother was unwell, Bassaine purchased a one-way ticket to Morocco. Giving her an address in Morocco and telling Miss Fitzgerald to send him press cuttings of any item that mentioned his name, Bassaine left on a flight from London Heathrow that departed at 3.10 pm that day.

On the Wednesday she read of Sessé's murder in the newspaper and telephoned Scotland Yard.

Without too much difficulty, Hensley and Davis found Bassaine's bloodstained shoes (the blood matched Sessé's blood group) and the over-large trousers in a dustbin at Tufnell Park and applied for a warrant for Bassaine's arrest the same day. Extradition was requested, although that was rather a forlorn hope, since no extradition treaty existed between Britain and Morocco. So long as Bassaine stayed in his own country, he was safe.

All of the documentation and exhibits were meticulously assembled, an appropriate entry was put into *Police Gazette* and the unfortunate Julian Sessé was largely forgotten. Lord Bernstein acquired a fresh butler (probably insisting on one with greater moral rectitude than his predecessor), and Hensley and Davis continued with subsequent investigations as their names came up 'in the frame' – although not always together.

'Ginger was a good guv'nor but he was a hard man', Davis told me. 'We were No. 1 in the frame and I asked for a few days off. He agreed, but told me, "If a job comes up, I won't take you." I told him if that did happen, I could be back at the Yard in time. A job did come up; it was to St Kitts and Nevis in the West

Indies, and he stuck to his word – he didn't take me. So he flew off with somebody else and I got the next murder enquiry with Reg Lasham – to Hull!'

Almost two years passed; and then Bassaine very foolishly left his homeland to travel to Holland. He was arrested for a minor offence in Rotterdam, where it was discovered that he was the subject of an international arrest warrant. Unusually in such a case, extradition was not resisted, and Bernie Davis went to Holland to bring him back.

On the return flight, the sight of Bassaine handcuffed to Davis moved the heart of one of the airline's stewardesses, who suggested that in the event of an emergency the handcuffs should be removed. It was a benevolent gesture although not a particularly pragmatic one, because as Davis told me, 'I said, "If the plane crashes, love, we're all in trouble!"'

The flight landed without incident, Bassaine was duly charged and committed to the Old Bailey where, before Mr Justice Forbes on 8 February 1973, he denied both murdering Sessé and stealing £80 from Lady Bernstein's bedroom.

The evidence was pretty overpowering, but Bassaine's defence was that although he had stayed with Sessé overnight on the night of 19 December, the butler was quite all right when he left on the Sunday morning. He had returned to the Tufnell Park bedsit and told Miss Fitzgerald of his previous night's encounter, whereupon she flew into a rage and, as he told the jury, 'She threatened to smash Sessé's face' and left the bedsit. When she returned, late that night, he said, 'I found her trembling. She told me she was sick.'

The jury spent little time considering this nonsense – Bernie Davis told me, 'Jean Fitzgerald wasn't involved in the murder in any way; she was a timid, unworldly Irish girl' – and the jury agreed. On 12 February, Bassaine was sentenced to life imprisonment. At the conclusion of his sentence, having served eleven years, he was deported to his homeland.

Which brings us to Jean Fitzgerald, who fortunately refused Bassaine's demands that she should go to Lord Bernstein's mansion on the day of the murder – for what reason? To help dispose of the body – or to put herself in jeopardy? And then, faced with irrefutable evidence, for Bassaine, who tried to blame her for the murder.

From these unfortunate beginnings, did the naïve, unsophisticated Miss Fitzgerald eventually find stability and happiness in her life? I hope she did; and if she reads these words, perhaps she'll let me know.

CHAPTER 11

An Exhumation in Acapulco

O n the same day that Julian Sessé met his untimely end, so did a seaman on board a British cruise liner, 5,712 miles away.

On the face of it, the facts were quite straightforward. Edward McLoughlin was a 33-year-old able seaman from Co. Wicklow, Eire; he was very experienced, having worked aboard ships since 1956. By comparison, Peter Charles Woolgar, also aged thirty-three, had only been at sea for eighteen months, but he was one of the ship's six quartermasters, whose duties led him to the ship's bridge and subsequent contact with the officers, something that annoyed McLoughlin. The antagonism was one-sided; there was no evidence that Woolgar felt any dislike for McLoughlin. But on 19 December 1970, McLoughlin had been drinking heavily, and by the evening he had begun riling Woolgar, telling him, in front of witnesses, that he (Woolgar) was not capable of doing his job; this hassling had been happening for much of the voyage.

The argument continued, then McLoughlin followed Woolgar to the latter's cabin, where the needling continued, until Woolgar had had enough; he punched McLoughlin – by his own admission – fifteen or twenty times around the head and body, threw him across the cabin, picked up a metal bunk ladder and hit him across the head with it. Since the ladder weighed 8¾lbs, was 4ft. 7¾ inches in length and 11¼ inches wide, it was a formidable weapon, and McLoughlin died as a result of the assault. Woolgar was immediately penitent, saying to a crew member, 'Why didn't you stop me, Charlie?' and 'Oh my God, what have I done?' But even though Woolgar had been extremely provoked verbally, the fact remained that McLoughlin had not offered him any physical violence.

Their ship, the 24,000-ton SS *Northern Star*, had anchored in Acapulco Bay, Guerrero, Mexico, 800 yards from the shore and clearly in Mexican territorial waters. However, the death had occurred on a British-registered ship, and the investigation had to be carried out by British detectives. Since Woolgar had been detained, having made verbal admissions to several crew members of his culpability, it looked very much as though everything was cut and dried.

Don't you believe it.

*   *   *

Detective Sergeant (First Class) Maurice Marshall was No. 1 'in the frame', together with Detective Chief Superintendent Don Saunders, on 24 December 1970, when they were informed of McLoughlin's death. Fortunately, this did not disrupt Marshall's Christmas arrangements, and he was able to spend Christmas Day with his wife and four children at his in-laws' home in Cheshire, although the next few days were spent arranging travel plans, travellers' cheques and visas for the USA – this being necessary for a short stopover – and Mexico. In addition, both officers were completely kitted out for work in the tropics at 'All Kits' in Leicester Square: a new suit, spare trousers, three shirts, underwear, pyjamas and even a couple of ties, all at the expense of the Metropolitan Police. 'I bet it doesn't happen now', Marshall told me, and it could well be he was right.

Saunders and Marshall were old friends; they had worked together in earlier ranks and different locations. Saunders – who later became Commander of the Metropolitan Police's No. 1 District CID – was an outstanding and much admired detective.

Marshall had joined the police in 1953 and served for eighteen years as a constable and sergeant, gaining a wealth of experience, both on division and in the Flying Squad and C1 Department before, during the next twenty-three years, shooting up to the rank of detective chief superintendent, collecting a clutch of commendations from Commissioners, judges and Directors of Public Prosecutions.

So both officers flew to Mexico City, and on 30 December, while Saunders remained at the British Embassy, Marshall travelled to Acapulco, where he was met by Derek Gore, the exceptionally helpful British Vice Consul. Apparently, the post of Vice Consul was not a full-time job; Gore was also deputy manager of the extremely prestigious Las Brisas, then rated one the world's top twelve hotels. On the wall near reception was an enormous plaque emblazoned with the Royal Coat of Arms. This was undoubtedly thrilling to the rich American tourists who flocked to the hotel, although not necessarily viewed with the same degree of enthusiasm by the Garter King of Arms.

With the New Year rapidly approaching, the hotel was full to bursting with wealthy Americans, but Gore – obviously a very enterprising deputy manager – not only managed to find accommodation for the Murder Squad officers, but also provided them with their own bungalow and swimming pool. They were even given (as were all the guests) a pink and white striped jeep, while breakfast was delivered by Mexican housemaids; the flasks of coffee, fruit and pastries were left on the bungalow's doorstep, while fresh blossoms were liberally sprinkled on the surface of the pool.

The friendliness of the American guests, who were enormously impressed by the presence of Scotland Yard detectives, plus the tequila and the hot sunny days, made a rather refreshing change from London, where during the last week of December their counterparts were experiencing sleet, snow and temperatures which varied between zero and 3° centigrade.

Meanwhile, the SS *Northern Star* had continued its journey, together with the witnesses among its 450 crew members, any of whom might join different ships travelling to anywhere in the world. Woolgar was locked up in a Mexican jail and McLoughlin had been buried in a Mexican graveyard; no post mortem had been carried out. At least, a doctor had certified that he was dead.

It was time to put lotus land on hold so that police work could begin.

At the Acapulco municipal offices, where a conference was held with the Mexican Government Immigration Inspector and the Federal District Attorney, Saunders dealt with the Mexican authorities in order to remove Woolgar from their territory, and after they considered a Consular Convention Agreement of 1964, the Extradition Treaty of 1886 and the Merchant Shipping Act of 1894, they agreed to waive their jurisdiction. Directly that was done, the British officers assumed jurisdiction on behalf of the Director of Public Prosecutions. Woolgar, having spent ten days in the local jail, offered no resistance to being returned to England, and on 1 January 1971, with the prisoner handcuffed to Maurice Marshall, they boarded a Quantas airliner; after twenty hours, with stopovers at Mexico City, Nassau and Bermuda, they arrived at London Heathrow, and on 2 January Marshall charged Woolgar at Cannon Row police station with murder. The following day, Marshall wrote down a long and detailed statement from him, and on Monday, 4 January, Woolgar appeared at Bow Street Magistrates' Court and was remanded in custody. The rest of that day was spent in Marshall updating the commander of C1, plus the Director of Public Prosecution's office, and obtaining airline tickets and a further visa at the Mexican Embassy.

On Tuesday, 5 January, Marshall flew to Acapulco via New York, finally arriving at 3.30 pm on 6 January; not that there was a chance to relax. Saunders had arranged for McLoughlin's body to be exhumed the following day and, as usual, exhumations were carried out early in the morning. Marshall now recounts what happened:

> At 5.30 am, while it was still dark, Don and I attended Las Crusas Cemetery near Acapulco together with Charles Tarrant, the Consul and Derek Gore, the Vice Consul. There we were met with Mexican officials including Señor De La Rosa from the funeral directors and Señor Cervantes of the Health Authority and others. There were approximately a dozen people, and the only ones who failed to turn up were the gravediggers. After waiting for about an hour and having established there were no volunteers in the company, Don and I decided there was nothing else for it but to do it ourselves. Using spades provided by the cemetery, we dug down and fortunately found the coffin only a couple of feet deep. We got it to the surface and then had to open it to establish we had the right body, which one of the undertakers present was able to confirm.
>
> The body had been in a shallow grave in a very hot climate for nearly three weeks and it stank. The stench was worse than anything I ever encountered, before or since. But that was not what concerned us. We discovered that no post mortem examination (as we would understand it) had been performed on the body and, to add to the confusion, the body had been liberally covered in some form of chemical crystals prior to burial, thus contaminating any future examination which would be performed in the UK. Such fears proved unfounded, as the UK pathologist, Dr Bowen, had no difficulty eliminating any effect the chemicals may have had from his conclusions.
>
> The body was then returned to the undertakers to be suitably packed for air travel back to the UK. This turned out to be an exact and lengthy procedure requiring three coffins, one inside the other. The first, an ordinary wooden coffin, was encased within a steel coffin which had to be welded shut and hidden inside a more ornate outer coffin. The whole was accompanied by reams of paperwork, inspections, permissions and authorisations from Federal and State departments and, of course, the airlines involved. Everything was in Spanish and had to be translated, which was time consuming but not so delaying as seeking the cooperation of the chief of the Municipal Police. This turned out to be the most bizarre contact I ever had with another policeman, anywhere.
>
> We were taken that same day to the local police headquarters by Derek Gore, the British Vice Consul, and after a short delay,

we were shown into the chief's office. We were not offered a seat
and stood before his desk while Derek Gore and he conducted a
conversation. We Brits could not understand a word of Spanish,
but it became apparent that this exchange was less than friendly.
After a short while, he must have summoned help, because
two burly police officers entered and he barked something at
them which I did not immediately understand. It would be
an exaggeration to say we were physically thrown out into the
street, but we were certainly bundled unceremoniously out of
the office and out of the building with helping hands behind
us. A very embarrassed and upset Derek Gore explained that
the post of police chief was a political appointment, and the
previous year, this man had been a taxi driver whom Derek Gore
had barred from the Las Brisas hotel for cheating. In order to
obtain the written statements we required from local policemen,
we enlisted the help of the British Ambassador and made a
formal complaint to the Federal District Attorney.

Later that day, we visited the doctor/medical examiner who
had pronounced McLoughlin dead. He now produced a large,
ornate certificate in Spanish which he had signed and sealed
and which apparently gave the cause of death as a blow to the
head. It was only later, when this document was translated,
that we discovered that it purported to be the details of the
doctor's post mortem examination of the body. We knew no
such examination had been made, although it transpired that
the Mexican's guess was right and agreed by Dr Bowen later
in the UK. It was explained by Derek Gore that the doctor's
official fee was so small it barely paid for the ornate certificate.
To do his job, he would normally expect someone else to pay
him, and as no one had, he didn't do it.

The following four days were spent interviewing local witnesses
and taking statements, making travel arrangements, supervising
the packing of the body and dealing with the Mexican regulations.
However, due to a delay in waiting for the federal police to arrive
from Mexico City to deal with the complaint against the local police,
it was with great regret that Saunders and Marshall were obliged
to spend the next four days lying on the beach, swimming and
snorkelling in the hotel's own sea lagoon and going on conducted
tours of all the visible sights in Acapulco. This came to an end
when a smartly suited official from Mexico City arrived, and after
he had a quiet word with the local chief of police, the matters
which should have been sorted out almost a week previously were
partially resolved. These were agents of the judiciary who had been
refused interviews with the Murder Squad officers and who had
brought ashore Woolgar, the dead man and the ladder which had

inflicted the fatal injury. They later made declarations through their district attorney.

Following the flight back to England, during which Marshall swore he could detect the smell of the corpse in the hold, the officers were fully engaged with the DPP, gathering exhibits and making arrangements to meet the *Northern Star* upon her arrival at Southampton. Next came the post mortem at Uxbridge mortuary, where Dr Bowen stated that the most likely cause of death was a subarachnoid haemorrhage – the type of haemorrhage brought about by a blow to the head – and then, on 16 January, the officers joined the ship and the same day, set sail for Las Palmas in the Canary Islands. By the time the ship docked, four days later, the remaining crew had been interviewed and statements obtained, and the cabin where the assault had taken place had been photographed.

Identification of McLoughlin was proved by the right thumb print from the body being identical with that in McLoughlin's seaman's discharge book.

The Met Commissioner personally wrote to Charles Hope, H.M. Ambassador to the United States of Mexico, expressing his thanks for the very great assistance which had been rendered to the officers by him and his staff; as Saunders would accurately state, 'Without the assistance so readily given, our task would have been nearly impossible.'

On 1 February, Marshall was promoted to detective inspector and posted to Islington police station, but he attended the Old Bailey on 27 May, when Woolgar pleaded guilty to the charge of manslaughter and, given all the circumstances of the case, received a twelve-month conditional discharge. This meant that as long as Woolgar kept out of trouble for the next year, it would be the end of the matter.

'It was', Marshall told me, 'probably the most expensive conditional discharge in history', and there was no doubt he was right. He was also concerned about the expenditure he and Saunders had incurred, telling me:

> We had been given a budget of some few hundreds of pounds but had arrived in a millionaires' paradise with costs to match, and our legitimate spend was ten times that amount and more. As it was part of my role to look after the financial side of the investigation, I was more than a little worried. 'Don't worry', said Don. 'As long as we can show we economised as far as possible, they can't complain.' So instead of dining at the super expensive Las Brisas Hotel, we ate dinner at the cheaper Hilton

instead. It worked, because Don used his charm on the ladies of F2 (Finance) Department and we never heard another word about it.

Except grumbles of envy from colleagues who were sent to investigate murders in places like Grimsby.

CHAPTER 12

Potpourri

W hat follows is a mixed bag of cases for the Murder Squad.

The tiny island of Diego Garcia (12 square miles) is set in the Indian Ocean, just south of the equator. Its history is interesting, as are its present-day circumstances, but suffice it to say, for the purpose of the stories that follow, that the island was transferred to British rule following the Napoleonic wars and between 1968 and 1973 its population was forcibly removed to establish an American military base there, including an airstrip and a communications station. Thereafter, the island was mostly inhabited by US and UK military personnel, and some overseas workers. But because it was a British dependency, the laws and regulations were administered by the British Indian Ocean Territory (BIOT), and the British contingent consisted of a Naval Commander, a company of Royal Marines and half a dozen ROPOs (Royal Overseas Police Officers, who were naval personnel). The combination of the UK and US forces were sufficient to deal with minor misdemeanours; for more serious matters, Scotland Yard needed to be called in.

One such incident occurred when there was a stabbing at the Royal Marines' Mess during a 'toga night'; US personnel had been invited, and both victim and perpetrator were Americans. The knife had nicked the victim's heart and he only survived because of the presence of qualified medics who provided immediate medical attention.

Detective Superintendent Graham Seaby was sent from the Yard and he told me:

> To get there, we had to hitch a lift on a US cargo plane out of Singapore and we lived with the troops once there, as there were no visitor facilities. The suspect was held in US custody and interviewing him was different, in that we had to satisfy the US Military Police (including their pastor) that we would treat him fairly and 'gently' and had the added complication that his solicitor was in Singapore. The whole investigation was done

against a background of the Americans thinking they controlled the island and the Brits seeking to prove that Britannia ruled; there were a few clashes!

★   ★   ★

There were clashes of a different nature when Detective Chief Superintendent Ken Davies and the late Detective Inspector Derek German were sent to the island; they travelled from Holland's Schiphol airport to Nairobi and thence on a US military cargo aeroplane to the island. The 'clash' in question is described by Ken Davies:

> A Brit Royal Marine was giving a lady American naval officer a seeing-to when he caught sight of one of the Philippino work force watching them. He gave the bloke a smack on the nose and the bloke ran off. He was not seen again and was reported missing. The island was searched, and he was not found for several days until his very decomposed body was found in a jungle area of the island. In the meantime, the Marine had reported the incident to the British authorities and had made a statement to the BIOT police. When the body was found, they charged the Marine with assault and then decided to call us via the Foreign Office. The Marine was shipped off the island and the Americans sent the lady officer home to the States before our arrival. The only pathologist we could get hold of was Colonel Bob Menzies of the Army, via the good offices of Professor 'Taffy' Cameron. He did a very professional job, but the situation was that having spent so much time in the jungle, the body (which was the worst I'd ever smelled) contained nothing apart from a thumbnail fragment of what was thought to be his heart. It had all been devoured by insects; consequently, no cause of death could be established. There was a mark on his nose which tied in with the Marine's account; the Marine was tried out there and was convicted of assault and got a couple of years.

However, a few months later, Davies was called back to the island (which, as he told me, 'could well be the remotest location that the Yard has ever carried out any investigation') to investigate a murder in which, following a dispute, one Philippino had fatally stabbed another, and this time it was more straightforward: there were witnesses, and the pathologist, Professor Hugh Johnson, had carried out a timely post mortem. The trial took place on the island some months later, and although the prisoner denied the charge of murder he was found guilty; but it was after the conviction that complications set in, as Davies explained to me:

> It was then found that the BIOT law (which mirrored English law) had not been updated and that the death penalty was still in being. So I guess I must have been the last murder investigating officer at the Yard to have had a trial with that penalty in place. Needless to say, the law was immediately updated and he was sentenced to life imprisonment. He was duly sent to Parkhurst, which I assume is the nearest of our prisons to Diego!

★   ★   ★

During the 1970s, John Spears was a detective sergeant (first class) on call in the Murder Office and acted as bag-carrier to a number of senior officers, one of whom was Detective Chief Superintendent Terry O'Connell (later Commander O'Connell QPM), a former wartime Royal Marine Commando, who had served for over nine years with the Flying Squad. During his 33-year career, O'Connell had collected twenty commissioner's commendations for arresting criminals who were variously described as 'troublesome', 'cunning', 'persistent' and 'violent'.

One investigation was on board a 17,000 ton P&O liner, *The Spirit of London*, where secret Admiralty documents had been stolen from the captain's safe. This had been the latest in a series of petty thefts from the passengers, and an investigation by Captain Gerry McGowan had been launched and the American FBI had been called in, but as a P&O spokesman had rightly observed, 'We decided to get an expert thief catcher and where better should we go than Scotland Yard?'

Escaping England's winds sweeping in from the north-west during February 1973, O'Connell and Spears flew to Acapulco, Mexico to catch up with the ship. It was quite possible that the thieves responsible for the onboard larcenies had mistakenly thought that the stolen papers were valuable securities, but at any event, on the first night the ship was in port, O'Connell came to the conclusion that a particular seaman was the culprit. He decided to use a little Flying Squad unconventionality in order to prove he was a thief. Spears takes up the tale:

> Terry asked me to wait on the quayside until a particular seaman came ashore. A US $100 bill had been planted where he could find it, and my job was to follow him to any bar he visited, grab the note and hightail it back to the vessel ASAP!

I was not happy about this as the Mexican police didn't know
we were there, and I was not happy to carry out his instructions
as I could have got into serious trouble, and my Spanish in
those days was very limited! Anyway, I was accompanied by
the staff captain from the vessel and we drank beers on the
quayside, and the suspect never came ashore. I didn't see eye to
eye with Terry over this case, as in my view he handled it badly,
but he was the boss.

Of course, Spears was quite right; nicking a $100 bill from a foreign
national on foreign soil where there was no British jurisdiction
could have led to a night in jug (or even several) for Spears, as
well as a diplomatic incident just as serious as the theft of secret
documents. During the next three weeks, the officers sailed to Los
Angeles, back to Acapulco, then back to Los Angeles; all of the
crew were interviewed, and although O'Connell and Spears were
initially introduced as P&O accountants, it soon became known
that they were officers from Scotland Yard and they were feted
by the mainly rich American passengers who were enchanted at
being in the presence of two such distinguished personalities.
What had initially been thought to be the work of Russian agents
or espionage by duplicitous crew members turned out to be
nothing of the kind; it was proved that a shore gang of thieves was
responsible.

And when the same officers flew out to Dakar, Senegal, where
the captain of a British ship, the *Rosewood*, had been stabbed, they
returned after the investigation had been successfully concluded
with the ship's bell, which found pride of place in the Murder
Squad office.

But the case which stuck most in Spears' memory occurred
not on the west coast of Africa or Mexico's Pacific coast but
in dear old Blighty – to be specific, Slough. It was not with
Terry O'Connell but with Detective Chief Superintendent Bill
Wright, who had successfully investigated a couple of murders in
Bermuda. And when the culprit had been arrested, it was Spears
who had to supervise the case at Reading Crown Court, because
Wright had to return to Bermuda in respect of one of his cases.
But the reason why this case was so memorable for Spears was
not necessarily because the murderer was a devil worshipper, but
because of what happened at court: a sequence of events that
occurred in the *Perry Mason* TV series on a weekly basis, but
hardly ever in real life. And it all started when Spears' Sunday
lunch was interrupted in July 1972 by a call from the Murder
office to say there had been a murder in Slough, and within

an hour a sleek black Austin Princess arrived outside his front door . . .

The body of 22-year-old Paul Anthony Duval had been found by two amateur sub-aqua divers in bloodstained grass, some 1,000 yards from Colnbrook bypass opposite the Riverside Café. Professor Keith Simpson was called, and within hours, at Slough mortuary, a post mortem examination revealed that the former public schoolboy had died as the result of being stabbed through the heart. Thames Valley Police had requested assistance from the Yard because they believed Duval had been a rent boy and that there was a London connection, although it transpired that London had nothing to do with the murder.

Duval was dressed rather distinctively in a grey striped shirt and pink and purple flared denim trousers. He had been seen in the company of another man dressed in dark, flared trousers and a safari jacket, and Al Bisley, the owner of the Riverside Café, recalled them because of their distinctive clothes. The area was carefully searched, and there was great local excitement after a helicopter was used for the first time in a Slough murder enquiry.

Several leads were followed up, resulting in the arrest of two men, one of whom was 23-year-old Douglas Geddes. The other man stated that he, his girlfriend and Geddes had driven from his home in Walsall to Birmingham, where they had met Duval. When they stopped in Slough, they got out of the car, and there was a fight between Geddes and Duval.

At Reading Crown Court in November 1972 both men pleaded not guilty to Duval's murder, with Geddes stating, 'I did not stab Duval. I was never there.'

But in the witness box, after Geddes told his defence counsel, Mr Maurice Drake QC that he was a devil worshipper and a 'nocturnal walker', there was a long pause before he said, 'It was the two of us. I can recall it . . . We walked some way from the car . . . I put the knife into his body once and then a second time.'

Returned to the dock, the charge of murder was put to him again, whereupon he pleaded guilty and was sentenced to life imprisonment; the second man was acquitted.

'I couldn't believe it!' exclaimed Spears to me, and he was right; witness box confessions seldom occur in real life – although they happen all the time on television!

★   ★   ★

But life in the Murder Squad office was seldom dull; taking their turn on 'stand-by' with passport to hand, and meanwhile dealing with blackmail and consumer terrorism ('or anything else that Division felt they couldn't deal with' as Graham Seaby told me, adding the acerbic comment, 'usually on a Friday afternoon!'), there were always odd adventures on the horizon, whether they be in rural Buckinghamshire or Trinidad and Tobago.

It was to the Caribbean that Seaby was sent to investigate allegations of corruption made in respect of an assistant commissioner of police and other high-ranking personnel but of course, matters were not straightforward, as Seaby explained:

> Investigation was wide-ranging, and one aspect involved the death of a policewoman shot in strange circumstances and the death of several people thought to have been shot by police but recorded as having other causes of death. When we started digging up a body, expecting to find bullets in it, the chief pathologist (who had done the PM and certified death) fled the islands and disappeared. As it was, we never found the right body as burial records were non-existent or totally inaccurate. My team spent nearly eighteen months in Trinidad, constantly watching our backs as we were not welcomed by either the police force or the Colombian drug cartels who shipped through Trinidad. We changed our cars every three weeks and we were armed. On one occasion, I very nearly mislaid my revolver!

That was fortunate; Scotland Yard will forgive many oversights, including misplacing a pathologist, a corpse or the correct burial records; but losing a revolver is something that displeases them greatly!

CHAPTER 13

L'Affaire Cartland

John Basil Cartland was a well-travelled man; by some considered extraordinary, and by others, eccentric. Born in 1912, he was a public schoolboy who gained a degree in history and economics at Oxford. After teaching for a year at Cranleigh public school, he took up a post with the civil service in India, Afghanistan and Egypt; he spoke French, Italian, Arabic and Urdu. He served in the Army during the Second World War and married; it would be the first of three marriages. Following demobilization, he managed and taught in a number of public schools, as well as working for the Kuwait Oil Company. From 1955 onwards, he either worked for or ran several schools, notably foreign language establishments in the Brighton area.

John Cartland was a raconteur and in common with that ilk, his wartime stories were often embellished, exaggerated or perhaps even complete distortions of the truth. He claimed to have been an intelligence officer with Wavell in Cairo, to have served with Lieutenant Colonel Vladimir Peniakoff in 'Popski's Private Army' (although there was no trace of him in that unit's rather shaky records), in the Sudan Defence Force and, back in London, in the Political Warfare Executive (the propaganda arm of the Special Operations Executive), which provided information to the Allies and disinformation to the Axis powers. When he arrived in Brussels as 'the first British officer to enter the city', the story he told was that he found 50,000 dossiers of French citizens who had collaborated with the enemy and set fire to the lot, a rather unconventional act for any intelligence officer – providing it was true. In fact, John Cartland had been a Second Lieutenant and an Acting Captain, although he used the full rank of Captain on his school correspondence. He was, in fact, a low-grade intelligence officer who did not have access to secret information.

So although there may have been a grain of truth in some of the stories he told, the tale of how, when he returned from Kuwait he detoured through Libya to meet his old chum referred to as 'Snusi', better known as King Idris I of Libya and who presented him with a suitcase stuffed full of dollars, is a little more difficult to swallow.

John Cartland taught at his language school, the Careers Tuition Centre in Brighton, until September 1972, when the school closed until the next term, which would have commenced in May 1973.

On 12 March 1973, Cartland crossed the channel to Le Havre, taking with him his Hillman saloon, as well as the son of his first marriage, Jeremy Brian Cartland, a poet and teacher born in February 1944. There were several reasons for John Cartland's trip. First, to travel to Javea, Spain to collect a caravan which he had purchased some two years previously. This was going to be taken to Jouques in Provence, where he owned a plot of land. Next, there was to be a recruiting drive, visiting contacts in several European countries to find new students for the school. There was also a third reason. There had been a serious disagreement between father and son and, as far as John Cartland was concerned, this trip was designed to bring about a reconciliation. Although Jeremy was keen to point out the loving relationship which existed between him and his father, this was not true. He loathed his old man and held him in contempt. But John Cartland was unaware of his son's antipathy towards him; he anticipated that upon their return, the rift between them would have healed and Jeremy would come to teach at his school. At least, that was the general idea.

*   *   *

On 18 March 1973, the couple had reached France, and the car and caravan were parked at a clearing by the Route Nationale 572 at a place known as Le Jas de Dane, in the parish of La Barben, near Pélissane, between Salon-de-Provence and Aix-en-Provence.

Jeremy's account of the subsequent events was as follows: after he lit the oil heater, he and his father fell asleep in the caravan at about 10.00 pm. The caravan was illuminated by a hurricane lamp and two candles; these he extinguished before going to sleep. He later awoke, having heard a noise outside, put on his trousers and shoes and woke his father, who sat up. When Jeremy went to investigate, he discovered a man inside the front passenger door of their car. He challenged the man, in his quite fluent French, only to be struck on the head from behind, whereupon he lost consciousness. When he came to, some yards away, he discovered he had been stabbed, sustaining a slight injury to the right side of his chest and another to his left abdomen.

He also saw that the caravan was on fire – it was completely ablaze – and having established that his father was not inside, he stopped a passing motorist, Frederic Delaude (who arrived between 12.30 and 12.45 am), who later took him to hospital. Other motorists stopped after the arrival of Monsieur Delaude, including a car containing three young men, who pushed the Hillman away from the blazing caravan. Several of the motorists and passers-by would give differing (and often contradictory) accounts of what they saw.

John Cartland's body was later found on some rough ground. He had sustained fatal injuries to his head and neck. An axe – which belonged to John Cartland and which was kept in the spare battery cupboard in the caravan – was found in the area, as was a knife.

*   *   *

The French National Gendarmerie were called and later, on 20 March the local examining magistrate (*Juge d'Instruction*), André Delmas, appointed Gregoire Krikorian, *Commissaire Principal* of the *Service Regional de Police Judiciaire* (SRPJ) at Aix-en-Provence to investigate the matter.

Initially, the police who attended the scene made a search of the area and at about 1.45 am found John Cartland's body in some bushes, about 5 metres from the caravan. He was dressed in a pullover and vest; his pyjama trousers were around his ankles and his slippers on his feet. After a doctor had certified death, unfortunately the body was moved to the mortuary at Pélissane cemetery. A further search revealed a knife with Jeremy's blood group on it, an axe and also a pillowcase containing a rock, both of which bore bloodstains which matched John Cartland's blood group. A Gaz bottle, purchased by Jeremy in Spain and used to fuel the stove in the caravan, which had been found under the towbar and disconnected by one of the motorists and placed 8 metres away, was found by one of the officers; but later, an unknown gendarme put it in the boot of the Cartlands' Hillman. It was not made an exhibit.

This demonstrated the differences between French and English policing. The French did not keep notebooks in the way that their English counterparts did; their statements were therefore made either from memory or from reports they had submitted. There were cases where officers submitted reports stating they had taken certain actions, but in fact they were taking responsibility for what they had instructed a subordinate to do, and the name of that subordinate was not always recorded. Furthermore, the French system did not appear to demand any record of persons finding exhibits or what happened to them thereafter. They had a good system of putting a label sealed with wax on an exhibit, but this was often done days after the exhibit had been found, and the packing could be done by someone other than the officer signing the label.

The police found that apart from the driver's door, the other three doors of John Cartland's Hillman, and the boot, were locked. This contradicted what Jeremy had said regarding the intruder being inside the front passenger door, as well as the interior light being illuminated; the police (plus one of the motorists) stated that the light did not work when the door was opened.

The Cartlands were only some 30km from Jouques; it seemed odd that they had not carried on to the site owned by John Cartland, but the answer was probably this: they had earlier stopped at Roubes Total service station at Pélissane, where John Cartland purchased petrol, being served by Mme Augusta Chauvet, and where there was a strong mistral wind blowing.

'I asked him if the wind did not bother them in towing their caravan', said Mme Chauvet. 'The father told me, "This mistral bothers us a lot. We will not be going far", and added they were going to camp a little further on.'

However, Mme Chauvet also stated that after she had been paid for the petrol, the two men sat in the car on the forecourt, apparently arguing, before driving off.

*   *   *

It was just 2km further on at La Jas de Dane that they parked up; it was the mistral which had concerned John Cartland that fanned the flames when the caravan was set alight.

The fire brigade was unable to give an expert opinion as to the cause of the caravan fire, and no examination was made by scientists. A local chemist employed by the Marseille police later examined the plastic paraffin container purchased by Jeremy in Spain and found at the scene. It contained a small amount of a mixture of paraffin and a light petrol, similar to white spirit and used for removing stains, that John Cartland kept in the car. When ignited, the mixture was volatile, causing the flames to spread.

*   *   *

The scene was not closed off after the first day and was swamped by sightseers and souvenir hunters; it is more than possible that some evidence may have been lost. This omission later came under intense criticism from the French press, not to mention from Scotland Yard. Only one fingerprint belonging to John Cartland was found in the car, and because of the rocky terrain, no footprints could be found.

The body of John Cartland was never formally identified in France, and there was no continuity from when the body was taken from the scene to when it was deposited in the unattended mortuary; identification was made by comparison with his passport photograph. The post mortem examination revealed a number of injuries, although the most important were three wounds to the head causing a fracture to the skull 6cm in diameter, as well as damage to the brain which would certainly have been fatal and which the pathologist, Doctor Jacqueline Jouglard, believed had been caused by the piece of rock inside the pillow case. Equally important was a gaping slit 15cm long to the left front of the throat, causing injuries (including the severing of the carotid artery) which would have proved fatal. This, Doctor Jouglard believed, was caused by the cutting edge of the axe, as were eleven smaller injuries above and below the main wound to the neck. She believed that the assailant was right-handed, as Jeremy was. The stomach contents suggested that he had died between four and eight hours after his last meal, which Jeremy stated had been at 7.00 pm.

John Cartland's bladder was full and there were also faeces in his rectum when he died, which indicated a need to relieve himself and might have explained the pyjama trousers around his ankles. Alternatively, the position of his pyjamas might have indicated he had been dragged to that spot. It was agreed by both the French and, later, English pathologists that the head injuries were inflicted first, but that Cartland was alive when the neck injuries were inflicted.

At Salon General Hospital, Jeremy Cartland was examined by a nurse, a medical intern and then a surgeon. There was a 2cm wound to his chest and a 3cm wound to the stomach, both described as superficial; both received two sutures. He complained of a pain in his right shoulder (believed to have been a pulled muscle), but there was no evidence of any internal injuries or concussion. More importantly, there were no injuries to the back of his head, where Jeremy said he had been struck, and no signs that he had suffered from unconsciousness. There were, however, scratch marks on his forehead that could have been caused by thorn bushes, which were present where his father's body was found. He appeared unaware of similar scratches on his legs and ankles and a long, thin scratch in his lumbar region which, the doctor stated, could have been caused by a thorny bush. The blood on his body was washed away and no fingernail scrapings were taken – there was no need to do so since, after all, he was regarded as a victim.

Initial examination of Jeremy's clothing revealed his own blood inside his right shoe, blood on the upper part of his left shoe and various blood markings on his pyjama jacket and trousers as well as on his corduroy trousers. The presence of blood on the bottom of his pyjama trousers did not fit Jeremy's account, since he had stated he had his corduroy trousers on top of his pyjamas when the attack took place.

*   *   *

The method of conducting interviews in France was as different as the way of recording exhibits. In England, an interview with a suspect was based on both questions and answers being recorded. In France, a system of recording statements – *procès-verbal* – was utilized, with a summary of questions and answers being typed on the form. Therefore, if a suspect was asked, 'Did you break into that house?' and the answer was 'No', it would appear on the form as, 'I did not break into that house' – which could make it seem as though the statement had been suddenly, guiltily, blurted out.

During the French police interviews, Jeremy reiterated that he had seen an intruder at the open front passenger door of the Hillman and that the interior light was on. He stated that only the rear doors and the boot of the car were locked; he was unable to explain how the front passenger door was locked. When it was pointed out to him that there was no injury to his head, he stated for the first time that he had also been struck on the jaw. However, no injury to his jaw was ever recorded.

Jeremy also said that before going to bed, he had filled the paraffin stove and lamp and had placed the almost empty container near the Gaz container under the front of the caravan. He said he had intended to put it in the car boot but had left the keys in the caravan, although following the attack, the car keys had been in his trouser pocket. (In a later interview, he amended his former statement, saying that he had put the car keys in his pocket.) He denied that he had ever seen the knife on which his blood had been found – it was of French manufacture, but a model seldom sold in France (nine dozen in four years), although frequently exported to England (1,000 dozen in four years). Interestingly, when Nicholas and Eileen Lyons, who had sold John Cartland the caravan, were shown the knife, they stated that it was similar to two knives missing from their home or boat, but were unable to positively identify it. Additionally, and before he was informed of his father's death, when two French officers showed him the axe, Jeremy turned his head away.

Although Jeremy had been treated as a witness and a victim, when he was next interviewed, the questioning became rather more pointed. He now stated that he had not been rendered unconscious by the blow on the back of his head but remembered being struck on the jaw, quite possibly by the man in the car. Therefore, he must have seen his attacker, not by the light in the car (which was not possible) but by the full moon. He had his shoes on, but when he was questioned about the blood on the sole of his foot, he replied that his shoe might have come off at some time.

He had all but been accused of the murder, and he denied it. However, he was now considered to be a suspect, which meant that all subsequent interviews would be conducted by the Examining Magistrate, André Delmas.

'I had not even realized that I was even suspected', exclaimed Jeremy.

But on taking legal advice from his French lawyer, the day following his accusation, Jeremy became a *Partie Civile*. This meant that he was taking a private action against an unknown person, known simply as 'X', for murdering his father and attempting to murder him. This meant that he was now a joint prosecutor with the State and entitled him to many privileges, including access to all official reports and statements. Now that he had been accused, it also meant that he could not be questioned by the police but only by the examining magistrate, and even then, not without his lawyer being present and the questions being presented to him in advance.

During the next interview on 28 March, no oath was administered, this being normal procedure for a *Partie Civile*. He stated that when he went to sleep at about 10.00 pm, the curtains of the caravan were drawn, and he could only describe the intruder as having dark hair and a white ear.

More statements were taken on 4 April when he was questioned regarding his relationship with his father. He said they were on good terms but had had '*discussions*' (which in French means debates, as well as altercations or disputes) regarding his (Jeremy's) relationship with a married woman; of which, more later.

He was adamant that there were no pillows in the caravan – this would have negated any inference that the pillowcase that contained the rock which caused the fatal blow to John Cartland had come from the caravan – and further stated that after the caravan had been parked, his father had gone for a walk and had spoken to someone in a car, asking directions to their destination, Jouques. However, two pillows were found nearby, both split open, one with an 'L'-shaped tear consistent with use as a defensive shield from a knife attack; and there were feathers on the dead man's clothing. On the other hand, there was a strong wind blowing that night, so theoretically, the feathers could have come from anywhere.

On 25 April, the magistrate, Delmas, interrogated Jeremy again as a suspect, but his lawyers objected to the procedure, some questions were ruled inadmissible by a higher legal authority and all record of it was destroyed.

After six hours of questioning, Jeremy told reporters, 'I'm out of the wood', adding, 'I think it impossible that I shall be charged now.' He also mentioned that he had issued a formal complaint against the French police for 'falsification of evidence and perversion of justice'.

Professor James Cameron had already physically examined Jeremy's injuries on 26 March in London – the results were never made known to the British police – but now it was stated that a secret file had been sent to the French authorities by Professor Cameron saying that as a result of that examination, he believed Jeremy to be a liar and that his word could not be relied upon. This caused some consternation after the London office of Interpol denied that they had sent that report to their French counterparts, and Professor Cameron categorically denied it, saying the report could not have been sent, because his notes of the examination were still on his desk and he had not compiled a report. A newspaper report later stated that Professor Cameron had had a meeting with Deputy Assistant Commissioner 'Jock' Wilson. Two weeks later, the French Ministry of Justice issued a statement 'deeply regretting' the controversy which had arisen. Six weeks after that, Wilson was shifted sideways to an administrative post.[1]

But further enquiries continued, and one vital piece of evidence came from Francis Caire, whose farmhouse at La Barben, 500 metres away, was obliquely opposite to the scene. At midnight – he had checked this with his watch – he got up because his dogs were barking. Through the trees he saw a small static light and when

---

[1] A further reference to 'Jock' Wilson's career can be found in *Scotland Yard's Gangbuster: Bert Wickstead's Most Celebrated Cases*, Pen & Sword Books, 2018.

questioned, stated that he felt sure that it was at the scene of the crime. After spending two or three minutes checking for prowlers, he returned to bed. After hearing of the murder, he reported what he had seen to the Gendarmerie the following day. This was put to the test on 20 April, when a substitute caravan was placed in the previous one's position, and a hurricane lamp was put in the caravan's window. Late that night, the lamp could be seen from Farmer Caire's doorway but not anywhere else in the vicinity. The interior light of a substitute car was then put on; that could not be seen from the doorway. The experiment was later repeated on 2 August by British police; again, the results were most convincing.

Additionally – and much later – René Salendre, a postmaster from St Cannard, the next village, recalled that he and his wife, Maryse, had driven past the caravan at 11.00 pm on the night, had noticed a light on in the caravan and remarked that caravanners had started early that year. Salendre had not realized the importance of his information and had only mentioned this to his cousin, a member of the Gendarmerie, in passing. There was no doubt that their account (which was thoroughly checked) was fully accurate. They had left a relative's home in Gard, 180km away, at 8.30 that evening and the journey time was later tested by car; it took almost exactly 2½ hours to reach the murder scene.

Therefore, according to the witnesses, although Jeremy had stated that the caravan's hurricane lamp had been extinguished at 10.00 pm, between at least 11.00 pm and midnight there had been a light coming from the caravan – and when the motorist, Monsieur Delaude, arrived at about 12.30 am, the caravan was alight.

On 17 May, Jeremy Cartland failed to attend France for further examinations, and an arrest warrant charging him with the murder was issued by the examining magistrate. However, it's fair to say that the evidence at that stage would have been insufficient under British law to warrant such a course of action. It seemed likely that that was a view shared by M Delmas who, referring to the strength of the case against Jeremy, stated, 'I am not certain, but it is a reasonable supposition.' When he was asked why the warrant had been issued at all, he replied, 'When the judge calls somebody, he is obliged to come. The fact he did not come has some weight.'

A senior British detective later referred to Delmas as 'a right prat'.

* * *

By now, the case had attracted massive publicity on both sides of the Channel. Rumours abounded, some more absurd than others. John Cartland had been involved in intelligence during the war; had he therefore been parachuted into enemy-occupied France and fought with the Maquis? And if so, were members of the Resistance responsible for his murder, in revenge for his destruction of the files of collaborators? The scene of the murder was some 60km away from where, twenty-one years previously, Sir Jack Drummond (coincidentally also driving a Hillman) had stopped while on a camping holiday and where he, his wife and their 10-year-old daughter had been brutally murdered. Gaston Dominici, a farmer who lived nearby, was arrested, found guilty of the murders and sentenced to death, although he was later freed on a presidential pardon. Also coincidentally, at the time of Cartland's murder, a film, *L'Affaire Dominici*, starring Jean Gabin in the title role, had just been released. M Dominici could be deleted from the list of suspects, since he had died in 1964.

When it was discovered that Sir Jack's secretary, Miss Jane Marshall, had died four years later in Dieppe, and then that in 1964, Sir Oliver Duncan had died in Rome, excitement in the conspiracy camp reached fever pitch, especially when it was claimed that both Sir Jack and Sir Oliver had been members of SOE – just like John Cartland. However, Miss Marshall had not been murdered, and Sir Oliver had died, after a short illness, in hospital. What was more, neither of the knights of the realm had been members of SOE, nor had they been employed in any military capacity during the war.

The waters were further muddied when anonymous communications arrived at the BBC's Paris office and also the Marseilles news agency, *Agence France-Presse*, similar typewritten letters addressed 'Letter to British Friends'. They alleged that Cartland's killing was an act of revenge by a French person in respect of Cartland's wartime activities, but the plot also involved British and Soviet Intelligence, the Gestapo, the Mafia, the French underworld and something referred to as 'Jewish-Arab antagonism'. The author was named as Henrico Polydeskis – also known as 'Sampaix' – a stateless Istanbul-born man of Greek origin who often made this type of allegation and who was rather kindly (and dismissively) referred to as 'an espionage crank'.

Enquiries had been made at two building sites in the vicinity; a gypsy site had been visited,; and the ne'er-do-wells in the area were spoken to. What was the motive, speculated the newspapers. Robbery? Revenge? Difficult to say.

★ ★ ★

Scotland Yard's involvement had commenced as early as 26 April, when Professor Cameron carried out an independent post mortem examination on John Cartland at the London Hospital. The examination had been at the request of Jeremy's London solicitor, Michael Relton, who had qualified in 1961. In 1970, he was suspended for six months by the Law Society's Disciplinary Committee for the misuse of money in a client's account. With friends in both the police and the underworld, he was regarded as a very tricky customer.

Present at the examination was Detective Chief Superintendent Ron Page of the Murder Squad, a very experienced investigator.

'He always had a pipe in his mouth', said Tony Yeoman (who later worked with him on a council corruption case). 'He was a deep thinker, not a great sense of humour and always seemed to be frowning.'

John Troon, then a detective sergeant, who was also present at the post mortem, would have agreed that Page was a 'deep thinker'. He told me, 'He was very honest and good to work with; he thought things through and paid attention to every detail and finer points.'

Troon spent much of his career at C1 Murder Squad (No. 1 squad as it was more properly known), starting as a detective constable in 1967. One of his first jobs was to get rid of the then redundant old-style 'murder bags' from the 1930s.

'I gave all the instruments which could be of any use to various pathologists', he told me, 'and with the exception of two of the bags – one went to the [then] Black Museum, the other to the Met. Historical Society – I threw the rest away; now I wish I'd kept one as a memento!'

* * *

The French authorities started to prepare papers for extradition, but it was decided at French Government level to request the UK to accept jurisdiction in this case.

It was just as well, because the British authorities would not have acceded to a request for extradition; if found guilty in France of the offence of *parricide* (the murder of one's parent), the penalty was death by the guillotine.

British jurisdiction was provided for under the provisions under Section 9, Offences against the Person Act, 1861, which stated that if any of Her Majesty's subjects were murdered in a foreign country, the perpetrator could be charged, tried and sentenced in England.

The French dossier was received by the Director of Public Prosecutions on 11 July, and following a conference with Page, he, Troon and other officers were directed to travel to France to carry out investigations under English law on his behalf. Between 25 July and 6 September 1973 the officers carried out their enquiries in France and obtained seventy statements; but prior to that, other enquiries had been carried out in England. Commissaire Krikorian had visited England between 7 and 11 May and together with Troon had carried out background enquiries regarding the Cartland family, to little effect.

Although the *Daily Express* exclaimed, 'A young Maigret flies in with murder on his mind', and the *Sunday Times* called him 'Le Superflic', this may have been a healthy dose of press hyperbole.

'My opinion of Krikorian was that he appeared out of his depth, although a nice enough person – I also believe he was honest', Troon told me. 'He held senior rank in the judicial police but appeared to be a product of university with very little practical experience; he certainly did not have any homicide experience.'

Krikorian therefore asked for his English counterparts to continue these enquiries on his behalf. They did, and what was discovered was ample evidence of motive and intent on the part of Jeremy Cartland to murder his father, details of which have never been previously disclosed; the file at the National Archives is closed, not to be opened for 71 years, until 1 January 2045. There follows a summary of this aspect of the investigation, in which the names of those involved in sensitive aspects of the case have been excluded.

⋆   ⋆   ⋆

During Easter 1972, Jeremy Cartland commenced an adulterous affair with a married woman, who left her husband in May 1972 to be with Jeremy but returned two months later, when Jeremy went to Brighton to assist his father in running a summer language school there. In November, the woman left her husband once more and, with her two children, went to live with Jeremy in Brighton; this infuriated John Cartland, something that was known to a number of people in his circle. In fact, in June 1972, John Cartland made a new will, excluding his two children and naming his housekeeper, Miss Janet Gibson (who Troon described as 'an old-fashioned Victorian housekeeper'), as sole beneficiary. During this time, Jeremy received some deeply unpleasant letters from his father about his adulterous relationship and these, police were told, so affected him that he intended to show them to his father on his death-bed in order 'to get his own back' when, he hoped, his father 'would be dying of an incurable disease'.

On 18 January 1973, the woman left Jeremy and returned to her husband, which delighted John Cartland. But this, she stated to police, had been a subterfuge; the plan was for her to pretend a reconciliation, then work for a divorce on the grounds of cruelty, so that as a wronged wife she would be in a better position to gain custody of the children. It was part of the plan that she and Jeremy should not communicate, although shortly after returning to her husband, she decided to abandon the scheme and remain with her husband and children, and the couple were reconciled. However, she did not inform Jeremy of this until after the murder.

Jeremy was unaware of the change in his father's will, because he often spoke to his lover about his expectations on the death of his father, detailing the values of the properties owned by him; he also mentioned to a friend the possibility of setting up a writers' commune in Scotland or Greece, funded by proceeds from his father's estate.

John Cartland had given Jeremy a house in Brighton by deed of gift in 1967 and a half-share of one in Eastbourne in April 1972, but bearing in mind death duties, Jeremy would have gained little financially by his father's death at that time. However, being unaware of the content of the new will, Jeremy might well have expected a share of other properties, plus whatever other assets his father possessed. John Cartland had transferred stocks and shares into Jeremy's name but kept the revenue from these assets; therefore, Jeremy's title to them was on paper only and of no value – until his father's death.

In September 1972, John and Jeremy Cartland had opened a joint building society account. The rent obtained by letting Jeremy's house in Brighton was paid into this account, but at John's insistence, both signatures were required for a withdrawal; an unusual practice, and one which suggested that John had little faith in his son's financial capabilities.

* * *

Jeremy's assertion that he loved his father was flawed; his lover told police that while the relationship between father and son was superficially cordial, he actually treated his father with contempt and described him as 'a joke'; this was corroborated by an entry in Jeremy's diary (another item which had not been made an exhibit by the French authorities) dated 13 March, during their trip to Europe and six days before the murder: 'The know-all has devious information about every subject, made thoroughly boring by his pedantic, smug delivery.'

She also told police of Jeremy's visit to a psychiatrist and of his irrational behaviour, including threats of suicide and violence towards her, plus his long, rambling letters and description of a nightmare he had experienced in the summer of 1972; when he woke up he was outside, in the grounds of the school with an axe in his hand. It was one of several nightmares; during others, he damaged his bedding, found himself howling like a dog, being pursued and defending himself with a knife; awakening from one such nightmare, found himself threatening his flatmate with a knife.

She spoke to Jeremy several times on the telephone after the murder, and in early July 1973, he suggested that her husband had paid someone to kill him but had mistakenly killed his father instead. He also mentioned that the case had cost him £15,000 and that he needed money desperately; he stated he had been offered £5,000 by the *News of the World* for his story and asked if she thought her husband would pay a similar amount to stop it being printed. When he asked to meet her, and she demurred, telling him not until after the case was over, he replied, 'There may be no afterwards.'

Other witnesses came forward. It appeared that Jeremy's detestation of his father was not limited to one emotional outburst to his lover; it had been mentioned to several other people a number of times over a substantial period.

One witness told police that Jeremy discussed pushing his father over a cliff, poisoning him or driving a nail into his ear; but his most favoured method would have been to kill him with an axe during a wood-chopping expedition and then report it as an accident.

Police obtained 125 pages of letters written by Jeremy which gave a good indication of his state of mind, as well as his mental deterioration. Other letters, including some from Jeremy to his father, were in the hands of Jeremy's solicitor; Jeremy had been advised to burn them because, in his own words, 'If revealed, they would prove conclusive.'

Those witnesses gave a rare insight into Jeremy Cartland's character, his torment and his mental deterioration, quite possibly fuelled by smoking cannabis. However, these statements were made by the witnesses with the greatest reluctance, and it was only after conferring with lawyers and a very senior officer at Scotland Yard, that they were made at all. Genuinely fearing retribution, possibly violence, from Jeremy, the witnesses wanted reassurances from Page that their statements would not be shown to Jeremy unless he was prosecuted; it was a reassurance that Page gave, and Jeremy and his solicitor were never given sight of those documents.

⋆   ⋆   ⋆

Several witnesses came forward to say that just prior to the continental trip, John Cartland – who was very enthusiastic about it – had said that he hoped that he and Jeremy could 'patch things up' but he was adamant that his son should give up his lover, which strongly suggests that he knew the liaison was still continuing – as indeed it was.

On 7 June, William Scales, the executor of John Cartland's will, gave details of it. Nothing was left to his son, John stating that he had made 'ample provision' for him. The estate, which was later proved at Brighton, left to his housekeeper, Janet Gibson, was valued at £30,046 (gross) and £27,931 (net).

Jeremy Cartland and his solicitor, Michael Relton, provided a great deal of coverage for the press, including stating that Jeremy was going to Oxfordshire to meet a man who might have new evidence; but what the result was of that meeting (if it ever took place) was never made known. There was a couple in France who supposedly held vital evidence; but whatever that was, it was not disclosed to either the French or British authorities, despite repeated requests.

⋆   ⋆   ⋆

The British officers returned to France between 23 November and 4 December 1973 and obtained fifteen more statements. A number of these were essential because Miss Margaret Pereira of the Metropolitan Police Forensic Science Laboratory discovered slight traces of the same blood group as John Cartland's on Jeremy's trousers. Therefore it was essential to strictly prove continuity in order to eliminate any possible contamination.

Unfortunately, a box containing Jeremy's clothing was taken into the primitive mortuary, a room measuring 16ft x 12ft and situated behind an undertaker's workshop, when the post mortem examination was carried out on the body of John Cartland. There was no evidence that Jeremy's trousers were ever taken from that box, but when Doctor Jouglard washed the blood from the body with rags and a basin of water she then tipped the contents of the bowl down the sink. Commissaire Krikorian was present and expressed the opinion that he could not see how the liquid could have come in contact with the clothing, but even though the sink was 6ft away from the box containing the clothing, the possibility (miniscule though it was) of contamination could not be completely eliminated.

★　★　★

Jeremy was interviewed by Page on 21 December 1973 in the presence of his solicitor; the questions and answers were recorded by John Troon. By this time, Jeremy, in his role of *Partie Civile*, had been issued with copies of all the statements and reports from the French police, which prior to the interview had helped as an aide-memoire.

Much of what he said corresponded with the account he had given the French police. However, now that the will had been read, Jeremy stated that he had no financial expectations from his father's estate; indeed, he had expected him to live 15–20 years longer. He asserted that he had not discussed with anyone his financial prospects in the event of his father's death, nor had he discussed different ways of killing his father with anyone. Of course, he had not been given sight of those English statements.

Jeremy signed the 89 pages of contemporaneous notes, written by Troon, as being correct. There was suspicion, but nothing more.

A conference was held at the chambers of Senior Treasury Counsel John Matthew QC; amongst those present was the pathologist Professor Keith Simpson, who felt very decisively that Jeremy's wounds were self-inflicted. There were so many inconsistencies in Jeremy's story that have already been mentioned, and improbabilities, too. But although there was evidence, much of it was circumstantial, and following a conference with the Director of Public Prosecutions, the Director's conclusion was that there was insufficient evidence to prosecute him; this information was passed on to Jeremy on the evening of 3 January 1974.

This relieved Jeremy, although it also infuriated his followers, one of whom wrote to the Attorney General, Sir Peter Rawlinson, demanding that the Director should reissue the statement, to the effect that that there was NO evidence on which Jeremy could be prosecuted. Sir Peter, obviously knowing rather more about the case than the writer, wrote back diplomatically stating that nothing could be properly added to the statement.

And that, more or less, was that. Jeremy had already co-authored *L'énigme de Pélissane. Jeremy Cartland, Coupable ou Innocent?* as a hardback in 1973; it was republished as a paperback in 2001. In 1974, he wrote *Laughter from the Watching Trees* and in 1978,

The Cartland File, into which he crammed every conceivable piece of information from the French authorities and took every opportunity to demonstrate his hatred of them. The British police were dealt with in a patronizing, condescending, contemptuous manner.

Two interesting points emerged from his book. In it, he stated that at no point during his English police interview, was he asked, 'Did you kill your father?' That, not to put too fine a point on it, is a lie.

On page 85 of John Troon's contemporaneous notes, the following question from Page was recorded: 'Is it possible that on the night of 18th and 19th March this year, you had a nightmare or sleepwalked during which time you killed your father?' to which Jeremy replied, 'No.'

The second point is despite the plethora of medical evidence contained in the book, Professor Cameron's diagnosis of his injuries was not included, nor was it ever disclosed to the French or British police. It was after the DPP's decision not to prosecute that Cameron confided to police that he believed that Jeremy Cartland's injuries were self-inflicted. At the time, Cameron had sought advice from the Medical Council's legal society as to what he should do. He was advised that he should not disclose this information to a third party, because of the confidentiality of the doctor/patient relationship. Cameron added that he had given his opinion to Michael Relton, and if that had indeed been the case, Relton would undoubtedly have observed solicitor/client confidentiality, in the same way that he had not disclosed to the authorities the letters that Jeremy had written to his father that had been thought so incriminating.

Michael Relton went on to other things and ran with the hare and hunted with the hounds once too often. In July 1988, for handling millions from the proceeds of the Brink's-Mat £26 million gold robbery, he was sentenced to twelve years' imprisonment.

Cartland became an acclaimed poet; he died on 4 June 2014, aged seventy.

John Troon's opinion of him?

> He was a conceited and vain character, full of his over-inflated importance, a liar (but not very good at it!) and I have no doubt of his guilt in relation to his father's murder. It's a great pity that due to the vast differences in law and procedure at that time in France and the UK, great difficulty was experienced by us in collating the evidence, etc. to comply with UK law, particularly the differing technicalities of evidence gathering, preservation

of the scene and interviews of both Cartland and witnesses that
he did not face trial at the Old Bailey for murder. He certainly
would have faced trial in France if they had continued with the
case. All the exhibits in the case are contained in a large trunk
contained in the Prisoner's Property Store (PPS). Just before
I retired, I submitted a report to the PPS, advising that the
exhibits be retained for at least 25 years. As far as I understand,
this was agreed. They may well be still there.

They may not be. Many exhibits in many cases have now been
destroyed, not necessarily at the PPS – if it still exists. And in any
event, if the custodians at the PPS did adhere to Troon's request,
the exhibits might well have been destroyed one year after Jeremy's
death.

It was indeed fortunate that Jeremy failed to attend the hearing
in France on 17 May; had he done so, he would certainly have
been remanded in custody. If he had then been found guilty, it
would have necessitated a close shave with Madame Guillotine,
since the death penalty in France by that means was not abolished
until 10 September 1977.

So what did happen on the March night in 1973? It's quite
possible that Jeremy and his father had a furious row in the caravan,
Jeremy hit him on the head with the rock in the pillowcase and,
whilst the old man was stunned, self-inflicted his own wounds
over his pyjamas. Then, pulling on clothes over his pyjamas, he led
the old man outside to the bushes five metres away, cut his throat
with the blade of the axe – he knew where that was stashed – returned
to the caravan and set it ablaze with the contents of the paraffin
can, to which he had added the accelerant, to destroy any evidence
of the struggle, and then waited for the first car to come along.

That's if you believe – as I do – that Jeremy was responsible
for his father's murder.

But as a defence barrister once brayed at me, in cross-
examination at the Old Bailey, 'You thought my client was guilty,
and that's why he's now in the dock, isn't it?'

To that, I replied, 'Your client is in the dock because of the
weight of evidence against him, not because I thought he was
guilty; because if I went out and arrested everyone whom I thought
was guilty of an offence, I can assure you, London's streets would
be a lot safer than they are now!'

Let the last words go to Jeremy's obituary in *The Times*, in
which it was said, 'Wherever [he] appeared, he seemed to become
involved in a fascinating or outrageous situation from which
only his extreme ingenuity could extricate him.'

CHAPTER 14

Murders in St Kitts

D r William Valentine 'Billy' Herbert Jr. LLB, PhD, three-times ambassador for St Kitts and Nevis, which are a tiny (101 square miles) pair of islands situated between the North Atlantic Ocean and the Caribbean Sea, set sail in his 24ft motorboat, *Maxi II*, on 19 June 1994. There were six other people on board – his wife, Cheryl, four men and a 6-year-old child – and they were ostensibly on an unremarkable fishing trip. They had not told anybody where they intended to fish, and when a coastguard saw the boat leave the harbour at 7.40 that morning, the weather was moderately rough, with swells of between 4ft and 6ft

The boat – built by the American company 'Welcraft' in 1984 – had been well maintained, and the two recently fitted 150 h. p. Mercury outboard engines had been reconditioned. They were fed by a single fuel line from a 100-gallon tank. So far, so good. At one time a radio had been fitted in the boat, but this had been taken out by Dr Herbert and not replaced; instead, the crew had two hand-held radios with, at best, a range of 8–10 miles. What happened regarding radio transmissions was highly confusing, but it seems certain that at 2.30 pm, one of the crew, Michael Blake, called the coastguard base on Channel 6 – the emergency channel – asking the coastguard to change to Channel 14, the channel open to anyone; and although the coastguard did so, he heard nothing more. It was initially thought possible that the *Maxi II* might have encountered engine trouble rather than criminal activity. In any event, Blake, who ran a boat chartering company, had good reason to return by 3.00 pm, since he had a booking at that time. His wife tried to contact him by radio, but without success, and raised the alarm.

The US coastguard, the French Marine Rescue, the Dutch air-sea rescue patrol and a Venezuelan naval aircraft, plus a whole convoy of aircraft, helicopters and boats, swept the area, covering 250,000 square miles and looking for signs of wreckage; they found nothing. Matters were made considerably more difficult by a mist coming down which lasted for several days.

Experts were hired to plot the pattern of wind and currents and try to ascertain where the boat might have drifted to, and the wife of one of the missing men offered a $50,000 reward for information – but still, nothing.

So had there been some kind of tragic accident – or something else? Since Billy Herbert was a controversial figure in the island's politics, having raised PAM (the People's Action Movement), the ruling right-wing party, and been previously investigated by the FBI, who suspected him of laundering drug profits on behalf of the IRA, 'something else' was considered more likely than a freak accident.

Although the islands had gained independence in 1983, it was requested that Scotland Yard should investigate, because they were part of the British Commonwealth with the Queen as head of state.

On 22 July 1994, Detective Superintendent Alex Ross from the Murder Squad travelled the 4,114 miles from London to St Kitts' capital, Basseterre, and commenced his investigations. Joining the Met in 1964, Ross had accrued a wealth of experience, working in some of London's toughest areas, as well as in postings with the Serious Crime Squad, the Regional Crime Squad, the Complaints Branch and the 3 Area Major Investigation Pool, before arriving at SO1 Department in 1993.

Over one month had elapsed since the boat's disappearance, and few statements had been taken. Certainly, the case had been the subject of a great deal of discussion amongst the islanders, but memories had become confused and some matters which may have started as rumours had now become 'fact'. There was also a general unwillingness among the islanders to talk to the local police. It would have been helpful if enquiries had been made to ascertain where and when Dr Herbert had purchased his fuel, and how much, to give an approximate idea of what was in his tank; then an idea of the boat's range could have been ascertained.

But Ross had not been called to try to solve a missing persons case; what he needed to resolve was if criminality had been involved in the boat's disappearance. For a criminal act to have succeeded, there were several things which the perpetrators would have needed:

1. To know at what time the *Maxi II* was due to leave the harbour.
2. To (a) follow them to the fishing ground or (b) know where they were headed.
3. To be able to approach the *Maxi II* without arousing suspicion.
4. To be able to dispose of all six persons on board and the boat without leaving any trace of either.
5. To be certain that their intended target(s) were, in fact, on board.

It did seem improbable, therefore, that the disappearance was the result of a criminal act; but if it had been, then it would have required a highly sophisticated conspiracy, something not within the capabilities of local gangsters – 'de Yout' as they were locally referred to – but perhaps carried out by the mafia, the Colombian drug cartels or those acting on their behalf.

Therefore, the officers needed to thoroughly research the background, the correspondence and the bank accounts of the missing persons, to uncover any possible motive and try to establish any justification for the murder of six people. All of the families were eager to help, save one: Herbert's daughter, Maxine, flatly refused permission for the police, be they local or from Scotland Yard, to examine her father's correspondence, telling them that she would provide answers to their questions. The officers felt that her answers were disingenuous. A letter signed by Ross was delivered to her by hand on 29 July; it was forwarded to the family solicitor. There followed a four-day public holiday on the island, during which time, on 3 August, Ross returned to London, and Ms Herbert took herself – and the rest of the family – off to Antigua, where her parents had a second home and Dr Herbert had business interests in the form of a bank and a lawyer's practice. And that was the finish of any consultation between Ms Herbert, her solicitor and Scotland Yard; not that it had really started.

So, unable to solve the conundrum of *Maxi II*, Ross would later say, 'The *Maxi II* and all aboard have disappeared without trace. There is nothing at this stage to tell us whether it was an act of God or a criminal act' – and that, for the time being, was that. Recommendations were made to the local police force: in the event of a suspicious death, the need to appoint an experienced detective as senior investigating officer (SIO) and a deputy to the SIO, to photograph the scene, obtain written statements from witnesses and background information on the deceased, to set up an incident room and record all messages – in fact, the bread and butter of a major investigation that every police constable walking the streets of Britain would be aware of. Unfortunately, giving that advice was rather like pissing in the wind.

*   *   *

But it was not too long before Ross was recalled to St Kitts. It appeared that the islands' sugar and fishing industries were being replaced with the importation of drugs, because on 24 September 1994, fishermen searching for turtles' eggs discovered one metric tonne of cocaine buried in the sand on a beach at Grange Bay, near the town of Cayon. The cache was wrapped in one-kilo blocks, and they were packed in fibre sacks. This discovery was not reported to the authorities, but its existence was spread by word of mouth. Two days later, one of the fishermen and a friend returned to the site, retrieved two or three of the fibre sacks (containing some sixty blocks of cocaine) and took them back to their homes, where they buried them.

Just before dusk the same day, four men drove to the site; they dug up all of the remaining sacks and carried them to their vehicle. The leader of the group was 38-year-old Dean Morris, one of the three sons of the island's Deputy Prime Minister, 59-year-old Sidney Morris.

About half the sacks had been loaded on to Morris' vehicle when car lights were seen approaching, and Morris and his companions fled; however, it's highly likely that his vehicle was spotted leaving the scene, and even more likely that the car lights belonged to those who had imported the drugs.

Dean Morris took the drugs to the house that he shared with his brothers, 31-year-old David and Vincent, aged thirty-six. The drugs were stored in a shed, David and Vincent were told about them, and Dean and David said they thought the best course of action would be to store the cocaine for several years, then dispose of it gradually. But Vincent decided that it would be far better to sell it immediately, and the following day, he sold several kilos in Basseterre. This, it transpired, was a huge mistake.

One of the potential customers whom Vincent unwittingly approached turned out to be the owner of the cache. The gang member requested a 'test purchase' to see if the cocaine was the real McCoy; it was, in every sense of the word. The packaging and identifying marks revealed the drugs as the gang's, and the following day, Vincent Morris unwillingly accepted an invitation from Glenroy 'Bobo' Matthew to accompany him to a house at Frigate Bay. The property was occupied by Charles 'Little Nut' Miller – originally known as Patrick O'Connor or Cecil Connor – who had been serving life sentences for two murders in Jamaica before escaping. Also present were Clifford Henry, Noel 'Zambo' Heath and two Colombians. The men were part of a gang strongly suspected of drug dealing on an industrial scale and considered highly dangerous; it was said that two other Colombians who had been employed to watch over the cache of cocaine on the beach, and who had failed dismally in their duties, had been duly executed.

Vincent was interrogated regarding the whereabouts of the rest of the drugs and he agreed to return them. The gang were not particularly surprised that he had capitulated; but what they were not aware of was that he had covertly recorded the conversation by means of a hidden micro cassette recorder.

So by the end of the meeting, matters appeared fairly amicable. Morris, who employed Matthew at St Kitts Freight Services, offered to falsify documentation so that the drugs could safely pass through the airport and on to Miami, Florida. Taken home by Clifford Henry, Vincent disclosed the whereabouts of the rest of the cocaine, which was duly retrieved; but this reclamation was discreetly filmed on his video camcorder. Therefore, it appeared that Vincent was by now working with Miller's gang to smuggle the cocaine into the United States. He may have been coerced – Henry had been in possession of a pistol – or it may have been of his own volition. But what was clear was that Vincent was playing a very dangerous game indeed.

Because the very next day, at 6.30 am, Vincent arrived home with seven large boxes, each containing 20kg of cocaine. Had he stolen them – or had they been given to him by the gang, to be flown out of St Kitts using forged documentation? Either way, for the rest of the day, Morris's home telephone was constantly engaged by callers asking his whereabouts, including one who spoke only Spanish. That evening, a vehicle containing four men, one of whom spoke with a Jamaican accent, was outside Morris' address, and the occupants demanded to know where he was. But Vincent was elsewhere; he was seeking the return of some of the cocaine which had been stolen by an associate, and the following day, it was retrieved, with the aid of a pistol and brother Dean.

By now, it was Friday, 30 September; Vincent Morris together with his girlfriend, 35-year-old Dominican-born Joan Walsh, had rented a white Nissan Sentra, registration number R3973, and that evening he was in possession of a very large quantity of dollars, both East Caribbean and US. It appeared that Miss Walsh was unaware of Morris' criminal activities; she would subsequently be referred to as one of those unfortunate people who was 'in the wrong company, at the wrong place at the wrong time'.

The next day, 1 October, was Vincent's birthday. Having stored the seven boxes of cocaine with an associate, he and Miss Walsh went out to celebrate; but although they were expected at a number of events and locations, they never appeared. Throughout the evening, Miller and his associates were in the Cayon area actively seeking Morris and using a number of vehicles, including a minivan owned by Michael 'Illa' Glasford. Various people were asked if they had seen Morris or his rental vehicle. It's likely that someone had, because it's believed that the gang caught up with the couple before midnight; it then appeared that they had vanished as completely as Billy Herbert and his crew had, some four months previously.

On Sunday, 2 October, the families of Morris and Miss Walsh reported them missing. There was no major police investigation at the time, but due to the political prominence of the Morris brothers' father, the islands' senior detective and head of Special Branch, 38-year-old Superintendent Jude Thaddeus Matthew, was put in charge of investigating the couple's disappearance.

The following day, Michael Glasford's minivan was deliberately set alight outside his house. Glasford was an associate of Miller; was this done to obliterate any bloodstains which might have been present? It was a strong possibility, especially when a burnt 'Michael X' watch – similar to one worn by Vincent Morris – was found. But the flames had done their job reasonably well, in as much as no further evidence was found.

Glenroy Matthew certainly had good intelligence as to the whereabouts of the seven boxes of cocaine, because he demanded them from Vincent's associate, who promptly informed Dean Morris. Extremely concerned for his brother's safety, Dean retrieved the seven boxes and returned them that evening to Clifford Henry, in the hope that this would be a bargaining chip in gaining the release of his kidnapped brother; but matters had gone too far for that.

Meanwhile, between 4 and 10 October 1994, Superintendent Matthew had arrested six men in connection with the couple's disappearance. Superintendent Ross had already been requested to return to the island, and by the time he arrived in Basseterre on 11 October, the sextet were banged up in four of the island's police stations. They were Noel Timothy Heath, Charles Emmanuel Miller, Kirt Anthony 'Ibo' Hendrickson, Glenroy Wingrove Matthew, Michael Lloyd Senrick Glasford and Clifford Nathaniel Henry. They had been charged, the previous day, with conspiracy to murder Vincent Morris and Miss Walsh. Not all of them had been interviewed, and no formal record was made of those who had.

On 12 October, Ross and his assistant had a meeting with Matthew, who briefed them on the case – it transpired that the same day, Miller had seen Matthew in the holding area and had told him, 'You're a dead man tomorrow morning' – and the two superintendents agreed to meet at Ross's hotel the following day.

Matthew was convinced he had the right people but he had been working virtually alone, and the evidence was weak.

At 7.50 am the following day, Matthew, married with four children, left his home at Franklands driving his Pajero jeep, and as he turned the vehicle towards Basseterre, he was hit and killed by eleven shots from an automatic machine pistol, initially fired from cover, then at point-blank range. The shots were heard by lawyer Constance Mitcham, who had been visiting Matthew's wife; she saw a man in a black ski mask with a gun and shouted 'Hey!', believing he would stop firing if he knew he had been seen. Instead, the gunman fired at her and then, as a bus approached, he fired two shots at it, puncturing a tyre. Several other witnesses saw the incident, and the police were called.

The culprit was 22-year-old David 'Grizzly' Lawrence, who had worked for Charles Miller, and he now fled on foot across country. Fortunately, members of the island's Special Services Unit (SSU) were nearby on an unrelated drugs investigation and were quickly on the scene. Lawrence was pursued to the main island road, near the village of Challengers; he was pointed out to the SSU by the occupants of a vehicle which Lawrence had tried to hijack at gunpoint and was arrested, still in possession of the murder weapon, a Tek-9 automatic pistol, together with a pair of infra-red binoculars and a large knife. The ski mask was found tucked down the side of one of his combat boots; at his home address, three pieces of cloth were found which fitted exactly the holes in the ski mask.

It appeared that Lawrence must have put up some form of resistance when he was being handcuffed: two of his teeth were missing, his forehead was bleeding and there were abrasions on his shoulder, forehead, back and legs; there were also lacerations and swellings on his lips, and one of his ribs was fractured. It was not until 16 October, when he had recovered sufficiently from his injuries, that Ross was able to interview him about the murder. Lawrence freely and fully admitted the murder and did so in a written statement. However, he declined to admit a motive or give the names of anybody else involved in the offence, and he was then charged.

The Met team was supplemented by local officers: three newly qualified detectives, a detective inspector and a typist. However, with Matthew's murder, the implied threat against Ross was considered so serious that the commander of SO1, Roy Ramm, took the unprecedented step of sending officers from the Met's elite firearms unit, SO19, plus reinforcements, an inspector, a sergeant and a constable.

The firearms team included the rather controversial officer, Police Constable Tony Long, who during the course of his career shot five men (killing three of them), and added a dog, belonging to a gangster, to his casualty list.

'Once it became apparent that there wasn't any real threat against me, the other guys from SO19 mucked in and became part of the investigation team and were extremely enthusiastic to be involved'. Ross told me. However, it was not too long before the threat aspect would change.

As Ross set up offices at the island's deep water port, Bird Rock, carried out house-to-house enquiries and set up roadblocks, the *Democrat* newspaper urged anyone with information to contact him, telling their readers, 'We cannot afford to allow the drug traffickers and gun-runners to take over the land with which God has so richly blessed us.'

Since St Kitts had no forensic facilities other than fingerprint retrieval, all of the forensic exhibits were packaged up and sent to the Metropolitan Police's Forensic Science Laboratory in London. Formal statements were taken, and the murder investigation was concluded in three weeks.

Ross now turned his attention to the disappearance of Vincent Morris and Miss Walsh. It was necessary to backtrack through the whole enquiry and re-interview witnesses. Even when statements had been obtained by Superintendent Matthew, they had been rushed and lacked depth. As Ross told me, 'Most of the evidence was in his head.' As matters stood, there was very little direct evidence to support a charge of conspiracy to murder.

'He [Matthew] had been working with the DEA [the American Drugs Enforcement Agency] and the CIA [the American Central Intelligence Agency], and covert tapes existed', Ross told me. 'Suffice to say, they were never handed to me, and a long drawn-out investigation ensued.'

Deputy Prime Minister Sidney Morris admitted that his sons were engaged in the drugs trade; on 9 November, Ross carried out a search at the home shared by the three Morris brothers. Drugs were found hidden on a nearby beach, and some were buried on a farm. Ross arrested Dean Morris for conspiracy to sell 57kg of cocaine and his brother David for possession of a gun and ammunition; both were bailed (£62,500 in Dean's case, £1,875 in David's) to attend court, and one week later, their father tendered his resignation to the Prime Minister, Mr Kennedy Simmonds. Since there had been fierce pressure from opposition parties and business leaders for Mr Morris to step down from posts which included the ministries of education, youth, social affairs and communications, as well as works and public utilities, Morris's resignation was accepted by the Prime Minister with alacrity; however, he immediately appointed him as 'special advisor' to all of the ministries he had vacated.

But the fact that the Deputy Prime Minister's sons had been granted bail for such serious offences was all the political opposition, the United People's Party, needed to whip up a vitriolic storm of protest.

The leading agitator was the exotically-named Dr Kuba Omoja Assegai, known to the police of North London by his baptismal name of Sebastian Godwin. He had skipped bail in 1988 after being charged with threatening to murder the Borough of Brent's director of education. Now the father of ten was back in St Kitts; originally, he had joined the Labour Party, but after its failure in the recent election, he joined the United People's Party. Hero-worshiping Colonel Gaddafi ('a great man') and denying the existence of Christ, Assegai referred to the Police Commissioner, Derrick Thompson, as 'brain-dead' and to Alex Ross as 'The Yard's Chief Bwana', who, Assegai claimed, was 'organising a cover-up'.

It was suggested in an opposition newspaper that Ross had issued 100 diplomatic passports to the Prime Minister and his cronies – including the two Morris brothers – in order that they might flee the islands. On the neighbouring island of Nevis an equally false rumour was circulated that Ross had arrested the manager and chief teller of the St Kitts National Bank.

Two days later, egged on by Labour Party activists – including a lawyer wearing a billboard inciting people to riot – a mob marched through Basseterre, and there was a disturbance at the town's jail; the inmates set it on fire and all of the 150 prisoners were released for their own safety. Some took the opportunity to escape, but many simply sat on a wall opposite the prison to enjoy the spectacle. Troops from the six neighbouring islands, forty-five members of the Caribbean Security Force, were flown in to restore order and capture the escaped prisoners. Ross now takes up the tale:

> However, one of those who escaped was Lawrence, and the local police contacted me to ensure I took extra precautions in case he tried something stupid. We normally went out as a group for our evening meals, but in the light of what was happening, we decided to stay in and eat in the hotel, which was on the outskirts of town. The SO19 guys took their responsibilities very seriously and so in addition to carrying

their revolvers, they brought their HKs (Heckler & Koch sub-machine guns) in holdalls to the open-air dining area. Picture the scene: a steel drum band playing for us and other guests, the flames of the burning prison silhouetted against the night sky and us guys dining whilst all this was going on! The next morning, things were very tense and a US cutter had come into harbour. We decided to visit on the off-chance we might have to arrange our evacuation. I know it sounds a bit dramatic, but things were not looking very good by then.

'Grizzly' Lawrence surrendered and returned to the jail – 'Apparently, he believed himself to be safer there', commented Ross. The British Government made £50,000 available to provide new prison facilities, since the prison was still minus its roof.

But on the day after the riot, 12 November, plantation workers discovered the burnt-out rental Nissan in a cane field on Rawlings Plantation, 20 miles from Basseterre; the remains of Vincent Morris and Joan Walsh were in the back of the vehicle. The fire had been so intense that there was no chance of establishing the cause of death. There was a single bullet hole in the boot of the car, and the burnt remains of a pair of handcuffs and a gold neck chain, later identified as belonging to Vincent Morris.

Ideally, Ross and his team wanted to use tried and tested British methods of evidence gathering: split the cane field into sections and carry out a systematic search for evidence, and leave the bodies and the remains of the car in situ until a scientific examination could be made – Ross had sent for a London pathologist to attend the scene – but the sugar cane was too dense to permit an inch-by-inch search on foot. 'We approached the US cutter to lift the car out with their helicopter', Ross told me, although this was unsuccessful.

Worse was to come. The cane field was in the middle of an opposition party stronghold, and word went round that the British officers had planted the bodies there to discredit the opposition.

Due to the fact that a mob several hundred strong was now approaching the cane field and threatening to burn it, members of the Special Services Unit brought the car into town.

The case against the six men charged with conspiracy to murder Vincent Morris and Joan Walsh dragged on until they were eventually granted bail after no attorney from the public prosecutor's office turned up at court, amidst howls of protest from the *Democrat* newspaper, who wondered 'if this was not stage-managed'.

The Met officers felt that there was convincing evidence to prosecute Charles Miller, Noel Heath, Glenroy Matthew and Clifford Henry for drug trafficking; but although the Proceeds of Crime Act 1993 had been passed by the St Kitts and Nevis Parliament, it had never been gazetted. This was quickly corrected, and a number of production and inspection orders under the Act were obtained from the High Court, in an effort to trace monies which had been put through bank accounts held by the four men. Large deposits had been transferred from their accounts to accounts held by their lawyer, Fitzroy Bryant. Further production orders were obtained to search the lawyer's accounts, whereupon Bryant obtained a High Court writ against the authorities, claiming that the Proceeds of Crime Act was an abuse of human and civil rights. At a subsequent hearing at the High Court it was held that no further action would be taken in respect of those production orders until such time as the matter could be fully heard in court. Couldn't make it up, could you?

So the four men were charged with conspiracy to import drugs, but there was one delay after another, with a jury being undecided in October 1995 and a further trial being scheduled for January 1996, before that fixture was abandoned and a re-trial was fixed for March 1996.

But in May 1996, the United States filed extradition requests in respect of Miller, Matthew, Heath and Henry for conspiracy to import a tonne of cocaine into the United States.

There were a series of court battles in St Kitts; Henry, believing a court victory in Basseterre was the end of the matter, discovered he was wrong when he tried to enter the United States, was arrested and later sentenced to life imprisonment. In 1998, Miller threatened to kill American students at St Kitts' Ross Veterinary University if he was extradited, but he didn't, and he surrendered to be extradited in 2000 – he was convicted on narcotics charges by a Miami jury in December that year and on 13 February 2001 he was sentenced to life imprisonment at the US Penitentiary, Terre Haute, Indiana.

Heath and Matthew were extradited in 2006. The same year, Heath pleaded guilty to conspiracy to violate the US Federal Narcotics Laws and was sentenced to four years' imprisonment; Matthew, after some plea-bargaining, on 29 January 2007 received eleven years and four months' imprisonment, to be followed by five years supervised release. Officers from the Yard's Murder Squad had found Vincent Morris's cassette tape of Matthew and others planning to import cocaine into Miami by aeroplane.

Back now to 'Grizzly' Lawrence who, if found guilty, faced the death penalty. He stood trial for the murder of Superintendent Matthew on three occasions; each resulted in a hung jury.

'It was impossible to find impartial jurors or people who were not afraid of Miller and his associates', Ross told me. 'I discussed at length with their Attorney General moving the trial off the island, but they wouldn't move it.'

During one of the trials of Lawrence for the murder of Superintendent Matthew, a local officer with limited knowledge of the case was put in charge; he ended up giving evidence for the defence. When the jury was sworn in for the final trial, Miller – on bail for the drugs charge – swaggered into court and did his best to intimidate the jurors and the bench by loudly declaiming that the trial was 'political' and the accused was innocent. He then proceeded to abuse the appeal judge and also Constance Mitcham, who had witnessed the shooting and was due to give evidence at the trial. Not one local police officer did anything to stop, eject or arrest him.

Fitzroy Bryant – whose bank accounts had been flooded with cash from the drugs deals mounted by Miller, Heath, Matthew and Henry – was one of the lawyers who appeared for Lawrence's defence. He alleged that when Lawrence was arrested 'he was given a good beating' by the SSU officers, a claim denied 'with some consistency' by the officers, according to the *St Kitts-Nevis Observer*. One British forensic scientist gave evidence that samples of Lawrence's hair were identical with hairs found in the ski mask; Bryant argued that his client was 'incoherent from the beatings' and could not have given consent for the samples to be taken. Kevin O'Callaghan, another British scientist, had examined bullets fired from the pistol and told the court that they 'could not have been fired from the barrel of any other weapon'. Bryant alleged that 'there had been a substitution of weapons'.

Lawrence was given the choice of either appearing on the witness stand, in which case he could be cross-examined by the prosecution, or making a statement from the dock, in which case he couldn't. He chose the latter course, saying, 'I did not shoot Superintendent Jude Matthew. I was not at Franklands on the morning Mr Matthew was killed.' He went on to suggest he was going to meet a drugs drop-off but when the shipment failed to arrive he encountered the police and, he whined, he had been beaten in the police van and at SSU headquarters. He concluded by saying, 'The gun the police have in evidence is definitely not my gun.'

Well, sometimes that type of defence wins a case, sometimes not; on this occasion, despite the highly professional way in which the Met had put their case together, Lawrence was freed.

However, in 2002 Lawrence was himself murdered, apparently following an altercation in a nightclub; he was chased out of the club and stabbed to death with knives and an ice pick. Six suspects were arrested (although two were released without charge) and appeared in court, where they were cheered by their fans. One newspaper reporter was so enthusiastic at what she perceived to be the prisoners' star-status that she wanted her editor's permission to refer to them as 'The Fantastic Four', The four were later acquitted, although two of them, plus three others, were arrested in 2006 for the murder of Michelle Weekes-Benjamin, whose body was found in a septic tank.

So it went on; the islands' population of 31,800 appeared to be diminishing week by week.

Ross and his team could not be expected to stay forever, and they left the island on 20 January 1995, although other Met officers remained; one month later, the local Commissioner, Derrick Thompson, resigned after two years in the post.

'The Prime Minister did ask if I would take on the Commissioner's role', Ross told me, 'but that was never going to happen as my family would never have moved.'

For Ross it had been an almost impossible investigation; quite apart from the lack of resources and scientific expertise, the islands were rotten with fear, corruption, political bias and drugs. As long as the Met officers held the reins, good results were forthcoming; they cultivated informants and, out of a spirit of assistance to the local officers, dealt with matters not included in their original remit. One such case was the arrest of a wanted drug trafficker for importing a metric tonne of cocaine from Colombia. The SO19 officers also undertook a training role with local police officers in tactical and practical firearms training.

But in the absence of the Met officers, matters started to crumble once more.

The trials of David and Dean Morris for drug dealing and possessing a firearm were adjourned *sine die* – in other words, indefinitely.

As always, the Foreign and Commonwealth Office billed the country concerned for employing the Met's expertise. St Kitts and Nevis were extremely reluctant to tender a prompt payment. Ross retired from the Met in 1995. He travelled backwards and forwards to the islands to give evidence in the trials. By 1996, he had still not been reimbursed for his daily rates; it took a series of faxes to the new Commissioner before the account was settled.

★ ★ ★

Noel 'Zambo' Heath was released from his four-year sentence having served just two years of it in a US prison and returned home to St Kitts in 2009, to a tumultuous welcome from friends and family. Not everybody was so rapturously inclined towards him, because on Friday, 14 October 2011, he died as the result of multiple gunshot wounds. It was felt in some quarters that he was an informant, and as one observer sagely commented, 'Snitches get stitches – in Z's case, bullets.'

Two years later, in August 2014, his son, Zamba 'Zambi' Heath, carried on the family tradition when for possession of cocaine and crack cocaine with intent to supply he was fined $75,000. His brother, Marlon Heath, was fined $500 for possession of cannabis.

A few days later, on 1 September 2014, Zambo's old sparring partner, Kirt 'Ibo' Hendrickson – they had both been arrested for conspiring to murder Vincent Morris and Joan Walsh – was shot at Fern Street in the Greenlands community of St Kitts and rushed to the Joseph N. France General Hospital suffering from wounds to his back and arms.

And another contender in the Morris/Walsh conspiracy plot, Michael 'Illa' Glasford, was shot dead on 30 June 2015 as he was sitting peacefully on a bench at Dorset Village, Basseterre. 'Remember', said the Royal St Christopher and Nevis Police Force, in their quest for information as to the assailant's identity, 'you do not have to provide your personal information and you may be eligible to receive a reward' – but it's doubtful if anyone spoke up.

In 1989, the then Prime Minister, Kennedy Simmonds, had opened a six-mile-long highway, which was named after him. He stated that two international hotel chains would be building luxury complexes there; but construction never even started. However, it was a useful road, a 'Gateway to Progress' as the Prime Minister called it, for the young gangsters – 'de Yout' – to drive along to collect their drug imports from Colombia.

On 20 September 2015, Dr the Right Excellent and Right Honourable Sir Kennedy A. Simmonds was elevated to the rank of 'National Hero' by the island's Prime Minister, Dr Timothy Harris.

Eleven days later, following a drugs bust in which one man was shot dead by police, Simmonds' son, Kenrick 'Rico' Simmonds, was one of three later convicted in St Kitts on 11 February 2017 on seven charges, including importation of drugs; he was fined $300,000 and given five months to pay, or face four years' imprisonment. He had been on bail throughout the proceedings. The sentence having been described in the press as 'a slap on the wrist', the Director of Public Prosecutions said he was considering an appeal.

It looked very much like a case of 'business as usual'.

★   ★   ★

Which really brings us full circle to where Alex Ross' investigations commenced, with the disappearance of 'Billy' Herbert.

He must have been an industrious lawyer and politician indeed to have left an estate valued at $20 million, and he would have made enemies, not only in the IRA but among those clients for whom he laundered the proceeds of drug trafficking from his office in Anguilla, because he had given their details to the authorities. This, it appeared, was after he was confronted with his misdeeds as a money launderer; in consequence, the authorities had been able to freeze those clients' accounts in the bank across the street, in which Herbert had a financial interest.

There was also a very strong rumour that Herbert, plus the rest of the fishing party, were buried under a swimming pool in St Kitts. Well, if that's the case, it would be easy to check the detailed planning applications, which I feel sure would have been scrupulously filed with Basseterre's Borough Council, to determine which swimming pools were under construction at the time of the fishing party's disappearance.

That is, if anybody wanted to.

Epilogue

At the conclusion of a book, readers often want to know, when referring to characters in the various chapters, 'Whatever happened to him?' – I know I do.

★　★　★

Charles Stockley Collins, who featured in the Stratton brothers case, was promoted to superintendent in 1908 to head the Fingerprint Department. After his retirement, he wrote two books on the detection of fingerprints.

Following the Stratton case, Fred Fox was permitted to head a small team of officers to detect counterfeit coiners anywhere in the Metropolitan Police Area. It was not a runaway success and nothing like it was repeated until the formation of the Flying Squad in 1919. Fox retired on 20 January 1907, having served 33 years in the Force.

Sir Melville Macnaughton retired from the Met in 1913 and died aged sixty-eight in 1921. He was much admired; his successor said, 'He knew the official career of every one of his 700 men and his qualifications and abilities.'

★　★　★

Chief Inspector Salisbury, who arrested 'The Monocle Man', had his career cut short after 23 years' service, when he was medically discharged due to bronchitis; he died in 1955.

Fred Cherrill retired in 1953 having solved more cases through fingerprint detection than any other officer. He died aged seventy-two in 1964.

★　★　★

In the Ransom case, Fred Smeed – more officially known as Francis Herbert Smeed – was promoted to superintendent and later became Chief Constable of Newport, Monmouthshire and was appointed OBE. He was described by one of his junior officers as being 'a truly sound and helpful man'.

Bert Tansill never married. He rose to the rank of detective chief inspector, was a well respected murder investigator and died aged eighty-one, after almost 33 years of retirement.

Beveridge spent the war years with the Flying Squad, investigating several more high-profile murders, and was promoted to detective chief superintendent, becoming one of 'The Big Five', having control of the Met's No. 2 District. He was appointed MBE and retired, having been commended by the Commissioner on thirty-eight occasions, after over 35 years' service. He died in 1977.

* * *

Before and after the Heys murder case, Greeno solved many baffling murders, rose to the rank of detective chief superintendent and, as one of 'The Big Five', headed the Met's No. 1 District. He retired in 1959, having served over 38½ years, collecting eighty-six commissioner's commendations and an MBE. Sadly, his retirement was short-lived; he died seven years later.

* * *

John Ball was promoted to superintendent and, after several more successful murder investigations, retired in Fulham, where he'd always lived, to enjoy the less exhausting pursuit of playing bowls.

* * *

Wilfred Daws only got a small mention in the Griffiths chapter, but a little more should be disclosed about him because he was what was known as 'a character', a type which the Metropolitan Police have since seen fit to ruthlessly eradicate. Like Capstick, he prided himself on his immaculate attire and was one of the few detectives to wear spats over his shoes. Nicknamed 'Flaps' because of his protruding ears, he was a model witness in court; his voice was quiet and well-modulated, but when roused, it took very little for the volume to rise by several decibels, and his language was described as being able 'to make a Billingsgate porter blush'. But he was a highly efficient Flying Squad officer and would go on to successfully investigate several baffling murder cases. One such was the murder of a prostitute, a case where, without exception, all of the female witnesses were also prostitutes. This was so unusual that it received a large amount of publicity, and 'Flaps' was photographed leaving the Old Bailey in the company of a woman; the picture was published in a newspaper the following day with the caption, 'Chief Inspector Daws leaving the court with one of the witnesses'. It turned out that the lady in question was a CID typist, who was duly awarded an exceedingly large sum in compensation.

Prior to retirement, Daws was promoted to the rank of superintendent.

★　★　★

Ernie Millen shot up the promotional ladder, serving three postings with the Flying Squad, on the last occasion as its chief. Known as 'Hooter', either because of his imperious nose or for his habit of bellowing orders down the corridors at the Yard, he was promoted to the rank of deputy assistant commissioner. He retired one month short of 35 years' service, was appointed CBE and died, aged seventy-six, in 1988.

Jack Capstick finished his distinguished career as Detective Chief Superintendent of No. 4 Area; he was still investigating murders when he retired. The death of June Anne Devaney continued to haunt him. When he retired after 32 years' service – astonishingly without being mentioned in the Honours List – he had just ten years left to continue his devotion to playing bowls and cultivating roses. When he died aged sixty-four in 1968, he had not lived long enough to collect his state pension.

★　★　★

Following the Bodkin Adams case, Bert Hannam was promoted to detective chief superintendent and retired from the Met's No. 3 Area on 27 July 1959. He went to his grave on 24 February 1983 convinced that Adams could have been successfully prosecuted for fourteen murders.

The Chief Constable, Richard Walker OBE, QPM, continued in his role until 1967, when the force amalgamated with another.

Detective Inspector Brynley Pugh died shortly after the trial, in early middle-age.

Charlie Hewett had a glittering career, rising to the rank of detective superintendent before retiring on 12 May 1968, having served 30 years and 18 days. But following Adams' death, rumours surged up again, now that there was no further chance of libel proceedings, and Charlie Hewett was in the forefront of them. Not only did he think that Adams was guilty, he believed that twenty-five murders could have been laid at his door and that he could have been successfully prosecuted for all of them. He also believed that Mrs Sharpe held the key to the case; not only that, but she was due to be questioned again by him and Hannam but died before they could do so – and Hewett thought it a possibility that Adams, knowing this, had 'speeded her on her way'. Hewett died aged eighty-eight of a massive stroke in 2003.

*   *   *

After 'The Body in the Trunk' case, Dave Dilley was promoted to the rank of commander, was awarded the Queen's Police Medal and remained in C11 until his retirement in 1976; he died nine years later. It's interesting to note that when he first went to C11 as a detective inspector in 1964 he had never been a senior investigating officer in a murder enquiry; yet the way he investigated the Coleman murder was exemplary. Allegations of serious misconduct were later made about him by serving officers, although none was ever proved. Not that Geoff Parratt will hear a bad word said about him. 'I thought he was great', he told me. 'He was very thorough and a great investigator; I learnt so much from him.'

Obviously, it rubbed off. Parratt reached the rank of detective superintendent and headed one of the Met's AMITs (Area Major Investigation Teams) before retiring in 1991. 'That Geoff Parratt's so bloody lucky', sourly complained one of his contemporaries (who was no slouch at murder investigations himself), but it was more than that. Former Detective Sergeant Tony Yeoman was Parratt's bag-carrier for about four years. 'During that time, he investigated 85 murders', he told me. 'Only two were unsolved.'

A success record like that requires a little more than luck.

*   *   *

Following the Bassaine case, Ginger Hensley retired in 1975 after 30 years service. Two years later, he died of cancer, fighting it, as Jack Slipper of the Flying Squad described, 'with a courage that brought tears to your eyes'.

Bernie Davis rose through the ranks to become a detective chief superintendent and retired from the Metropolitan Police's 4 Area in 1989. He spends his days gardening at his home on the south coast.

★   ★   ★

Maurice Marshall eventually recovered from his strenuous exhumation exertions in Acapulco and retired in 1984. Living in Buckinghamshire, he goes sailing and for over 20 years was the popular president of the ReCIDivists' Luncheon Club.

★   ★   ★

From the potpourri of cases, Graham Seaby retired in 1994 and Ken Davies in 1986; he plays golf and gardens.

★   ★   ★

Following the Cartland case, Professor Cameron died in 2003, Ron Page retired, then died in 2009 and John Troon was promoted to detective superintendent as a murder investigator, retiring in 1990 from SO1 – the renamed C1. He spends his days shooting in what he describes to me as 'Poldark Country'.

Bibliography

Arrow, Charles	*Rogues and Others*	Duckworth, 1926
Bedford, Sybille	*The Best We Can Do*	Penguin Books, 1989
Beveridge, Peter	*Inside the CID*	Evans Brothers Limited, 1957
Browne, Douglas G. & Tullett, E. V.	*Bernard Spilsbury: His Life and Cases*	George G. Harrap & Co. Ltd., 1951
Browne, Douglas G.	*The Rise of Scotland Yard*	George G. Harrap & Co. Ltd., 1956
Capstick, John, with Thomas, Jack	*Given in Evidence*	John Long, 1960
Cartland, Jeremy	*The Cartland File*	Linkline Publications, 1978
Cherrill, Fred	*Cherrill of the Yard*	George G. Harrap & Co. Ltd., 1954
Devlin, Patrick	*Easing the Passing*	Faber & Faber Ltd 1986
Fido, Martin & Skinner, Keith	*The Official Encyclopedia of Scotland Yard*	Virgin Books, 1999
Frasier, David K.	*Murder Cases of the Twentieth Century*	McFarland & Co. Limited, 1996
Frost, George	*Flying Squad*	Rockliff, 1948
Godwin, George (ed.)	*The Trial of Peter Griffiths*	William Hodge & Co. Ltd., 1950
Greeno, Edward	*War on the Underworld*	John Long, 1960

Hallworth, Rodney & Williams, Mark	*Where There's a Will ...*	The Capstan Press 1983
Hatherill, George	*A Detective's Story*	Andre Deutsch, 1971
Honeycombe, Gordon	*The Complete Murders of the Black Museum*	Leopard Books, 1995
Honeycombe, Gordon	*Murders of the Black Museum*	John Blake Publishing, 2009
Hoskins, Percy	*No Hiding Place!*	A *Daily Express* publication, 1951
Hoskins, Percy	*Two Men Were Acquitted*	Martin Secker & Warburg Ltd 1984
Keily, Jackie & Hoffbrand, Julia	*The Crime Museum Uncovered: Inside Scotland Yard's Special Collection*	I. B. Tauris & Co. Ltd., 2015
Kirby, Dick	*The Guv'nors: Ten of Scotland Yard's Greatest Detectives*	Wharncliffe True Crime, 2010
Kirby, Dick	*The Sweeney: The First Sixty Years of Scotland Yard's Crimebusting Flying Squad 1919–1978*	Wharncliffe True Crime, 2011
Kirby, Dick	*Scotland Yard's Ghost Squad: The Secret Weapon against Post-War Crime*	Wharncliffe True Crime, 2011
Kirby, Dick	*Whitechapel's Sherlock Holmes: The Casebook of Fred Wensley OBE, KPM, Victorian Crime Buster*	Pen & Sword True Crime, 2014
Kirby, Dick	*London's Gangs at War*	Pen & Sword Books, 2017

Kirby, Dick	*Operation Countryman: The Flawed Enquiry into Police Corruption*	Pen & Sword Books, 2018
Kirby, Dick	*Scotland Yard's Gangbuster: Bert Wickstead's Most Celebrated Cases*	Pen & Sword Books, 2018
Lock, Joan	*Scotland Yard Casebook*	Robert Hale, 1993
Long, Tony	*Lethal Force*	Ebury Press, 2016
Martienssen, Anthony	*Crime and the Police*	Secker & Warburg 1951
McKnight, Gerald	*The Inside Story of the Murder Squad of Scotland Yard*	W.H. Allen & Co, 1967
Millen, Ernest	*Specialist in Crime*	George G. Harrap & Co. Ltd., 1972
Millen, Paul	*Crime Scene Investigator*	Robinson, 2008
Moss, Alan & Skinner, Keith	*Scotland Yard's History of Crime in 100 Objects*	History Press, 2015
Read, Leonard with Morton, James	*Nipper*	Macdonald, 1991
Robins, Jane	*The Curious Habits of Doctor Adams*	John Murray 2013
Simpson, Keith	*Forty Years of Murder*	George G. Harrap & Co. Ltd., 1978
Slipper, Jack	*Slipper of the Yard*	Sidgwick & Jackson, 1981
Swinden, D., Kennison, P. and Moss, A.	*More Behind the Blue Lamp*	Coppermill Press, 2011
Tullett, Tom	*Strictly Murder*	The Bodley Head 1979

| Wade, Stephen | *The Count of Scotland Yard* | Amberley Publishing, 2018 |
| Wensley, Frederick Porter | *Detective Days* | Cassell & Co., 1931 |

Index